Ending Teacher Shortages

ENDING TEACHER SHORTAGES

TUAN D. NGUYEN AND
CHRISTOPHER REDDING

JOHNS HOPKINS UNIVERSITY PRESS | *Baltimore*

First printed in the United States of America on acid-free paper
9 8 7 6 5 4 3 2 1

Johns Hopkins University Press
2715 North Charles Street
Baltimore, Maryland 21218
www.press.jhu.edu

Library of Congress Cataloging-in-Publication Data

Names: Nguyen, Tuan, 1984– author | Redding, Christopher, 1985– author
Title: Ending teacher shortages / Tuan D. Nguyen and Christopher Redding.
Description: Baltimore : Johns Hopkins University Press, 2026. | Includes bibliographical references and index.
Identifiers: LCCN 2026006007 | ISBN 9781421455419 hardcover | ISBN 9781421455426 ebook
Subjects: LCSH: Teachers—Supply and demand—United States | Teacher turnover—United States | Teachers—Selection and appointment—United States
Classification: LCC LB2833.2 .N485 2026
LC record available at https://lccn.loc.gov/2026006007

A catalog record for this book is available from the British Library.

Special discounts are available for bulk purchases of this book. For more information, please contact Special Sales at specialsales@jh.edu.

EU GPSR Authorized Representative
LOGOS EUROPE, 9 rue Nicolas Poussin,
17000, La Rochelle, France
E-mail: Contact@logoseurope.eu

To teachers

TUAN D. NGUYEN—To Kate, Mira, Ella, and Ruth
CHRIS REDDING—To Julie, Elliot, and Sylvia

CONTENTS

ACKNOWLEDGMENTS

We thank Susan Kemper Patrick, Tiffany Tan, JR Funk, and two anonymous reviewers whose thoughtful feedback on earlier drafts strengthened this work. Chris Redding is deeply grateful to the University of Florida College of Education for granting him a sabbatical that provided the time to support the development of this project. Similarly, Tuan Nguyen is grateful for the University of Missouri's Provost Great Books Program for granting him a course release that provided time for the development of this project.

Introduction

TEACHER SHORTAGES ARE ONE of the most critical issues currently facing public education. According to the US Department of Education, nearly every state has listed teacher shortages. Across the country, schools have an estimated 50,000 vacant teaching positions.[1] If we assume that each of these teachers has just one class with 20 students, this means their absence would affect at least a million students annually.

The inability to fill vacant positions is not the only aspect of teacher shortages of concern to educational leaders, policymakers, and families. Vacancies are often filled by teachers who are underprepared for the roles they are assigned, such as those who have a short-term or emergency teaching certification or those teaching outside their field of expertise. Nationwide, as many as 400,000 teachers are underqualified. With roughly 3.5 million public school teachers, this represents more than 10% of teachers—a number that has only grown in recent years.

Though a substantial portion of vacancies are filled by teachers moving from one school to another, school staffing also requires hiring beginning teachers. Evidence indicates that finding enough new teachers to fill vacancies is a growing challenge for many school systems, particularly in high-demand subject areas such as special education, mathematics, science, and English as a second language. Though the United States saw a decline in the number of people getting a teaching degree throughout the 2010s,[2] this decline does not affect all schools equally. The teacher labor market can be extremely segmented by urbanicity, by school poverty levels, and across district and state lines. These challenges for teacher recruitment result in localized teacher shortages that can vary by subject area and by school within the same district—and even within schools themselves.

Shortages are not only a result of too few people coming into teaching but also a result of the large number of vacancies caused by high levels of annual teacher turnover.[3] Similar to vacancies, turnover rates are significantly higher in higher-poverty schools and schools enrolling more students of color than schools with more affluent, white students. The National Center for Education Statistics reported that teachers who work in schools in which 75% of students or more are eligible for free or reduced price lunch are nearly twice as likely to turn over than teachers from schools in which 25% of students or less are eligible for free or reduced price lunch (22% versus 12%).[4] Teacher turnover is also incredibly high among new teachers, with roughly a third of teachers leaving within their first three years.[5]

Because teacher shortages have existed for so long, we worry that they have come to be seen as a natural part of public schools in the United States. Moreover, the increased turnover rate after the COVID-19 pandemic has only exacerbated the number of teacher vacancies and the hiring of underqualified teachers. Though steps have been taken around the margins to increase teacher recruitment and to retain more teachers, we have not made significant strides, as a field, in addressing teacher shortages in recent decades. The overarching purpose of this book is to lay out a vision of the steps that would need to be taken to actually end teacher shortages.

Underpinning this book lies a central question: Is there a future in which teacher shortages are not a normal part of schooling in the United States? Toward answering this question, we first characterize the nature of teacher shortages from the past to the present. We document the dramatic changes to the compensation and training of teachers throughout the twentieth century that brought much greater stability to the teacher workforce. Yet our exposition of teacher shortages shows how the historical progress made in reducing teacher shortages has stalled and that shortages remain a concern for many schools. We then describe the highly localized challenges related to both teacher recruitment and turnover and how the two are deeply intertwined with one another. With an understanding of the causes of teacher shortages, we describe the need to shift the focus from preventing turnover to intentionally creating school environments where teachers will want to stay because schools have developed teacher-centered policies that support their teachers well.

We come to this topic from the vantage of former teachers and education policy researchers. As former teachers, we each bring insight into how satisfying the work of teaching can be, but we also admit the challenges it entails. These include teachers recognizing areas for professional growth but not receiving the coaching they need to improve and teachers seeing administrative decisions made that affect their classrooms without their input.

We are also fortunate to have been part of an active education research community that studies teacher shortages and turnover. Since 2008, there have been more than 25,000 research studies on this topic. In this book, we review and synthesize our own work and the research of others who study teacher shortages. We believe it is of critical importance to provide a single book-length treatment of this topic, given that, over the past couple of decades, educational researchers have developed an increasingly nuanced understanding of the factors that shape teacher shortages and the steps that can be taken to reduce them.

Ending teacher shortages requires an understanding of their varied and localized nature. To this end, a large purpose of this book is to synthesize the most current research on teacher recruitment and retention to help guide readers in understanding the ways in which teacher shortages are a problem in their local community. In so doing, we review evidence-based policies and practices that have been shown to increase teacher recruitment and retention. With knowledge of the localized nature of teacher shortages and evidence of policies most effective for specific problems, educational leaders and policymakers can work to end teacher shortages.

This targeted approach much be augmented by deeper changes in how teachers are valued and respected in their schools and beyond. Such an approach begins with increased salaries, not only to improve teachers' material conditions but also to symbolize to current and prospective teachers that teaching matters and is worthy of much higher compensation. Though improved compensation is an important starting point, it must be accompanied by systems that help to support the work of teachers, whether this occurs in the schools in which they work, their school district, unions or professional organizations, their preparation program, or organizations that provide professional development for teachers or support them in advocacy efforts. Such a system includes comprehensive pre-service preparation that is critical for developing the skills, attitudes, and dispositions needed when assuming their role as a classroom teacher. Under a career model of teaching, teachers' development continues throughout their career, with opportunities not only to continue to hone their instructional skills but also to make broader contributions to their school, district, and the profession writ large. In addition, we argue that the teaching profession would benefit from much greater involvement in education policy decision-making.

Despite the complex causes of teacher shortages and their persistence, we do not view them as an unsolvable problem. To skeptics of this goal, we point to historical precedent. Throughout the twentieth century, teaching moved from a short-term, itinerant job for most teachers to one in which the overwhelming majority had a career dedicated to teaching. Improvements in how teachers were compensated, prepared, and supported dramatically improved the conditions of being a teacher in the United States. Unfortunately, progress in this direction has stalled in recent decades, as is evident in declining interest in becoming a teacher, lower enrollments in teacher preparation programs, and elevated attrition rates, particularly among beginning teachers.

This book is our attempt to put forward a vision of the system-level changes and targeted strategies that will reinvigorate a career model of teaching poised to end shortages. To this work, we bring the fundamental assumption that teaching can be deeply satisfying work. Teaching is dynamic and challenging, and it affords an ultimate societal responsibility in getting to shape future generations. For too many teachers, however, the conditions needed to have a fulfilling career in teaching are in too short of supply, whether because they were allowed to enter teaching without the training and support to be successful, they are expected to make astronomical strides with their students without the instructional resources to do so, or they do not think themselves fairly compensated for their labor. We believe that concerted efforts from federal, state, and district policymakers and leaders can create work environments where teachers are well supported. There needs to be a shift from applying short-sighted responses to addressing ongoing teacher staffing challenges (e.g., hiring underprepared teachers to fill vacancies). Instead, efforts should focus on making teaching a more attractive and sustainable career where teachers want to stay. Only then will teacher shortages truly be addressed.

A Note on Definitions

One difficulty in writing this book was that, even among education scholars, there is a lack of clarity regarding the key concepts and terms used to describe the teacher workforce. The term *teacher shortage* has come to be used as shorthand for varied and complex challenges related to staffing all schools with high-quality teachers. For some schools, high annual turnover rates make it challenging to fill all vacant teaching positions for the next school year. In others, too few applicants or underprepared teachers preclude schools from ensuring that all students are taught by a qualified and effective teacher. Moreover, the schools most likely to be affected by teacher shortages are those enrolling more students placed at risk by society and its institutions. With shortages caused by challenges related to teacher recruitment and retention, we share the definitions we will be using in this book.

Labor economists define labor shortages as an imbalance between the demand for workers in a particular occupation and the availability of qualified individuals to fill vacant positions. From this starting definition, we emphasize that shortages can be understood in terms of unfilled teaching positions (i.e., vacancies) or in terms of the qualifications of teachers who apply for or are hired to staff a vacant position (i.e., teachers who lack a standard certification or are teaching in a grade or subject area for which they are not fully prepared). These underqualified positions encompass roles filled by teachers with short-term or emergency certifications or by teachers teaching outside their field of expertise. Having many teacher vacancies often leads to underqualification as school and district leaders may prefer having someone without all the right qualifications over leaving the position empty or filled by long-term substitutes. To summarize, when we speak of shortages, we are referring to sustained labor market disequilibrium between the supply of workers and the demand by schools. From there, we specify the nature of shortages, whether in terms of the number of vacancies or the underqualification of teachers.

As shortages are focused first and foremost on filling vacancies, there is often the impression that doing so would require the recruitment of new teachers. Though the overall supply of new teachers is part of this equation, most vacant teaching positions come to be filled by either current teachers moving between schools or districts ("switchers" or "movers") or teachers in the reserve pool. The reserve pool includes newly prepared teachers who did not go into teaching at first, delayed entrants who are waiting on a preferred school or grade level before taking their first teaching job, and re-entrants—teachers who took temporarily leave from teaching with the intention of returning at some point. When we speak about *teacher recruitment*, we are referring to teachers being recruited into the teaching profession. We then refer to the teacher hiring process to describe the multitude of ways in which teachers come to fill vacancies.

The final set of terms includes teacher turnover, attrition, and retention. When we discuss *teacher turnover*, we refer to the rates at which teachers exit their school. This may include switching schools within the same district, switching districts, or leaving teaching—which we also refer to as *attrition.* For our purposes, turnover is a concern not only because of its impact on students and schools but also for the close connection between turnover and vacancies. A critical and often overlooked way to reduce vacancies is to retain teachers in the first place. *Retention*, then, can be seen as the inverse of turnover, in that it refers to the rates at which teachers stay in their school.

A Note on Sources

In the process of writing this book, we examined and reviewed thousands of studies, and each study comes with its own strengths and weaknesses. In the early chapters, we relied primarily on descriptive quantitative studies, supplementing them with historical monographs and qualitative research when relevant. This body of work helps us address our first aim of establishing a baseline understanding of the nature of teacher shortages.

Later in the book, when we begin making prescriptive policy recommendations, our standards for evidence shift. Our primary consideration is the degree to which a specific policy or practice changed teachers' labor market behaviors. This focus is needed so that we do not misattribute the underlying cause when recommending policies for reducing shortages. An example is helpful here. If researchers are trying to assess the degree to which paying teachers more reduces attrition, they may study districts that have raised salaries to see whether this led to lower attrition. These districts may have other unobserved factors, however, that drive both salary levels and attrition (e.g., school funding or cost of living). If high attrition rates are what drive the salary increases, researchers also need to be concerned about reverse causality; that is, salary alone may not be affecting attrition, but attrition might be influencing salary too. Privileging research studies where we can infer causation is critical to providing policy-relevant guidance for readers.

Throughout the book, we take care to emphasize studies that are rigorously designed (i.e., where causality can be inferred). We have denoted these rigorous studies with a star (*) in the references. In this way, readers can see for themselves which studies we consider more rigorous and decide the extent to which they may trust the other studies' results. We wanted a way to designate measures widely believed to reduce teacher shortages but for which there is not rigorous evidence, and thus they should be treated with caution by policymakers. We supplement this with reference in the text to policies for which there is more or less rigorous evidence to support our recommendations.

We anchor our vision to the evidence that exists, particularly with our comprehensive examination of the literature around teacher recruitment and retention. In writing this book, however, it became clear that if we relied strictly on rigorously designed studies, our recommendations would be too narrow in addressing the underlying structural challenges currently shaping teacher shortages. For instance, the impact of financial incentives on teacher retention has been studied far more extensively than the impact of instructional coaching. This does not mean that instructional coaching does not increase teacher retention but rather that rigorous evidence is not available to support this assertion. We added this framework to clearly differentiate rigorous research that exists while ensuring our aspirational ideas and vision are grounded in evidence.

The Plan for the Book

We begin in chapter 1 with a history of teacher shortages spanning roughly the past 150 years. Beginning with this historical perspective allows us to document how current teacher shortages are low by historical standards. In the late nineteenth and early twentieth centuries, teaching was a highly transient occupation for all but a small group of teachers. Throughout the twentieth century, the material conditions of teachers' work improved drastically, driven by higher salaries, the availability of pensions, and other job protections. Increasing teacher pay and improving job protections were adopted with the explicit goal of reducing teacher shortages. With improved compensation and greater job security, teachers had more of an incentive to invest in their formal teacher preparation. By undergoing more comprehensive professional preparation, teachers had newfound expertise and a greater commitment to their work that helped them to negotiate the challenges of teaching. We describe these shifts as moving toward a career model of teaching. That improvements in teacher recruitment and retention have been made at points in the past suggests to us that more active steps could be taken to reduce teacher shortages in the future.

Upon this historical foundation, chapter 2 characterizes the teacher shortages that continue into the present. We begin by dispelling the myth that teacher shortages are a challenge for all school systems. Instead, we put forward a more nuanced argument about the need to identify the schools experiencing shortages, whether in terms of vacancies or underqualification. To accomplish this goal we begin with a state-level scan of the variation in shortages across the United States. We then elaborate on how, even within a single state, teacher shortages are a function of a labor market that is not uniform across grades and content areas; rather, there are many teacher labor markets distributed across grades and content areas, and the dynamics in each of these labor markets can be quite different from one another. We conclude this chapter with a discussion of the connection between teacher recruitment and retention to warrant the next two chapters.

Chapters 3 and 4 describe the "revolving door" in teaching, with many entering the teaching profession for only a short period. These chapters summarize research on teacher recruitment and retention to help readers understand the multiple causes of shortages. In chapter 3 we synthesize recent research describing the variety of ways in which teachers come to be hired in a given year. This includes a description of the three predominant ways in which beginning teachers enter teaching: traditional university-based teacher preparation programs, alternative certification programs, and no formal preparation. We then detail the hiring process for teachers to highlight how schools work to fill vacancies and how this process varies across schools facing different staffing challenges. We conclude this chapter with a brief discussion of the teacher reserve pool to underscore the extent to which filling vacancies is a growing problem for many schools.

When discussing teacher turnover in chapter 4, we describe the factors that drive teacher turnover: background characteristics and qualifications, school conditions, and external factors, such as state policies. In characterizing the predominant factors related to teacher turnover, we focus readers' attention on the circumstances in which turnover is most elevated, including among early-career teachers, teachers in particular subject areas (e.g., special education or math and science), and in higher-poverty schools enrolling more students of color. The basis for teachers' decisions to turn over can be quite varied, so describing both the scope and variation in teacher turnover can help educational leaders and policymakers better understand how turnover is (or is not) detrimental in their setting and, more importantly, what can be done to retain teachers.

Chapters 5–7 shift attention from describing the nature of teacher shortages to recommending policies and practices that can break the cycle of teachers churning in and out of the profession. A throughline of these chapters is the argument that addressing teacher shortages will require a deep shift in how we view the teaching profession and how we frame teacher staffing challenges. We present system-level, teacher-centered policies and practices that create supportive work environments supportive of the values that drive teachers to enter the teaching profession in the first place. Ending teacher shortages requires affirmative strategies that attract more people to teaching and create schools where teachers want to stay. For conceptual clarity, we focus first on policies designed to increase teacher recruitment before examining corresponding policies related to teacher retention in the next chapter. In these chapters we prioritize policies with a track record of success. We then build on these research-based recommendations with a chapter that sketches out an aspirational vision of how these and other policies and practices could end teacher shortages.

Specifically, in chapter 5, we discuss a variety of policies aimed at increasing teacher recruitment, both overall and for teachers in key shortage areas. These include teacher salaries, financial incentives (e.g., TEACH grants, loan forgiveness, free tuition to attend teacher preparation programs, and recruitment bonuses), licensure exams, and licensure requirements that shape the design of teacher preparation programs—including traditional university-based preparation programs, alternative certification programs, teacher residency programs, Grow Your Own programs, and teaching apprenticeship programs. We also home in on district-level practices, including those related to teacher hiring, teacher leadership, and teacher involvement in local decision-making. We pay careful attention to policies and practices aimed at diversifying the teacher workforce, including racially minoritized teachers, in key subject areas such as STEM (science, technology, engineering, and mathematics) and special education, as well as across school contexts such as economically disadvantaged schools, majority-minority schools, and geographically isolated schools.

Next, in chapter 6, we explain the array of teacher-centered policies related to teacher retention. We distinguish among three main approaches: financial incentives, preparation and support, and improved working conditions. There are many financial incentives that can be used to retain teachers, including salary increases and bonuses. The second category—teacher preparation and support—include pre-service preparation and in-service supports (e.g., mentoring and induction, professional development, and instructional coaching). The last category is the school conditions in which teachers work. This expansive category ranges from the number of courses assigned to teachers to the support provided to them by administration. In each of these categories, we discuss where policies have been implemented and the extent to which they have been evaluated and found effective. Then we examine how these policies have been used to target the retention of specific types of teachers (e.g., STEM or special education) and teachers working in hard-to-staff settings.

In chapter 7, we put forward our aspirational vision to end teacher shortages. There are no silver bullets in education, and there is no one-size-fit-all approach to end teacher shortages. We strongly believe in a mix of bigger and bolder approaches to ensure a robust teacher supply and to increase teacher retention along with targeted strategies to address specific shortage challenges. This vision includes ways in which educational systems could be established that center teachers and their work to a much greater degree than happens currently. Though salary increases are a critical step in this work, we emphasize how increased compensation must be accompanied by approaches to teacher recruitment and retention that begin with increasing public interest in teaching and extend through career-long supports for teacher development. In response to an education policy ecosystem that often has failed to involve teachers, this vision includes much greater agency among teachers in shaping their broader working conditions.

We conclude with the importance of teaching and teachers, why we should care about teacher shortages, and how complicated teacher shortages can be. While teacher shortages are a complex problem, we do not believe they are unsolvable, as we have laid out the evidence for specific and discrete policies having improved teacher recruitment and retention as well as our aspirational vision to end teacher shortages. We articulate our goal to create a sustainable teacher workforce that is needed to ensure that all children will have the best opportunities to learn and can become the best versions of themselves.

We end this introduction in the same way we will end the book, by making this statement: Ending teacher shortages requires affirmative strategies to create schools where teachers want to stay—not simply preventing some teachers from leaving.

CHAPTER 1

The Teaching Procession or Teaching Profession?

A Historical Perspective on the Nature and Magnitude of Teacher Shortages

> *There has long been a feeling in educational circles that the number of public school teachers leaving their position each year is inordinately high; that this high rate of turnover has a very undesirable effect upon the school systems concerned. . . . It is this feeling which has given rise to the not inappropriate epithet, "the teaching procession."*
>
> —WILLARD SLINGERLAND ELSBREE, 1928

IN HISTORICAL TERMS, the rate at which teachers turn over in American schools today is low. An average of 8% of teachers leave teaching and another 8% move schools yearly, a statistic stable for decades except for the years after COVID-19. In contrast, during the late nineteenth and early twentieth centuries, most teachers did not view teaching as a permanent career. Average years of teaching experience is a helpful proxy for the longevity of a teaching career. The average teaching experience at the turn of the twentieth century was three years. A century later, teachers had an average of 15 years of experience.[1]

Describing this historical shift toward a career model of teaching—the goal of this chapter—allows us to contextualize a few defining features of the teacher workforce that shape teacher shortages in the present. This begins with different forms of labor market segmentation that emerged during the Common Schools era, including the feminization of teaching and sharp urban-rural divides in schools. Throughout the late nineteenth and early twentieth centuries, teaching was a highly transient occupation. Men would often use teaching as a secondary job or a springboard to a higher-status occupation. Those that did make a career out of teaching were still highly mobile, often moving schools after a year or two in efforts to seek out higher pay or better working conditions. Women, on the other hand, tended to teach for a few years before they married or had children. In short, teaching was a career for only a fraction of teachers.

This changed quickly during the early decades of the twentieth century, when many of the job structures emerged that still shape teachers work.[2] In this chapter, we first focus on how teachers organized to improve their material conditions, whether through higher salaries, pensions, or other job protections. Educational administrators became increasingly sympathetic to these appeals as a transient teacher workforce was seen as inhibiting efforts to centralize and standardize school operations. Higher salaries and improved job protections were adopted with the explicit goal of improving teacher retention.

The second shift that brought greater stability to the teacher workforce was the formalization of teacher expertise through changes in teacher preparation and licensure. Though formal teacher training emerged in normal schools in the middle of the nineteenth century, most teachers at that time had little more education than the students they were charged with educating. Again, this changed rapidly in the first half the twentieth century, with 88% of teachers having attended college by 1940.[3] This period was also marked by more centralized teacher licensure. These changes formalized a career model of teaching in two ways. They created entry barriers that reduced transience in the teaching workforce. By undergoing more comprehensive professional preparation, teachers not only had a greater commitment to their work but also a newfound expertise that helped them negotiate the challenges of teaching, thereby contributing to an extended career in teaching for a growing number of educators.

The greater stability in the teacher workforce was also due to changes from outside education. A variety of economic and social forces contributed to decreasing employee turnover throughout the United States during the twentieth century. Wages increased and employer-provided benefits became more generous. The design of compensation systems promoted long-term tenure (through seniority-based compensation and pensions). Hiring and firing decisions were increasingly centralized, helping to reduce arbitrariness in staffing decisions. By the latter half of the twentieth century, federal civil rights legislation prohibited employment discrimination based on race, gender, age, religion, or national origin. Workers were increasingly covered by unions to collectively bargain for improved working conditions. With improved compensation and greater job security, employees had more of an incentive to invest in industry-specific job training—further embedding employees in a career occupation.[4]

At times, efforts to improve teachers' material conditions and to professionalize their knowledge were complementary to one another. Teacher pay schedules were linked to both teaching experience and educational attainment, which encouraged more teachers to earn an education degree. At other times, the goal of establishing teaching as a profession akin to medicine or law was undercut by teachers' efforts to improve their material interests. When teachers became more active in advancing their collective material interests through unionizing after World War II, it became difficult for teachers to maintain an image of a noble helping profession.[5]

There were also limits on how successful a career model of teaching could be. With the Great Depression as perhaps the only exception, there were never enough people who sought out teaching to eliminate teacher shortages, whether this stemmed from material conditions such as low salaries or barriers to entering teaching. As a result, efforts to establish high standards for all teachers have never been fully realized.[6] Thus, it is difficult to argue that all teachers should have sufficient expertise and preparation when many teachers have entered the classroom without the full professional preparation they need.

Teacher Labor Market Segmentation

One of the defining features of the teacher workforce that extends into the present is its segmentation. This notion of labor market segmentation is useful in anticipating a point we develop in greater detail in the next chapter: there is not a singular teacher labor market. In the past and into the present, teacher labor markets were segmented geographically and by school features. Who became a teacher and how long they remained in teaching also varied by teachers' background characteristics. Arguably the largest development shaping the teacher workforce toward the turn of the twentieth century was the feminization of teaching, whereby women came to constitute the overwhelming majority of teachers—a pattern that still exists in public schools today. Schools were also segmented by urbanicity. As urban schools were often better resourced and had better working conditions, teachers tended to move to schools with more favorable conditions. Though this urban-rural divide dissipated as school management became more centralized, this trend anticipated the labor market segmentation by school working conditions that continues at present.

Gender and Teacher Workforce

Scholars speak of the feminization of teaching to describe its swift transition into the female-dominated occupation we see today. Amid a sharp increase in student enrollments during the Common School movement of the mid-nineteenth century, the gender makeup of schools changed rapidly. Scholars attribute this transition to a number of factors: the emergence of gendered conceptions of women as superior teachers, a longer school year that limited male teachers' opportunities to work multiple jobs, women's increasing educational attainment, changing gender norms facilitating working outside the home, and the financial benefits afforded to school districts by paying women an estimated half to a third what men were paid in the same teaching position. Some women built lasting careers in teaching, often for the independence and autonomy it afforded. By one estimate, 20% of women teachers in Boston in the late nineteenth century taught for their entire careers. More common, however, was for women teachers to teach for a few years prior to marriage. When three-quarters of teachers were women by the turn of the twentieth century, the short tenure of female teachers was a primary contributor to the high attrition rates within the teacher workforce.[7]

The job tenure of male teachers was slightly longer in the latter half of the nineteenth century, particularly in the South, where the feminization of teaching was delayed among Black teachers. Teaching was still temporary work for many male teachers. Some taught for a few years as a springboard into more prestigious long-term careers in the law, ministry, or medicine. Others moved schools annually in efforts to improve their pay and working conditions. The high rates of mobility across schools speaks to how challenging it was to work in nineteenth-century schools, particularly those in rural areas. Teachers not only needed to ensure some semblance of learning and order—often in an ungraded one-room schoolhouse—but also helped with school upkeep (e.g., chopping wood, drawing water, and repairing the building).[8]

Though no national estimates of teacher turnover existed during the nineteenth century, teaching was clearly a transient profession for the majority of teachers. These patterns were shaped by emergent gender norms shaping who went into teaching and how long they remained. For the women who filled a growing number of teaching roles, teaching was a lifelong career only for a small subset, with most exiting teaching after marrying or having their own children. That more and more teachers were women would shape the structure of teachers' work—and efforts to improve it—in manifold ways during the twentieth century.

An Urbanizing Teacher Workforce

The teacher labor market during this period was not only segmented by gender but also urbanicity. The statistics on rural teacher turnover are extreme by contemporary standards. In Princeton Township High School, a 200-student high school in Illinois, only 8.6% of teachers remained in the same school after five years from 1867 to 1892.[9] Administrators at one school in Quincy, Massachusetts, in the 1880s remarked that for its five teaching posts, "Not a single teacher remains who was there ten months ago."[10] As a result of high levels of turnover, it was estimated that between 25% and 30% of rural teachers were new to teaching each year.[11] A 1911 study showed that rural teachers had only two years of experience, on average.[12] Tyack and Hansot summarized the situation: "Teachers in . . . rural schools could hardly be considered members of a profession. . . . They were young, poorly paid, and rarely educated beyond elementary subjects. . . . Turnover of teachers . . . was extremely high."[13]

Teachers did not necessarily leave teaching outright. Many of them moved from rural to urban schools. Urban schools appear to have experienced lower turnover rates and also benefited from the recruitment of career-minded teachers with prior teaching experience who had moved to more urban areas. For instance, in New York state in the early 1900s, the median annual turnover rate was 11% in city schools and 16.8% in rural schools.[14] Compared with the average rural teacher who had only 2 years of experience, women teachers in urban schools had an average of 7 years while male teachers had 12 years of experience.[15] Higher pay and better working conditions appear to have shaped these locale-based mobility patterns, as did the social and cultural amenities of larger towns and cities. Even if teachers earned higher salaries and experienced more favorable working conditions in towns and cities than in rural areas, teaching was still not supported as a lifelong career for the majority of teachers.[16] In the next section, we develop the steps teachers took, often organized through labor unions and education associations, to improve their professional standing, whether through better material conditions or formalized expertise.

Improving the Material Conditions of Teachers

The turn of the twentieth century was marked by growing concerns over the need to structure teachers' work and compensation in ways that would "mold the teaching profession into an island of stability."[17] Teachers became increasingly organized, arguing for higher salaries and greater job security.[18] School administrators' views of teachers also appeared to shift during this period. Amid rapid social transformation, teachers were increasingly viewed as critical to the efficient management of schools. In 1881, Thomas M. Balliet, the superintendent of schools in Springfield, Massachusetts, summarized this emergent perspective: "The present social unrest among all classes of people . . . [will] before long force upon us, in a very practical way, the necessity of securing men and women of first-rate ability to direct the work of the public schools. . . . Good salaries, better social recognition, permanency of tenure, and a certainty of being above want after the years of efficient service are over, are the only means by which such talent can be secured for this work."[19] Increasing the material well-being of teachers and the prestige of teaching was seen as a way to increase stability so that teaching could serve as a bastion against social upheaval of the time. We focus on the ways in which higher pay, pensions, and tenure and other job protections all helped to turn the tide on teacher turnover during the twentieth century.

Teacher Salaries

Low pay deterred many Americans from pursuing teaching as a career. In 1902, the average monthly salary of men teachers was $42 ($1,536 in 2024 dollars) and $39.77 for women ($1,454 in 2024 dollars), though there appears to be significant variation by school level, teacher characteristics, and across schools.[20] For instance, in a 1905 study by the National Education Association, the base annual salary for male elementary teachers in New York City was $900 ($32,064 in 2024 dollars), with an annual increase of $105 until a ceiling of $2,400 was reached ($85,504 in 2024 dollars). In contrast women in the same position had a beginning salary of $600 ($21,376 in 2024 dollars) with only a $40 annual raise.[21] Though low teacher salaries were generally justified based on broader labor market conditions, pay was also determined by contemporary social mores—mores that were discriminatory toward women and people of color.

Wages might have also been driven down by popular views of teaching as an act of moral transfer.[22] The motivations for teaching were widely understood not to be financial but to serve a larger societal purpose instead. As one Boston school reformer stated, "If you merely want high wages, and teach only because you can get your living by it, you are not a teacher in any high sense of the term."[23] Kafka explains further that "school districts' hesitancy to increase women teachers' salaries was buttressed by the perception that women teachers were supported by their families and essentially worked for 'pin money.'"[24]

At the same time, higher pay was seen as necessary to address the perceived shortages of male teachers. The solution was to develop a differentiated salary schedule. These pay schedules were not only determined by teachers' experience or features of the job (e.g., primary versus secondary) but along gender and racial/ethnic lines as well, with white male secondary teachers earning the highest salaries. As women teachers organized around the labor demand for higher salaries, it was not only to increase salaries. Equally important was to move toward a uniform salary schedule, with standardized pay grades and incremental increases tied to experience as opposed to ascriptive identities or school level. Single salary schedules spread quickly, with 97% of districts having adopted one by 1950.[25]

Regardless of the levels of teacher pay, a single salary schedule promoted a career model of teaching in important ways. First, all teachers had access to pay raises under a transparent, uniform system. By linking teacher pay to both experience and educational attainment, this system encouraged more teachers to earn an education degree and remain in teaching longer to earn incremental pay increases. This compensation structure also changed teacher-administrator relationships. The adoption of a single salary schedule curtailed administrators' oversight of teachers' work and granted teachers greater autonomy in the classroom.[26]

Under the single salary schedule, teacher pay increased rapidly in the first few decades of the twentieth century. Increased salaries appear to be one factor that helped to reduce teacher turnover. Following the adoption of a single salary schedule in New York in the early 1920s, Elsbree's survey of superintendents about the amount of and reasons for teacher turnover showed turnover rates that were similar to current estimates. By the 1920s, the average teacher working in a school in the city had an estimated 10 years of experience—a sharp increase from just a couple of decades prior.[27]

Following pay cuts, if not outright loss of employment, during the Great Depression, teacher shortages during World War II and the postwar baby boom were a boon for teacher salaries. Still, increased teacher salaries were often less than the salaries available in wartime industries. In the years following World War II, teacher salaries did not rise fast enough to meet the sharp increase in the cost of living or to compete with wages possible outside education, contributing to ongoing teacher shortages. In response, a number of high-profile teacher strikes aimed at increasing teacher pay occurred in the 1940s, only to be met with state bans on public employees' striking. Throughout the 1950s, strikes were virtually nonexistent amid the political climate of the Red Scare that equated teacher protests with a subversion of the postwar order.[28]

Aside from the shift to a single salary schedule, arguably the most impactful change to teachers' salaries during the twentieth century was the opportunity for teachers' unions to collectively bargain teacher contracts. Collective bargaining requirements mandated that local school boards bargain with teachers' unions. Collective bargaining agreements (CBAs) are the resulting contracts negotiated by unions. CBAs are consensus contracts that govern district and school operations, including teacher compensation. The first CBA covering teachers was won in New York City 1962 following a high-profile strike. As legally binding contracts, CBAs were a powerful tool in stabilizing teacher salaries. Unlike earlier efforts to secure teacher pay raises, which were contingent and often reneged upon by district officials, teachers would now be compensated regardless of city finances. In the following decades, CBA become the *modus operandi* in all but a few states, with a primary goal of unions being to establish protections for teachers' compensation.[29] As we detail in the next section, CBAs also included increasingly generous pension plans for career teachers.

Teacher Pensions

Another labor demand was for pensions. In contrast to the efforts to increase salaries, which were generally viewed as inadequately low for attracting a high-quality, stable teacher workforce, numerous concerns were voiced about pensions, including how they would dampen teacher pay, bring financial burdens for school districts, and change the composition of the teacher workforce in undesirable ways. Regardless of said concerns, public pensions spread quickly for teachers. In 1911, at least twenty large school districts had pension plans for their teachers. Two decades later, nearly half of states had pension plans for their teachers and another five allowed school districts to create plans. Their rise was a result of teachers' organizing efforts, which also benefited from the fact that women teachers who continued working into old age were often unmarried—as marriage frequently led to dismissal—and often lacked the financial means to support themselves after years of low pay as teachers.[30]

Still, their adoption was not without challenges, chiefly the financial difficulties they posed. In response, the reliance on defined-benefit pension plans likely contributed to age discrimination in both teacher hiring and layoffs. There were numerous reports of older teachers being laid off and preference being given to hiring younger teachers who would contribute more to pensions than older teachers nearing retirement age. By the 1960s and 1970s, antidiscrimination laws and the expansion of collective bargaining rights brought defined-benefit pension plans to the overwhelming majority of teachers—90% by some estimates.[31]

Defined-benefit plans were another factor in progressing toward a career model of teaching, because "the structure of the traditional [defined-benefit] plans treated teachers well if they work a full career in teaching."[32] By backloading benefits and rewarding teachers for factors such as years of experience and final average salary, longer-serving teachers benefited in the long term from these plans—further supporting the development of a career model of teaching.

Teacher Job Protections

To this point, we have focused on teacher-initiated attrition as a main driver of teacher shortages. Teacher dismissals, which were often discriminatory or politically motivated, also determined who could make a career in teaching during the first half of the twentieth century. There were numerous ways in which teachers' hiring and continued employment was at the discretion of school and district administrators. This pattern is perhaps most evident with school desegregation efforts outside the South in the late nineteenth and early twentieth centuries. When schools were integrated, it was usually followed by contract nonrenewal or firing of Black teachers. Though research has documented how desegregation after *Brown v. Board* resulted in a loss of teaching positions for Black teachers, northern cities were not immune to this trend in decades prior.[33] White parents and teachers challenged the hiring of Black teachers in many schools and districts with predominantly white student enrollments.[34]

In both rural areas and large cities with active political machines, teachers could be hired because of personal relationships, religious affiliation, or even the spoils system. In such a system, political patronage could also cost teachers their job when political control shifted. Many districts also maintained marriage bars, whereby many female teachers were fired if they disclosed or were found out to be married or pregnant. Teachers could also be fired for other political motivated reasons, including political activism and union activities.[35]

Teachers often had little autonomy over routine classroom decisions, such as how to discipline a student or plan a lesson. Teachers frequently reported intimidation without the ability to voice concerns. When William Maxwell—the superintendent in New York City in the early 1900s—was asked, "Do you think that there are no conditions which might justify a teacher in complaining of his superior?," his response was "Absolutely none."[36] Teacher job insecurity was, thus, widely used as a tool to ensure that teachers conformed to administrative expectations. Though scholars have not documented the exact rates at which teachers were dismissed during this period, many teachers lacked due process in employment decisions and were subject to some high-profile dismissals.[37]

In response to what often amounted to capricious employment practices, teachers' unions in the first half of the twentieth century were dedicated to expanding teacher job protections once protections for teachers' compensation were solidified. Arguably less controversial at the time was the introduction of tenure for teachers, which was typically earned following a three-year probationary period. Tenure required that employers show a "just cause" as the basis for termination. District administrators had warmed to tenure protections given that it served as a cost-saving measure that could ensure a stable corps of public school teachers. In the face of the high annual costs of rehiring teachers amidst high turnover rates, tenure was viewed by administrators as improving the desirability of teaching without an attached cost. The greater stability also helped support administrators' efforts to develop the increasingly bureaucratic organizational structures that were emerging at the time, efforts that were not seen as possible with a highly impermanent workforce.[38]

Beginning first in New Jersey in 1909, tenure rights were intended to ensure that teachers' employability was shielded from undue political influence. Over time, teacher contracts increasingly included provisions related to teachers' due process and rights to a fair dismissal. An estimated 70% of teachers had some type of job protections by the 1940s.[39] Though tenure protections appear to have reduced arbitrary dismissals, teachers could still be dismissed for a variety of reasons. Perhaps the best example is the persistence of marriage bars—limits on women's careers as a teacher following marriage or pregnancy—which persisted into the 1950s in many districts. As it initially emerged, tenure protections did not protect teachers' academic freedom or increase their autonomy. So union leaders at the time pushed for greater protections. They argued that the "the perfunctory kind of tenure which is more or less in existence" that "avoids the frequent turnover of teachers under ordinary circumstances" was of benefit to school leaders "but deprived teachers of respect."[40] The starkest evidence of the limits of the tenure protections that existed at the 1940s came from state-led efforts at removing teachers who were suspected of having been members of the Communist Party or had socialist views, which were commonplace in districts in the 1940s and early 1950s.[41]

Unions took steps to strengthen tenure protections, including grievance procedures that guaranteed due process and allowed for union representatives to call meetings and defend members. As a result, teachers were subject to less centralized control over their work and found new autonomy in the classroom. They experienced enhanced rights in the classroom and were also less subject to administrative discretion in school operations (e.g., last-minute meetings or spur-of-the-moment classroom walkthroughs). While some observers have bemoaned the loss of principals' authority to run their schools effectively, these changes insulated teachers from external threats to their employment. As a result, these job protections served as an additional means to improve teachers' materials conditions in support of a career model of teaching.[42]

Final Thoughts on Material Conditions

On net, teachers' material conditions improved greatly during the twentieth century. Though reliable teacher turnover data did not exist until the late 1980s, estimates from the middle of the century suggest that approximately 10% of teachers left teaching annually, only slightly higher than contemporary levels. Though improved compensation and greater job security likely had a direct effect on retention, enhanced job protections made teaching a more attractive career, which in turn incentivized teachers to invest in furthering their education. In the next section, we talk about the ways in which efforts to formalize teacher expertise through certification, education, and professional development also helped to solidify a career model of teaching.

Improving Teacher Expertise

At the same time that teachers were taking steps to improve the material conditions of their work, school administrators and teacher educators were working to formalize and centralize the professional knowledge that was deemed necessary to teach. Having a defined body of knowledge that all teachers were familiar with was seen as critical in establishing a career model of teaching. If successful teaching required certain expertise, dilettantism must be replaced by teachers who are dedicated to developing their professional knowledge. These efforts started within normal schools, the educational institutions that emerged in the middle of the nineteenth century to train teachers to work in Common Schools, and later spread to university-based teacher education programs. As normal schools never supplied enough teachers to meet local demand, certification processes were designed to determine who was fit to be a teacher, first at the local level and later at the state level. This determination was not only based on perceived academic competencies but also on the moral character of the candidate. Given that a professionalized body of knowledge and a screening mechanism to determine who is granted the authority to belong to an occupation are key markers of any profession, these two mechanisms played an important role in shaping who became teachers and how long they remained in teaching.[43]

It cannot be understated the degree to which these efforts were not spearheaded by teachers themselves but by administrative reformers, such as superintendents and school administrators. Their push for an educated teacher workforce was intimately connected with the emerging career model of teaching. As Murphy summarized, "Teachers were not just to have jobs, they were to have careers commanding a much greater and absorbing commitment."[44] Educational administrators' interest in a committed teacher workforce aligned with their broader goals to centralize and rationalize schooling. The outset of this vision of a teaching career was matriculation at a teacher preparation program, where teachers-to-be completed the coursework needed to earn the credential to teach. Though many teachers derided this formal preparation as less beneficial than experience as a means of learning how to teach, the increasing educational standards for entry into teaching throughout the twentieth century and pay increases tied to a four-year college degree contributed to teachers being one of the most educated occupations in the United States during this period.[45]

Formalizing Teacher Education

We have painted a picture of the teaching profession as characterized by transience and amateurism at the turn of the twentieth century, with few teachers having received any formal education before becoming a teacher. This began to change with the expansion of normal schools through the nineteenth and early twentieth centuries and with universities beginning to offer teacher education. Though the curricular focus of normal schools and university-based teacher preparation programs differed, they each, in their own way and in competition with one another, promoted teacher professionalization. First, they each put forward a formalized professional knowledge base for teaching. Second, they contributed to the rapid educational attainment of teachers.

Normal schools were established in response to a growing need for adequately prepared teachers amid growing public school enrollment. They aimed to provide a more standardized teacher preparation, which emphasized pedagogy and proficiency in school subjects. The overarching curricular emphasis was on practical knowledge for teaching, with "experience as an important source of educational knowledge."[46]

Normal schools were also characterized by their close ties with the local community. As an illustration, Pawlewicz describes how district administrators worked closely with the Normal College of the City of New York (later Hunter College) to meet staffing needs. This included quality control—"excluding from the profession unworthy and incompetent members," in the words of Commissioner John Eaton—but also maintaining a supply of teachers that met demand.[47] In periods when the supply of teachers exceeded local demand, this could result in the addition of new course requirements in an effort to extend the period to graduation. More commonly, however, programs were under pressure to enroll more students, given that they were heavily dependent on student tuition. As a result, many normal schools were plagued by low admission criteria and watered-down content meant to reduce attrition from their programs. Programs also faced pressures to prepare student teachers quickly and efficiently, both from school districts and teacher candidates themselves, who had new educational opportunities outside the preparation programs themselves.[48]

The vision of an appropriate university-based teacher education placed greater emphasis on subject-matter expertise and objective, scientific knowledge than on the practical, pedagogically focused orientation of normal schools. This approach was spearheaded by teacher educators at universities who sought to develop an empirically grounded understanding of teaching. Their claim for teacher professionalization rested on the development of a distinct knowledge base. By the Great Depression, university-based programs adopted a more vocational focus, while normal schools were increasingly transitioning to teachers' colleges before becoming state colleges and universities. This "mimetic tendency" was further promoted by professional associations, which insisted on greater uniformity for practitioner-based preparation.[49]

The result was a model of teacher education that many teachers themselves deemed necessary for their professional advancement but not particularly helpful for their professional preparation. Many believed college education was not as useful as experience in learning how to teach but did see the upside of broader professionalization efforts given how teaching would be viewed more favorably if teachers were highly educated. This was especially true after a growing number of districts tied permanent teacher licenses—and the associated pay increase—to the completion of an education degree.[50]

These efforts to centralize teacher education cannot be divorced from administrators' efforts to reformulate teaching around middle-class values. Murphy writes that "a college education was not just a certificate of [middle-class] culture; it acted as a barrier to working-class women."[51] The gradual formalization and expansion of postsecondary education requirements changed who could became a teacher. This centralized model of teacher preparation positioned teacher professional standards as being defined by experts within universities or normal schools as opposed to the local community. This shift in teachers' professional preparation was also linked with racial/ethnic discrimination, as notions of class were tied to Americanization efforts that increasingly restricted immigrants and African American descendants of slaves from becoming teachers. Over time, this resulted in teachers being much more likely to come from white-collar families. It was only during the push for community schools amid desegregation efforts that the discriminatory nature of this system was challenged. That said, this critique was never resolved, as experience levels and educational attainment remained the main factors in determining teacher pay levels.[52]

It should also be noted that, in an irony of history, the different approaches to teacher education ultimately proved inadequate to the goal of fostering a more professionalized teacher workforce. For one, the emphasis on practical knowledge did not provide a basis for teachers to establish specialized knowledge—a core marker of professionalized occupations. Moreover, while medicine and law became more specialized, teacher preparation leaned heavily on practice-based knowledge. In doing so, teaching was portrayed as a practical activity without the expertise and status of a true profession. Many teachers themselves attested to this view, thinking they could have simply learned their craft in first few years on the job rather than through their college education.[53]

When teacher educators put forward a vision of the importance of subject-matter expertise and scientific knowledge of teaching, it emboldened teacher educators, administrators, and policymakers, often at the expense of teachers themselves. A traditional *producer-user* knowledge paradigm was solidified, whereby those outside the classroom with more training and expertise managed the work of teachers, undermining teachers' autonomy in the process. This view also contributed to a deficit model of teaching, where teachers lacked something that must be supplied by those outside the classroom.

In addition, it also risked discounting the social and emotional dimensions of teachers' work in favor of the objective, decontextualized evidence of experts.[54]

Patriarchal views clearly shaped the underwhelming efforts to professionalize teachers' work through greater education. The feminization of teaching corresponded with the bureaucratization of schools, whereby school administrators aimed to standardize and control teachers' work. Such efforts further served to devalue women's skills and knowledge as educators, discounting the knowledge that women teachers had access to through experience. Instead, scientific knowledge obtained through university training—training that was disproportionately available to men—justified administrators' roles and the associated monitoring and scrutiny of classroom teaching. As control over one's work is a hallmark of one's professional identity, these efforts further undermined teacher professionalization efforts.[55]

Another marker of professionalization that has not applied to teachers is exclusivity of membership. Teachers' educational attainment increased sharply over this period. By 1940, 56% of teachers had earned a bachelor's degree or higher, with another 32% having completed some college but not earning a degree. Still, teaching was not able to attract enough candidates to achieve the goal of a highly educated workforce. When a nonnegligible share of teachers had not completed an education degree, it further reified the view that teaching was a job that could be done without specialization skill or training.[56]

In summary, a college-based education became a critical step in the career model of teaching. Becoming a teacher in the late twentieth century required a much greater investment of time and resources—a sharp departure from the amateur model of teaching that was the norm a century prior. Though greater preparation prior to entering the classroom was likely a factor in increasing the longevity of teachers' careers, the emphasis on university-based credentials had consequences that remain unresolved to this day (e.g., class-based and racialized barriers to becoming a teacher; devaluing of practical teaching experience). Moreover, increasing teachers' educational attainment did not serve to establish teaching as the true profession that many reformers envisioned.

Formalizing Teacher Certification

Prior to the expansion of formal teacher education, schools and districts still needed a way to ensure that the teachers in their classrooms were fit for their role. Teacher certification came to fill this role. At the turn of the twentieth century, the certification of teachers still tended to be a local decision. In 1898, only a few states issued teaching certificates. In others, it was a mix of states setting rules but counties grading tests and issuing licenses or states and counties both controlling teaching licenses. Even as the authority of state superintendents to issue teacher certificates grew, most certificates were still local. When certification decisions were made locally, there was a widespread perception that any teacher was certified who was deemed fit by community members. The result was that there were no universal standards for the qualifications to become a teacher, with wide variation in the credentialling of teachers even within the same state. This haphazardness is captured by Rugg's remarks in the 1933 National Survey of the Education of Teachers: "probably the greatest single obstacle to making teaching a profession . . . is the present chaos in certification practices."[57]

The next few decades saw a slow transition from the geographically varied certification system to a state-centered certification process centered on state-level examinations and education requirements. School administrators shifted from the oral examinations that had been conducted informally by local officials to a system of increasingly standardized written examinations administered at the state level. These tended to be core knowledge examinations designed to assess candidates' proficiency in the Common School curriculum, including reading, writing, mathematics, geography, and history. These exams were generally used to assess the academic qualifications of teachers who had not completed postsecondary education, which represented the majority of new teachers in the early decades of the twentieth century. Even if graduates of normal schools were exempt from teacher examination in half of the states, not enough teachers graduated from these schools to meet local demand.[58]

In determining who was fit to be a teacher, certification exams appear to have been exclusionary in many regards. Though the exams were often portrayed as objective measures of the academic competencies needed to teach, they often measured cultural differences or disparities in access to educational opportunities. As a result, certification exams further restricted access to teaching among lower-class candidates and people of color. Moreover, the use of oral examinations, which continued into the twentieth century, provided another way for educational administrators to discriminate against those that fell outside the dominant culture. As one might expect, these assessments excluded immigrants and racial/ethnic minorities, among others.[59]

These efforts to centralize teacher licensure essentially went out the window amidst World War II–era shortages. In 1945, over 100,000 teachers held emergency certificates—roughly the number of newly hired teachers. Though the large number of emergency-certified teachers continued into the 1960s, states still took steps to raise the standards for earning a teaching license—with 25 states requiring a four-year college degree for a teaching license and nearly all states requiring it if the teacher was working in a high school. Professional organizations, including the National Commission on Teacher Education and Professional Standards, which was created by the National Education Association, and the National Council for the Accreditation of Teacher Education, worked to galvanize support for states to improve the standards of preparation and of admission to teaching. Efforts at the state level to take over the approval of teacher education programs were underwhelming. This was particularly true by the 1960s and 1970s when teachers could demonstrably improve their wages and working conditions through the newly gained collective bargaining process. Thus, professional autonomy was supported less through strict entry standards for teaching and more through other characteristics of a highly educated and credentialed workforce.[60]

Final Thoughts on Expertise

One of the primary markers of a professionalized occupation is an established knowledge base that guides professional practice. The model of teacher professionalization that was promoted over the twentieth century was one in which a baccalaureate degree came to signify how teachers possessed such knowledge. This development often corresponded with increased teacher licensure standards that, over time, required a degree from an accredited teacher preparation program for a full teaching license. This shift in teachers' professional preparation established teacher preparation programs as the gateway into teaching. Though it became a key foundational step in a teaching career, the historical question remains of whether it promoted career longevity in the same way that improved materials conditions did. We suspect that the investment in time and resources to complete a degree, along with improved preparation, helped to improve teachers' commitment to a career in teaching—though perhaps not to the degree that improved compensation and working conditions did. We return to this question in chapter 4 when discussing factors linked to teacher turnover.

Conclusion

The twentieth century brought clear changes in the responsibilities and rewards of public school teaching. System-level improvements to compensation and job security created additional incentives to invest in teacher training, further embedding employees within a career occupation. Teachers' work environments also shifted, as tenure protections and grievance procedures granted teachers more autonomy over their work. Set against a backdrop of feminization of teaching, urbanization, mass immigration, and racial segregation persisting under Jim Crow, the design of the teacher's job changed in ways that made teaching a more attractive career for Americans who had access to the profession and that also improved teacher retention.

By the 1980s, however, questions remained as to how well the career model of teaching was meeting the needs of American schoolchildren. Though perhaps no longer the procession-profession of the early twentieth century, challenges remained to recruiting a high-quality, stable teacher workforce. *A Nation at Risk* of 1983 described pervasive shortages in teachers of math, science, foreign languages, English as a second language, and special education, with many who filled these positions being woefully underprepared. Teacher salaries were also described as too low, with many teachers supplementing their income with secondary employment. The solution, summarized in the follow-up report of 1986, *A Nation Prepared*, was to improve the selectivity and quality of teacher preparation programs, to increase teacher salaries, and to offer additional opportunities for career development. Of note, these proposed policy solutions emerged not from teachers—no teachers were included on the National Commission on Excellence in Education, which authored these reports—but from the educational administrators and policymakers that had worked to centralize the preparation and licensure of teacher over the prior century.

That a panel commenting on the work of teachers did not include a single teacher is a telling sign of the status of teaching in the latter decades of the twentieth century. Regardless of whether reforms to create a career model of teaching helped to do so, they had the effect of centralizing control among those overseeing the preparation and the work of teachers rather than directly empowering teachers themselves. The question is whether centralized strategies to improve the preparation and support of teachers are sufficient for reducing shortages or if approaches that further elevate teachers themselves in leading this work are needed. Before developing these recommendations in more detail, we turn in the next chapter to the matter of teacher shortages and review the factors that shape who enters teaching and how long they remain in the profession.

CHAPTER 2

Schools in Crisis?

Characterizing Teacher Shortages

KHON, A JUNIOR in an urban high school, has been hoping to take Advanced Placement (AP) classes in science so that she can potentially save some time and money when she goes to college. Unfortunately, her school serves mainly low-income families and has had trouble recruiting teachers in the past few years. The school was unable to hire a qualified science teacher who can teach AP Chemistry or AP Physics, so Khon winds up not being able to take them in her junior or senior year. A few hundred miles away, Johnny, an eighth grader, is in Algebra I, but his teacher is not fully licensed to teach mathematics. His teacher has an alternative certification from an online for-profit institution, has not taken a college-level math course in 20 years, and never even earned a degree in mathematics. As unfortunate as this situation is, it marks an improvement over what Johnny had the year before—a constant rotation of substitute teachers.

These stories are not uncommon in many schools and districts across the United States, and, as was noted in the last chapter, they are not new. Many classes are taught by teachers who lack a standard license to teach, either overall or in their assigned subject area. Even before the COVID-19 pandemic, state departments of education across the country had granted thousands of emergency and provisional certifications to teachers in order to fill classrooms every year.[1] Many of these teachers received no training in pedagogy (i.e., how to teach) and lacked subject-matter expertise in their content area, such as having no background in math even though they were paid to teach mathematics.

When schools lack enough adequately prepared teachers, the result is adverse outcomes for both students and the educational system. Not only is it detrimental to student learning when teachers lack proper teaching skills or subject-matter expertise, but these teachers are also more likely to leave their current school or quit teaching altogether, which they do at significantly higher rates than their counterparts who are fully certified to teach by an accredited higher institution of learning.[2] Consequently, schools and districts end up investing significant resources each year to replace these rotating novice teachers who typically stay for only a year or two.

Even more concerning is the prevalence of schools and districts struggling to recruit teachers to staff every classroom. Echoing *A Nation at Risk*, countless headlines today announce districts and states facing challenges in finding enough teachers, particularly in critical subjects like special education and STEM (science, technology, engineering, and mathematics) or in schools that tend to be more difficult to staff, such as majority-minority schools or those with high poverty rates. For instance, in the 2020–21 school year, about 30% of public schools were unable to fill a teaching position for biology or life sciences, and about 32% mathematics positions went unfilled.[3] Relatedly, one estimate in 2022 posited a shortage of between 15,000 and 23,000 physics teachers nationwide.[4] In the same year, more than half of high-poverty schools had at least one teaching vacancy, and about 58% of schools with more than 75% students of color had at least one vacancy.[5]

The COVID-19 pandemic exacerbated these issues. Some states have reduced the requirements for becoming a teacher, asking for only a high school diploma or enrollment in a teacher preparation program. Retired teachers have been asked to return, school administrators are being utilized for teaching roles, and in extreme cases, the National Guard and police officers have been called upon to assist in schools.[6] These are all stopgap gestures disconnected from our call for teacher-centered policies that intentionally create school environments where teachers want to stay.

Teacher shortage, consisting of both unfilled positions and underqualified teachers, has prompted extensive research into strategies for attracting more individuals to the occupation and retaining them in the classroom. Significant gaps in understanding persist, however, regarding the problem. For instance, it is uncertain whether there is a nationwide shortage of teachers or whether it is confined to specific regions or subject areas. Conflicting reports exist about shortages nationwide, as numerous districts and states apparently do not encounter issues with teacher shortages.[7] For example, Memphis–Shelby County Schools and Spokane Public Schools indicated their school districts experienced no difficulties in recruiting teachers in the 2022–23 school year.[8] As a state, Utah has experienced little to no teacher vacancies for multiple years and reported very high teacher retention rate in the early 2020s.[9] Furthermore, some schools receive hundreds of applications for a handful of available positions, whereas others receive merely a few applications.[10] These contrasting reports make it difficult for the public and policymakers to understand the degree to which teacher shortages are a concern.

The goal of this chapter is to help readers wade into the discourse around teacher shortages. Doing so is a critical step in understanding the nature of teacher shortages and how they affect schools. It also has important implications for our recommendations for how to end teacher shortages. If teacher shortages are a universal phenomenon affecting all schools, then the policy priority should be system-level changes that aim to create school environments supportive of the values that attract new teachers to the profession and make existing teachers more likely to stay. If teacher shortages affect only some schools or groups of teachers, then targeted policies would likely be more beneficial to ending teacher shortages. Or, as we will argue, if teacher shortages affect many schools, though some to a greater degree than others, there is a need for both system-level changes to the structure of teaching and targeted strategies aimed at high-shortage areas.

We want to dispel the picture of teacher shortages as a general deficit of schools and of teachers everywhere. We push back on the closed-ended question of "Do we have a teacher shortage challenge?" and pose a more nuanced one: "To what extent do we have teacher shortages, where, and for whom?" Indeed, intricacy in conditions remains a pivotal element in the ongoing discourse about teacher shortages, even among experts on the topic.[11]

To accomplish this aim, we pick up on arguments from chapter 1 with a brief introduction of long-standing debates about the nature of teacher shortages. From there, we work to establish why the field of education lacks robust information systems on the nature of shortages. Accompanying this aim is our establishment of greater definitional clarity for the term *teacher shortage*. This leads to a discussion of two different meanings of shortages: teaching vacancies and the hiring of underqualified teachers. We then provide data that help to establish a series of empirical facts about the prevalence and scope of teacher shortages.

The Teacher Shortage Debate

Given uncertainty surrounding the nature of teacher shortages, it is not surprising that there is an ongoing debate over whether there is a national teacher shortage in the United States and, if so, has it worsened in recent time. There are also questions about whether teacher shortages primarily affect specific types of schools (e.g., economically disadvantaged schools) and groups of educators (e.g., in specific subject areas) or instead tend to vary with changing conditions in schools and in the broader labor market. The situation is sometimes described as an imbalance in teacher distributions across geographic locations and school characteristics. Some experts argue that there is an insufficient number of teachers based on the number of open positions.[12] Conversely, others suggest, when looking at the broader picture, there might not be an actual shortage since the number of graduates from teaching programs has increased over time except during the 2010s.[13]

Shortages are also connected to the job tenure of teachers. To this point, some researchers emphasize that the problem lies in insufficient numbers of teachers remaining in the teaching profession after becoming certified.[14] They focus on overarching issues affecting whether people decide to become teachers or to stay once in the profession, such as salary concerns and working conditions. In other words, shortages are due to an inadequate supply of qualified teachers. The other side argues that the problem pertains more to which teachers are needed and where. This latter group highlights difficulties in finding teachers in specific locations or for particular subjects, citing rules and obstacles that hinder teachers from moving to areas where they are most needed. In this telling, the real problem is not a shortage, per se, but the uneven distribution of teachers.

Understanding the factual basis behind teacher shortages is, unfortunately, no easy matter. Observers have debated the nature and magnitude of teacher shortages for at least the past century, if not more. As we saw in the last chapter, how shortages were conceived shaped the types of policies adopted. For instance, efforts to improve the material conditions of teachers' work did not simply focus on salaries but instead on a suite of reforms that made progress toward a career model of teaching. We find it of critical importance to identify the nature of the problem and potential solutions in the current moment. As an example, addressing a generalized teacher shortage might include policy responses such as raising salaries, reducing requirements to entering teaching, and allowing for-profit organizations to supplement staffing. These responses stand in sharp contrast to more targeted approaches to tackling shortages (e.g., offering salary incentives for teachers with specific expertise, for working in extremely rural or urban environments, or for working in schools with high poverty rates). Moreover, solutions designed for a general shortage might inadvertently generate new issues in the same way teacher unionization distanced teachers from the professionalized vision of teaching that other reformers had worked to foster. As a result, we may perhaps end up producing too many elementary education teachers, leading to oversupply and thus leaving some teachers without positions or else necessitating they teach subjects or in schools where they lack certification. In summary, while it is undoubtedly tempting to implement policies to combat teacher shortages, misdirected solutions could fail to address the actual problem and, worse yet, create unforeseen challenges.

What Do We Know About Teacher Shortages?

In order to formulate policies that can appropriately address teacher shortages, we need to know the extent to which there are teacher shortages (i.e., the magnitude of the problem), the geographical distributions of the shortage (i.e., specific states; rural or urban areas), and shortages according to school and teacher characteristics (i.e., high-poverty schools; STEM or special education teachers). Unfortunately, there is no standardized way that US states measure teacher shortages, nor does the federal government collect the information needed to identify whether a shortage is generalized or localized or is generalized *yet* worse for certain kinds of teachers in certain schools. Although the federal government queries states about so-called shortages in specific areas, it allows individual states to report any combination of unfilled positions, positions filled with nonstandard certification, or certified teachers teaching outside their subject area. Consequently, while we are aware that numerous states report shortages in STEM or special education, the data do not specify whether they lack a single STEM teacher or a hundred special education teachers. Without uniform ways to measure and report shortages, the magnitude and character of the problem remain unclear. Essentially, the information collected by the federal government does not elucidate the extent of shortages in any specific area; it merely confirms the existence of a shortage of some form.

Some states independently monitor their teacher workforce in public schools, documenting turnover rates annually. Yet many fail to track teacher shortage information, such as the demand for teachers in a specific subject area or the number who are teaching without standard certification. Notably, some populous states have inadequate reporting. New York, for one, offers no insights into the presence of teacher shortages. In California, state data regarding vacant teaching positions are altogether absent. Numerous states lack such information entirely, and where available, it may be several years old, offering minimal value for individuals interested in going into areas of shortage or for policymakers looking to devise solutions to shortages.

Conversely, some states excel in generating this critical information, which sometimes is discouraging. Florida, for example, annually publishes a comprehensive report on its teacher labor market data.[15] In the 2022–23 school year, Florida explicitly outlined at least 5,000 unfilled teaching positions and a minimum of 22,000 teachers lacking full certification. Overall, due to the disparate nature of US state reporting systems, the public, researchers, policymakers, and other stakeholders have access to inadequate data on the extent of teacher shortages in the country.

When we talk about teacher shortages, we should be clear about how we are defining and measuring these shortages. Sometimes, calling a teaching position *unfilled* can mean different things: it might refer to a job that is empty or to a position filled by someone lacking proper qualifications. Different groups might use the term *shortage* in different ways too. For example, economists might see a shortage if there are not enough teachers applying for available positions, while school administrators might see a shortage if they are not happy with the quality or quantity of applicants. The term *underqualified* teachers, often used to indicate teacher shortages, can also be a tricky concept because it covers various situations. For instance, a teacher with an alternative certification (such as completing their preparation while teaching) might have different effects on students compared with someone with an emergency waiver (often having no preparation for teaching at all). This matters because research has shown that having certain qualifications can signal differences in effectiveness, particularly among beginning teachers.[16] Being precise in discussions about teacher shortages can help us compare different states more accurately.

To confront these challenges, we need to tackle this problem in two ways: (1) by establishing clear definitions of teacher shortages and (2) by establishing effective and reliable ways to measure shortages.

Establishing Clear Definitions of Teacher Shortages

From our perspective, a teacher shortage can be defined in two main ways. By one definition, a shortage refers to unfilled teaching jobs, commonly known as vacant positions. This occurs when schools have posted open positions before the start of the school year (usually in late spring and summer), and by the start of the school year, these positions remain unfilled. In a second definition, a teacher shortage can also happen when schools employ teachers without the appropriate credentials or for a subject they are not fully prepared for, both of which are known as underqualification. Underqualified positions include those filled by teachers with irregular, provisional, or emergency certifications or by teachers certified in areas other than their field of expertise (for instance, an English teacher in charge of a biology course). To be clear, teacher vacancies may lead to underqualification as districts and schools would prefer to have someone without all the right qualifications than to leave the position empty or filled with long-term substitutes. Since vacancies sometimes lead to underqualification, this relationship can conflate the two issues in public discourse. In sum, teacher shortages comprise both vacancies (positions unfilled after the school year begins) and underqualification (positions occupied by inadequately qualified teachers). As much as we are able to, we need to differentiate these two issues.

As each type of shortage carries distinct implications for schools and students, it is crucial to distinguish them. Schools grappling with numerous vacant positions likely face different circumstances from schools contending with multiple underqualified positions, with differing impacts on student learning. In the first case, high vacancy numbers mean there are not enough prospective candidates who want to teach in that district or that state. As for students, they may not be able to take a desired class since there is no one to teach it, or it is taught by a long-term substitute teacher, or the only option is a large class combining multiple sections. Conversely, underqualification scenarios could involve an oversupply of certain types of teachers and a deficiency of others, such as secondary education teachers working in elementary schools or non-STEM teachers instructing STEM classes, potentially leading to a lack of pedagogical expertise or content knowledge to the detriment of students. Given these fundamental differences between vacancies and underqualification, we should distinguish between them as much as possible.

As previously mentioned, no existing national database contains data on the extent of teacher shortages that distinguishes vacancies from underqualification. To compensate for this, we conducted two systematic and simultaneous internet searches aimed at gathering vacancy and underqualification data for every state, including the District of Columbia. Specifically, we utilized a common search string in Google to locate news reports detailing the number of vacant positions in each state. Additionally, we thoroughly examined the website of each state's department or board of education for this information. If no information existed on a website, we corresponded with state officials to acquire these data.

Vacancies and Underqualified Positions in the United States

After years of collecting data on vacancies and underqualification across all states—from news coverage, published reports, state department websites, and academic publications—we compiled the most comprehensive overview of teacher shortages in the country. We gathered underqualification data for all 50 states plus Washington, DC, and vacancy data for almost every state. Given the considerable interest in teacher shortages and the evolving nature of this situation, we made these data available on a website, www.teachershortages.com. Table 2.1 and figure 2.1 summarize key findings for the 2023 and 2024 school years. (Interested readers can find more recent data on the website.)

The map in figure 2.1 represents the number of vacant teaching positions using different shades of gray. The map demonstrates that most reported vacancies are in the Southern and Atlantic regions, especially in states like Mississippi and Florida. Other nearby states like Tennessee,

TABLE 2.1 **Teacher vacancy and underqualification in the United States by state plus DC**

State	Vacancy	Under-qualification	Teachers	State	Vacancy	Under-qualification	Teachers
AL	1,343 (2022–23)	6,125 (2022–23)	42,022 (2022–23)	MT	443 (2022–23)	353 (2022–23)	11,036 (2022–23)
AK	355 (2022–23)	1,928 (2022–23)	7,160 (2022–23)	NE	203 (2022–23)	1,718 (2022–23)	23,910 (2022–23)
AZ	2,230 (2023–24)	6,748 (2022–23)	49,202 (2022–23)	NV	1,078+ (2024–25)	5,324 (2022–23)	23,076 (2022–23)
AR	unknown	4,956 (2022–23)	38,815 (2022–23)	NH	unknown	467^ (2020–21)	14,731 (2022–23)
CA	552+ (2022–23)	32,252 (2022–23)	267,659 (2022–23)	NJ	196+ (2022–23)	11,417 (2022–23)	117,643 (2022–23)
CO	618 (2023–24)	1,420 (2023–24)	53,553 (2022–23)	NM	751 (2023–24)	4,474 (2022–23)	21,572 (2022–23)
CT	1,221 (2022–23)	1,178 (2023–24)	44,002 (2022–23)	NY	unknown	18,302 (2022–23)	215,752 (2022–23)
DE	~500 (2023–24)	2,242 (2021–22)	9,991 (2022–23)	NC	5,242 (2024–25)	11,136 (2022–23)	99,975 (2022–23)
DC	276 (2022–23)	848 (2022–23)	8,052 (2022–23)	ND	418- (2022–23)	96 (2023–24)	9,581 (2022–23)
FL	4,767 (2022–23)	23,825 (2022–23)	156,787 (2022–23)	OH	unknown	3,932 (2021–22)	96,741 (2022–23)
GA	410+ (2023–24)	21,042 (2022–23)	121,301 (2022–23)	OK	1,019 (2022–23)	9,916 (2022–23)	42,124 (2022–23)
HI	166.00- (2024–25)	3,169.00 (2022–23)	11,984 (2022–23)	OR	44+ (2023–24)	3,517 (2022–23)	30,752 (2022–23)
ID	134 (2022–23)	1,102 (2022–23)	18,121 (2022–23)	PA	865 (2023–24)	19,502 (2021–22)	127,034 (2022–23)

IL	4,096 (2023–24)	9,114 (2022–23)	135,363 (2022–23)	RI	239+ (2023–24)	848 (2022–23)	10,778 (2022–23)
IN	1,170– (2023–24)	5,907 (2021–22)	65,565 (2022–23)	SC	1,380 (2023–24)	8,223 (2023–24)	55,947 (2022–23)
IA	1,013 (2023–24)	1,826 (2022–23)	36,138 (2022–23)	SD	96 (2022–23)	1,151 (2023–24)	10,261 (2022–23)
KS	671 (2024–25)	1,578 (2023–24)	37,885 (2022–23)	TN	1,009 (2022–23)	2,888 (2022–23)	65,781 (2022–23)
KY	277 (2022–23)	2,957 (2022–23)	43,023 (2022–23)	TX	546+ (2023–24)	83,620 (2023–24)	373,332 (2022–23)
LA	1,145 (2022–23)	16,195 (2022–23)	41,110 (2022–23)	UT	12+ (2022–23)	3,358 (2022–23)	31,164 (2022–23)
ME	665– (2023–24)	431 (2022–23)	15,168 (2022–23)	VT	unknown	594 (2022–23)	7,934 (2022–23)
MD	1,935 (2023–24)	12,506 (2022–23)	62,237 (2022–23)	VA	3,650 (2023–24)	18,519 (2023–24)	92,651 (2022–23)
MA	75+ (2023–24)	5,927 (2022–23)	76,978 (2022–23)	WA	1,810 (2021–22)	6,416 (2022–23)	63,272 (2022–23)
MI	530 (2022–23)	6,894 (2022–23)	85,668 (2022–23)	WV	1,500 (2023–24)	2,581 (2023–24)	18,670 (2022–23)
MN	~946 (2023–24)	5,485 (2022–23)	56,124 (2022–23)	WI	467+ (2022–23)	4,507 (2022–23)	60,011 (2022–23)
MS	2,775 (2023–24)	2,082 (2023–24)	33,768 (2022–23)	WY	~140 (2024–25)	404 (2023–24)	7,312 (2022–23)
MO	873 (2023–24)	3,969 (2022–23)	69,838 (2022–23)				

NOTE: + denotes a subtotal of the state's total teacher vacancies; – denotes the number of teacher openings instead of teacher vacancies, or a sum of vacancies from more than one school year; ~ denotes a rough estimate of the state's teacher vacancies; ^ denotes underqualification counts retrieved from the US Department of Education, Civil Rights Data Collection (2018), to supplement data unavailability in the primary searched results.

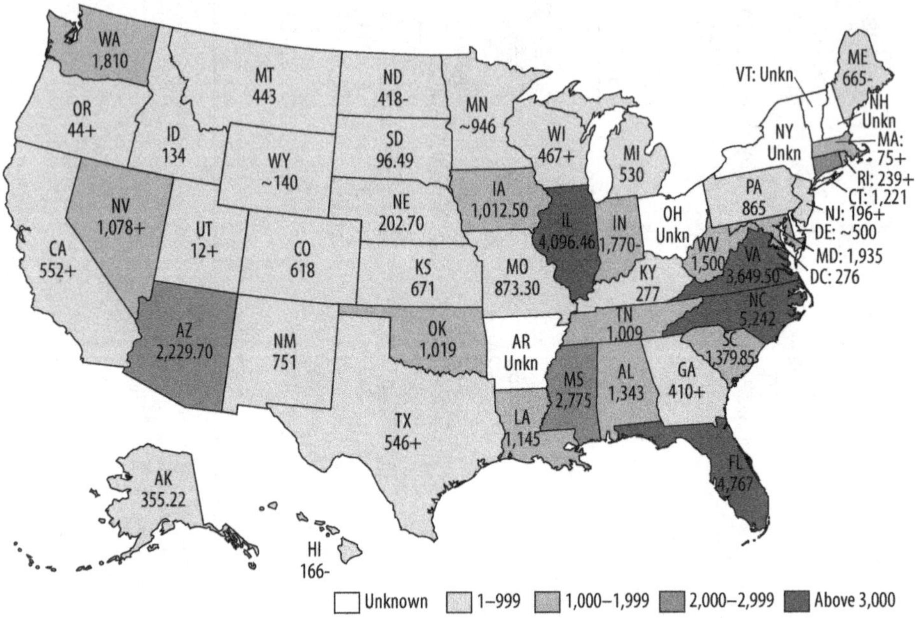

FIGURE 2.1 Teacher vacancies in the United States in 2023–24. + denotes a subtotal of the state's total teacher vacancies; – denotes the number of teacher openings instead of teacher vacancies, or a sum of vacancies from more than one school year; ~ denotes a rough estimate of the state's teacher vacancies. *Source*: https://www.teachershortages.com

North Carolina, South Carolina, Virginia, West Virginia, and Maryland also report a high number of vacant teaching positions.

During the 2023–24 school year, when we added up the reported vacancies for each state, there were at least 50,000 vacant positions in the whole country (up from 39,700 in the 2021–22 school year). When we compared the same 37 states plus DC where we have vacancy data for both school years, we found an increase of about 30%. The Southern region accounts for the highest number, followed by the West and the Midwest regions, with the Northeast region having the lowest raw number of vacant positions. Overall, these data illustrate two key findings. First, teacher vacancies vary substantially across the country; second, teacher vacancies increased after the onset of the COVID-19 pandemic.

To consider the number of vacancies per state is crucial, but it is not the sole way to compare vacancies across states. It is equally important to consider the size of the school system and the student population, given

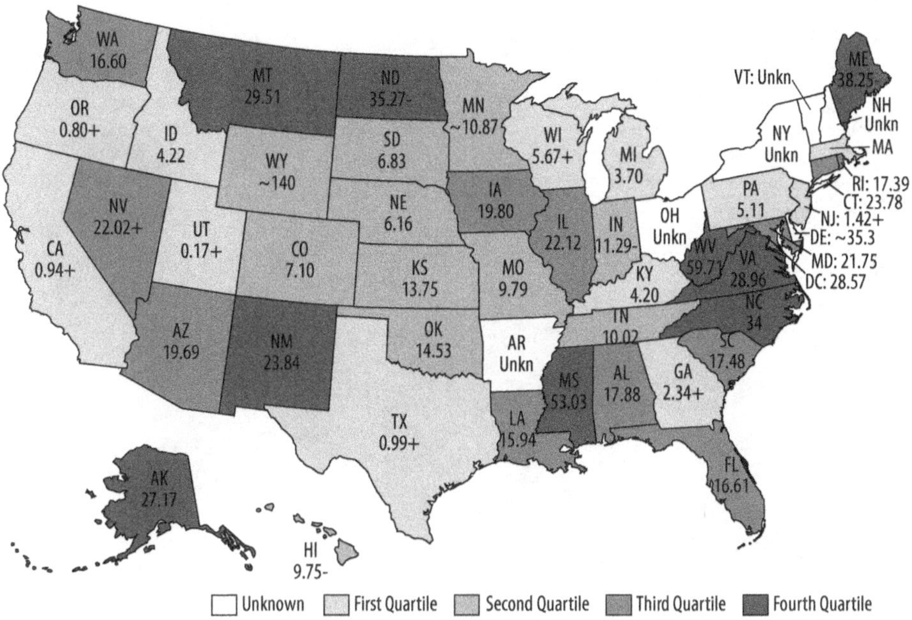

FIGURE 2.2 Teacher vacancy rate per 10,000 students in 2023–24. + denotes a subtotal of the state's total teacher vacancies; – denotes the number of teacher openings instead of teacher vacancies, or a sum of vacancies from more than one school year; ~ denotes a rough estimate of the state's teacher vacancies. *Source*: https://www.teachershortages.com

states' substantial differences in population size that lead to varying teacher-to-student ratios. Expressing numbers as a ratio, such as the number of vacancies for every 10,000 students or as a percentage of total teaching positions, could provide more meaningful insight.

When we look at the number of vacancies relative to the number of students in figure 2.2, the distribution changes substantially. The geographical concentration of high vacancies is less pronounced. West Virginia and Mississippi exhibit the highest rates of teacher vacancies, with approximately 60 vacant teaching positions for every 10,000 students. Put differently, in Mississippi, the number of vacant positions accounts for nearly 10% of the state's existing teacher workforce. Additionally, other states in the top quartile for vacancy rates are Alaska, North Carolina, Virginia, New Mexico, and Maine. Though some states like New Mexico having a low raw count of vacancies, they exhibit high vacancies relative to the student population or the existing teacher

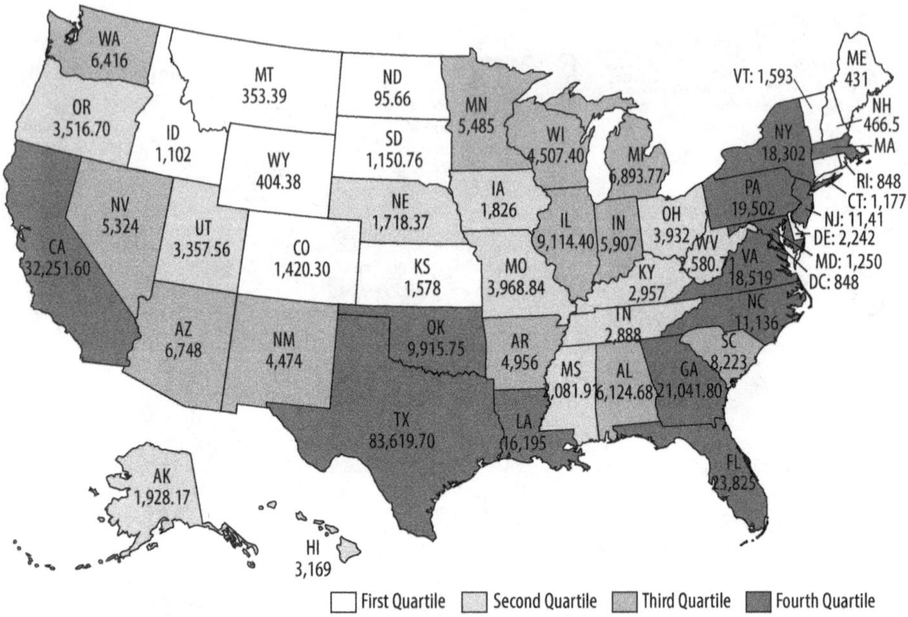

FIGURE 2.3 Teacher underqualification in the United States in 2023–24. *Source*: https://www.teachershortages.com

workforce. This points to disparities in teacher shortages when viewed from different perspectives. Therefore, journalists, parents, and stakeholders following this issue should always seek additional data to contextualize raw numbers, as they might not accurately represent the actual situation (a point we develop further toward the end of this chapter).

Next, we examine teacher underqualification in the United States. In figure 2.3 we observe that more than 20 states had more than 5,000 underqualified teachers in 2023–24. Overall, there are at least 400,000 underqualified teachers in the country (according to each state's own definition of who is a qualified teacher, not according to our own). Note that many states with low or unknown raw vacancy numbers, such as California, Louisiana, Texas, and New York, have high numbers of underqualified teachers.

Similar to vacancies, we also compare the number of underqualified teachers per 10,000 students in figure 2.4. Twenty-eight states have at

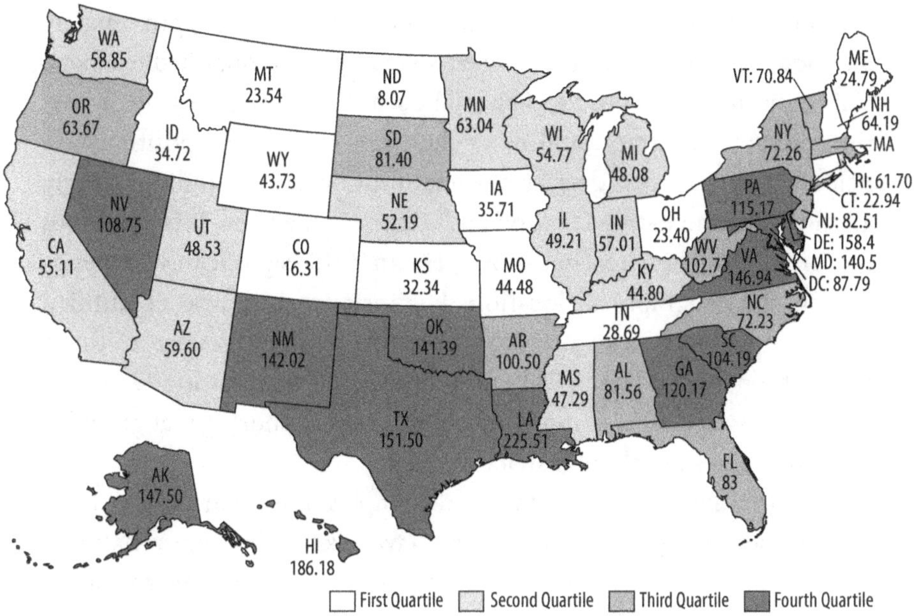

FIGURE 2.4 Teacher underqualification rate per 10,000 students in 2023–24. *Source*: https://www.teachershortages.com

least 60 underqualified teachers per 10,000 students, most of which are located in the South or Southeast. Eight states have fewer than 30 underqualified positions per 10,000 students, and 15 states have between 30 and 60 underqualified positions per 10,000 students. We observe that relative underqualification ranges from 8 position per 10,000 students, or 1% of the workforce in North Dakota, to 226 positions per 10,000 students, or 39% of the workforce in Louisiana. Hawaii has the second-highest relative underqualification rate at 186 positions per 10,000 students. These results illustrate how we must take into account the number of students, or the size of the state's teacher workforce, when comparing vacancy and underqualification across states.

Asking the Right Questions

Let us sum up here some key points we discovered from our research into teacher shortages across the nation. First off, we calculated at least

50,000 vacant teaching positions nationwide. Moreover, approximately 400,000 positions were currently occupied by underqualified teachers. This indicates that about 2% of all public school teaching positions across the country are vacant, and more than 10% of teaching positions are held by teachers lacking necessary qualifications; these findings closely align with some national estimates.[17] At the same time, it is crucial to recognize that these teacher shortages can differ significantly depending on the geographical location. For instance, the rate of unfilled teaching positions per 10,000 students in Louisiana is over 28 times higher than that in North Dakota. This difference across locales would likely be larger if we had more information about shortages at granular levels like cities or school districts.

Even though teacher shortages are complex and nuanced, our findings do beg the question that many have asked: "Is there a national teacher shortage?" We do not think there is a straightforward way to answer this question for two main reasons.

First, there is no established threshold for what can be considered a "national" teacher shortage. If a vacancy rate of 2% is compared with that of other professions, one could say that teaching faces relatively few vacancies.[18] Many have argued that this rate simply reflects the present state of the job market, and given the higher average pay of other occupations and other employment opportunities available to teachers, this vacancy rate is not an outlier in the overall economy. It can be counterargued, though, that teachers are more indispensable than many other jobs. The 50,000 vacant positions imply that millions of students do not have access to the classes or the quality of instruction they should have, which has implications for their learning, postsecondary choices, and eventual life outcomes.

Second, unlike many other professions, such as nursing, where there are national standards and requirements, there is no single national teacher labor market. Due to different state standards and certification requirements, teachers who are certified in one state are not automatically certified in another. As such, we do not have a single national teacher labor market but rather 50 such markets, where the movement of teachers from one state to another is rather restricted. Additionally, teachers are certified to teach in specific grades (e.g., elementary versus secondary) and with different content expertise (e.g., STEM, special education, social studies). In other words, even within a single state, the teacher labor market is not uniform across grades and content areas; instead, there are many teacher labor markets distributed across grades and content areas, and the dynamics in each of these labor markets may differ markedly. For instance, STEM teachers have many job opportunities apart from teaching, and most of these tend to pay more and offer a better working environment.[19] Special education teachers, likewise, have specialized skills that may enable them to work in non-teaching roles.[20] As a result, it is not clear how helpful it is to speak about a national teacher shortage when there is no national teacher labor market by which to fill teaching vacancies.

Complicating this picture further is the fact that teachers also have preferences for where they teach. Teachers have been shown to have a strong preference to teach at schools in geographic proximity to where they completed their student teaching, where they earned their degree, or near their hometown.[21] These preferences are individually reasoned, but collectively they present a complex scenario of unaccountable pulls affecting how schools and districts recruit and retain qualified teachers. This underscores the localized nature of the teacher labor market, implying not even a statewide teacher labor market but rather multiple teacher labor markets within a state shaped by geographical considerations and school characteristics.

A few recent studies speak to how varied teacher shortages are. For instance, in Illinois, teacher shortages have been shown to be more pronounced in rural districts, in districts serving more minority students and low-income families, and in high schools more so than in elementary schools.[22] Research in Tennessee similarly shows that looking at the state level would mask considerable variation between schools and subject areas.[23] In Washington state, researchers have examined teacher job postings and found more job postings for STEM and special education positions than elementary education positions. Moreover, schools that enroll more students of color, experience higher turnover, or are more rural tend to post more job openings than do schools with more white students, with lower turnover, or with an urban or suburban location.[24] In sum, there are wide variations in job postings and vacancies within states and between districts. There is no singular national teacher labor market; instead, all teacher labor markets are highly localized.

Conclusion

In summary, this chapter has demonstrated how teacher shortages in the United States are a complex and often poorly defined problem. We suggested that the problem is not just about the number of teachers but also about how shortage is defined. Teacher shortage should be delineated clearly into *vacancies*, where teaching positions are advertised but not filled by the start of the school year, and *underqualification*, where teachers are employed in positions for which they lack appropriate credentials or subject-matter expertise. Shortages, both vacancies and underqualification, are particularly acute in specific subjects like special education and STEM and in schools that serve economically disadvantaged students and majority-minority schools.[25] Despite concerted efforts by many organizations and researchers, the data on teacher vacancies and underqualification are still limited,[26] but being clear in how we define shortage, as either vacancy or underqualification, can help us understand where shortages are most concerning.

Acknowledging the nuances on multiple levels, we conclude this chapter by returning to the question we posed near the start: Is there a national teacher shortage? We do not think that a yes or no answer to this question matters very much. If teacher labor markets are highly localized, then there is limited use in proclaiming a "national" teacher shortage. However, when we consider vacancy and underqualification together, we find that the majority of states have as much as 10% (or more) of their teacher workforce in a state of vacancy or filled with teachers who, by each state's own standards, lack the qualification to teach in their classroom. In California, for instance, about 10% of the teacher workforce is underqualified, and in Mississippi, the vacancy rate is nearly 4% of the teacher workforce. In Florida, the situation is even more critical, with about 14% of the teacher workforce underqualified and over 3% of teaching positions vacant. This is a serious issue, and we do not want to minimize that or claim that teacher shortage is found in only a handful of states. An added complication we discuss elsewhere in this book is that the supply of new teachers has dwindled in recent years, and teacher attrition has increased substantially since the COVID-19 pandemic. In short, with vacancy and underqualification increasing over the last few years, declines in the teacher supply, and increases in teacher turnover, we need to move beyond the rhetoric of what constitutes a "national" teacher shortage or whether it is a "crisis." We need instead to focus on what we can do to fix this problem by promoting conditions that will attract a sustainable teacher workforce that can secure the educational foundations for our children's future.

The teacher shortage challenge is not simply an issue of the supply of new teachers; it is also an issue of teacher retention. We have to think about how to attract talented and racially diverse teachers in the face of obstacles such as declining enrollment in teacher preparation programs and the appeal of alternative career paths offering competitive compensation and benefits.[27] At the same time, we also have to think about breaking the cycle of teacher churn, where experienced teachers are leaving the profession and new teachers are constantly being hired to replace them. Teacher retention is the other side of the coin of teacher recruitment. The next chapter picks up on the issue of recruitment by considering the pathways of preparation by which teachers become eligible for hire.

CHAPTER 3

Where Shall They Come From?

Characterizing the Diversity of Pathways of Newly Hired Teachers

IMAGINE YOU ARE THE PRINCIPAL of a school tasked with hiring the teaching staff for the next school year. For most school leaders, this process begins months before the start of the school year. In the spring, it is common for school and district leaders to begin polling their teachers—both formally and informally—about their plans for the next school year. The overwhelming majority of teachers tend to remain in their school from one year to the next. For the others, career transitions include retirement; transferring to another school, either inside or outside the district; taking a leave of absence; or leaving teaching outright. Assessing the number of vacancies, as well as any specific subject area needs, is the critical first step in the teacher hiring process for the upcoming school year.

With an estimate of the number of vacancies, school and district leaders then embark on a lengthy process to fill vacancies, whether through teachers transferring within the district or by hiring new teachers. Schools and districts with low rates of turnover and thus few vacancies tend to be fully staffed at the start of the school year. These schools and districts are characterized by a large reserve pool of teachers as well as teachers from outside the district who transfer into schools of the district, often seeking better working conditions or higher salaries.

A high level of teacher turnover, on the other hand, places a significant burden on school and district leaders working to staff their schools. Hiring is a time-intensive activity, made all the more difficult when additional teachers resign over the summer, resulting in new positions being posted in the last weeks of summer or after the start of the school year. In addition to the disruption to students who begin the year without a permanent teacher, late hiring often results in a poor job match between teacher and school, which further contributes to a cycle of higher turnover for these schools. As elevated rates of teacher turnover, vacancies, and late hiring tend to be concentrated in schools and districts enrolling more economically disadvantaged students and students of color, teacher staffing poses yet another constraint to equity in public schooling—a point we return to at the end of this chapter.[1]

In what follows, we first describe teachers' pathways into their current role by reporting data on their main activity in the previous school year. This brief analysis illustrates two important facts about the teacher labor market: (1) that most teachers remain in their school from one year to the next and (2) that most vacancies are not filled by beginning teachers. Though we urge readers not to lose sight of these facts, we spend the bulk of the chapter discussing the different pathways into teaching, as most policies for teacher recruitment are targeted toward new teachers. Specifically, we describe the three predominant ways by which beginning teachers enter teaching: traditional university-based teacher preparation programs, alternative certification programs, and no formal preparation. We then detail the teacher reserve pool to underscore the extent to which filling vacancies is a growing problem for many schools. We conclude this chapter with a brief discussion of the teacher hiring process to highlight how schools work to fill vacancies and how this process varies across schools facing different staffing challenges.

Evidence reported in this chapter should further orient readers to one of our central arguments: namely, that it is likely to be more effective to focus on current teachers when designing policies to address shortages. At the same time, describing the varied pathways into teaching provides readers with some indication of not only the comprehensive preparation that many teachers receive but also the growing ways in which "band-aid" solutions are used to fill vacancies that do not necessarily address underqualification.

A Snapshot of Teacher Staffing

To contextualize the scenario we started with, we draw on data from the National Teacher and Principal Survey, a federally administered survey used by researchers to understand key features of the workforce of K–12 public school teachers in the United States. We report data from the two most recent surveys at the time of this book, the 2017–18 and 2020–21 school years. Figure 3.1 represents teachers' main activity during the previous school year. Note that the overwhelming majority of teachers in public schools remain in the same school from one school year to the next. In the 2017–18 school year, 86% of teachers were teaching in the same school they had the year prior. In the 2020–21 school year—the first full school year during the COVID-19 pandemic—a remarkable 91% of teachers were teaching in the same school. Data going back as far as the 1987–99 school year tell the same story, with just shy of 90% of teachers continuing in the same school from one year to the next.[2]

Among the teachers who were not working in the same school they had the year prior, most were working in another teaching position or position in the field of education. For instance, in the 2017–18 school year, 4% of teachers had transferred to a different school in the same district, 3% moved from a public school in a different district, 1% had another teaching position (i.e., teaching in a private school, preschool, or college/university), and 1% were working in the field of education but not as a teacher. Taken as a whole, these data illustrate how approximately 95% of teaching positions are filled by educators who already belong to the field. Though we spend much of this chapter focused on beginning teachers' varied pathways into the classroom, we urge readers not to lose sight of the point that most open positions that get filled

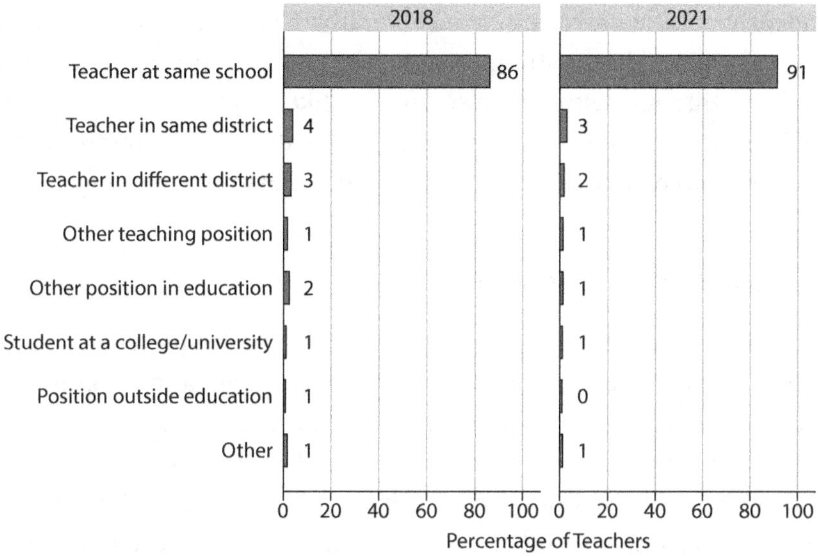

FIGURE 3.1 Public school teachers' main activity in the prior school year, for school years 2017–18 and 2020–21. *Source* of data: Authors' calculations from data published by the US Department of Education, National Center for Education Statistics, National Teacher and Principal Survey Sample restricted to full-time teachers

are not filled by new teachers. We cannot emphasize enough how retention of the existing teacher workforce is critical to reducing teacher shortages. Likely the single best way to reduce teacher shortages, we contend, is to ensure that fewer teachers are leaving teaching.[3]

The next data we share are on new teachers' preparation pathways. Figure 3.2 affirms the central role of university-based traditional preparation programs (TPPs) in the training of new teachers. Approximately 60% of public school teachers were prepared in a TPP in recent years. Teachers in these programs complete coursework and field experiences designed to meet the requirements for a teaching certificate en route to earning their bachelor's or graduate degree. Around 30% of public school teachers were prepared through an alternative certification (AC) program. These programs expedite entry into teaching by offering individuals with a bachelor's degree a way to serve as the teacher of record while completing certification requirements, including those from independent and university-based programs. Not all teachers enter from these formal routes, with approximately 10% indicating they entered teaching through neither pathway and are likely teaching as an uncertified teacher on a short-term contract. These data help to motivate the next sections on new teachers' pathways into classroom teaching.

Pathways into Teaching

The pathway into teaching can be described as both a professional and bureaucratic process.[4] Though formal teacher preparation begins in a teachers' preparation program, many teachers' career aspirations are formed during their time in K–12 schools.[5] This view of teaching is in line with the concept of *apprenticeship of observation*.[6] Unlike professional socialization in other careers, aspiring teachers enter with numerous preconceptions of what teaching entails based on their experiences as students in the classroom. Thus, professional preparation builds on pre-service teachers' preexisting knowledge, ability, skills, and mindsets to prepare them to be successful with students in the classrooms where they can expect to find themselves.[7]

There is extensive variation in the design of preparation programs.[8] Most variation in the design of TPPs is across state lines—indicating the primary role that states have in setting requirements for teacher licensure. State requirements for the design of university-based TPPs are often extensive and include everything from required courses and/or standards that must be taught within an accredited program in the state to the duration or design of pre-service teachers' clinical experience (i.e., student teaching). Even within states, there is variation in the nature and timing of requirements, particularly for traditional and alternative preparation programs. For instance, in New York, alternatively certified teachers must meet the same requirements as teachers in TPPs, but they complete coursework and licensure exams while they are teaching.[9] In Texas, however, AC programs have much more flexibility in program design.

It is also important to emphasize that, as mentioned in chapter 1, states have long tried to ensure that instituting licensure standards will mean

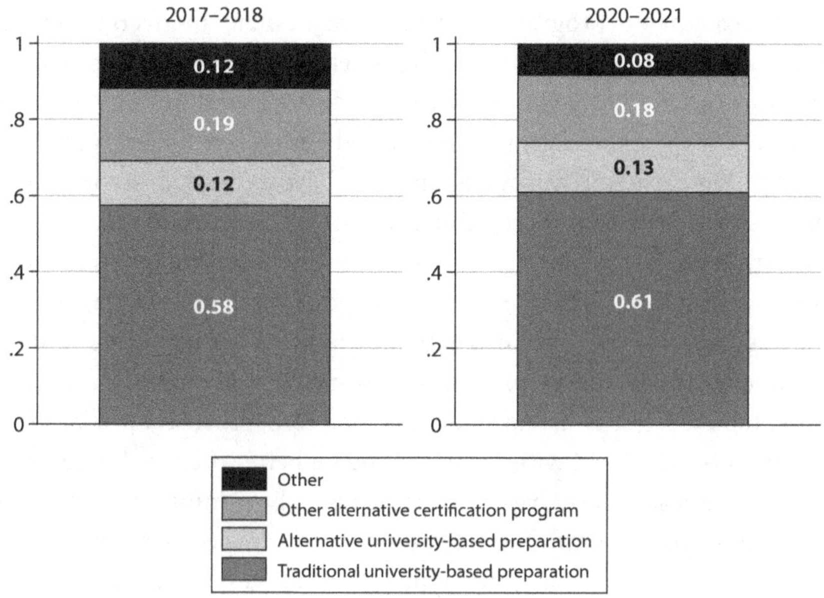

FIGURE 3.2 First-year public school teachers' main activity in the prior school year, for school years 2017–18 and 2020–21. *Source* of data: Authors' calculations from data published by the US Department of Education, National Center for Education Statistics, National Teacher and Principal Survey Sample restricted to full-time teachers

that all new teachers meet a minimum quality threshold. However noble, this goal has often been elusive. As recently as the 1999–2000 school year, as many as one in seven early-career teachers was uncertified. While uncertified teachers virtually disappeared in the wake of No Child Left Behind, some states have begun hiring uncertified teachers again.[10] In the next sections, we discuss both TPPs and ACs as well as those pathways without any formal licensure requirements.

Traditional University-Based Teacher Preparation and Teacher Supply

Traditional university-based training is the principal pathway of new teachers for most subject areas in most school districts across the country. This includes aspiring teachers in both undergraduate and postbaccalaureate programs. Though we hesitate to overgeneralize about the design of TPPs, we highlight here how a comprehensive curriculum and clinical teaching are two key features of the design of TPPs that appear to be most strongly connected with teacher shortages.

Over time, the topics covered in TPPs have expanded—reflecting a professionalized view of teaching requiring significant pre-service preparation.[11] For instance, contemporary TPP curricula often include training in subject-area knowledge, pedagogy, classroom management, curriculum development, instructional planning, data analysis, differentiation, student development, and working with families, among other topics. There is strong evidence that a comprehensive preparation program is associated with feelings of being better prepared to teach.[12] This relationship is perhaps unsurprising as beginning teachers who have undergone significant training have developed a repertoire of teaching techniques that can support their successful transition into the classroom. The improved preparedness that comes from attending a well-designed TPP is generally assumed to be a predominant factor in the elevated retention rates among traditionally prepared teachers.[13]

Another critical feature of TPPs is clinical teaching. Somewhat surprisingly, the research evidence linking clinical teaching experiences and retention writ large is not particularly strong. For instance, a National Research Council report from 2010 found no rigorous evidence showing a relationship between student teaching and retention. Since then, the number of rigorously designed studies has accumulated, with evidence showing that the benefits of clinical teaching suggests that the presence of clinical teaching alone does not improve teacher supply and retention but that key experiences need to be present in clinical teaching to have these benefits. In one study using national data, an increase in the number of weeks of student teaching had no association with teacher retention.[14] Clinical experiences in schools with supportive professional learning environments appear to be most beneficial to beginning teachers' labor market outcomes.[15] Pre-service teachers assigned to classrooms with more effective cooperating teachers report feel more prepared upon graduation and are more effective once they enter the classroom.[16] Some evidence also suggests that the presence of similar characteristics in the school where a student teacher has their clinical experience and the school where they land their job is associated with improved retention. Specifically, student teaching at the same school level and working in schools with students of similar racial demographics have both been shown to have a strong relationship with labor market stability among early-career teachers.[17] These studies suggest an important role for the effectiveness of cooperating teachers in the pre-service experience and an alignment between the environments of clinical practice and a teacher's first job for improving teacher retention.

Having described key distinguishing features of TPPs most strongly tied to new teacher recruitment and retention, we now describe in greater detail how these features relate specifically to the supply of new teachers. Though obvious perhaps, it is worth stating that many, but not all, pre-service teachers become full-time K–12 teachers. The exact rate at which pre-service teachers are hired seems to vary by local labor market conditions at the time of graduation. Specifically, fewer pre-service teachers become full-time K–12 teachers in periods of tighter labor markets. Longitudinal data from Washington state show that anywhere between 30% and close to 80% of pre-service teachers are hired the year after completing their clinical teaching. When looking out three years after completing student teaching, anywhere between 55% and 85% of graduates from TPPs are working teachers.[18] Data from a large TPP in Texas indicate that 78% of pre-service teachers become full-time classroom teachers.[19]

The rate with which pre-service teachers make this transition into full-time teaching also varies by subject area. Candidates in subject areas of greater shortage, including STEM subjects and special education, are considerably more likely to be hired than candidates with an elementary endorsement.[20] This pattern reflects a long-standing concern that colleges of education overproduce teaching candidates with an elementary education specialization and underproduce those in other subject areas.[21]

Arguably the most important and often understated way in which TPPs supply new teachers to school systems relates to their geographic proximity to school districts throughout the country. Data from the US Department of Education showed that there were 1,453 TPPs in 2019.[22] Our own analysis indicates that 82% of public schools are located within 30 miles of a TPP. As teachers tend to work closer to their hometown than do those in other professionalized occupations, geographic dispersion is a critical factor related to teacher supply and helps explain why some schools have more or less difficulty in filling vacancies.[23] For instance, in California, the proximity of TPPs and school districts is associated with a lower rate of teacher vacancy.[24]

Research from Washington state indicates that, while the location of a TPP is important for where teachers begin their career, the district in which pre-service teachers conduct their student teaching strongly influences where they start their career. More than three-quarters of teachers' first job is within 50 miles of where they completed their student teaching. Fifteen percent of pre-service teachers begin teaching in the same school in which they conducted their student teaching.[25]

Access to Traditional University-Based Teacher Preparation Programs

University-based TPPs fill a critical role in preparing a clear majority of teachers in the United States. At the same time, the core features of TPPs can limit access to teaching among students of color. For instance, clinical teaching is not only time-intensive but is also often uncompensated. For pre-service teachers of color, who work in college at disproportionately higher rates, it can be challenging to complete this central requirement.[26] Given that many TPPs disproportionately enroll white female teachers, their design often reflects the background knowledge and experiences of this group, often marginalizing pre-service teachers of color in the process.[27]

Research paints an increasingly rich portrait of a racially stratified pathway into teaching.[28] One recent study from a large TPP in Texas found that white high school seniors were only slightly more likely to express an interest in teaching than students of color when controlling for other background characteristics. Even with similar initial interest in teaching, at every juncture of the college and teacher preparation process, white applicants progressed at higher rates than applicants of color.[29] The authors note that there is no single "leak" in the pipeline toward a more diverse teacher workforce; rather, admission to college, enrollment, graduation, and completion of teacher preparation all served to limit the potential pool of teachers of color.[30]

The resulting racial disparities in the fraction of college graduates who earn a bachelor's of education is stark. One national study of college graduates showed that 9% of white graduates earned a bachelor's in education compared with 5% of Black and Latinx students.[31] Even among survey respondents who expressed an interest in teaching, stark racial disparities were observed for key teacher preparation activities. For instance, half of white graduates with an interest in teaching had entered a TTP compared with 20% of Black graduates and 28% of Latinx graduates. These findings suggest that improving access to and completion of TPPs could significantly increase the diversity of the teacher workforce. Another approach would be to expand AC programs for those interested in becoming teachers who already have bachelor's degrees but not necessarily in education.

Alternative Teacher Certification

We have explained thus far why university-based TPPs continue to be the predominant way in which teachers are prepared in the United States. Still, questions remain about whether more or different individuals would come into teaching if the credentialing of teachers were further divorced from these TPPs. This argument has been developed in a couple of different ways.

First, university-based preparation programs have never fully supplied public schools with a sufficient number of teachers to fill the vacant teaching positions not filled by current teachers. In many ways, this challenge is not the fault of TPPs themselves but of larger dynamics in the teacher labor market. For one, it is difficult to project with any reasonable certainty the teaching needs within a particular locale across all grades and subject-area expertise. Moreover, even if such projections could be accurately made, sharing this information with high school and college students with an interest in teaching is no easy pursuit.[32] Even if this information were shared with aspiring teachers, the degree to which they would respond to this information is an open question. At present, those who decide to become teachers clearly have a preference for elementary education.[33]

Broader critiques of TPPs tend to focus on the ways in which the bureaucratized nature of TPP-based teacher licensure increases the opportunity and financial costs to become a teacher, time that could be used to earn money elsewhere and money that could be invested in other ways.[34] That is to say, meeting all the milestones in a well-designed, comprehensive TPP is a significant investment of time and resources. In many states, it has become the norm for teacher preparation to take years and include the candidate earning both a bachelor's and master's degree. Despite the benefits of attending a TPP in terms of the development of specialized pedagogical and content knowledge, the question remains, At what cost to teacher supply?

Findings from several rigorous research studies support the view that more stringent licensure requirements reduce teacher supply. As licensure testing became more widespread, researchers showed that requiring a teacher test reduced the probability of majoring in education by 30%.[35] More recently, the rollout of the performance-based assessment known as the edTPA reduced enrollment in undergraduate TPPs.[36] The cost and time to complete the assessment added new burdens related to completing a TTP for a pre-service candidate. Licensure requirements appear to disproportionately deter academically talented individuals, people of color, and those interested in teaching an in-demand subject.[37] For instance, as the number of years required to become a licensed teacher increases, undergraduate students at selective institutions were less likely to take the steps to become a teacher.[38]

These varied data points suggest the potential benefit of expanding alternative entry pathways into teaching as a means to improve the supply of new teachers. Waves of federal policy have tried to incentivize the creation of innovative teacher preparation programs. For instance, one of the criteria in state applications for Race to the Top was the provision for having alternative routes to certification for teachers.[39] The

Every Student Succeeds Act allowed states to put Title II funds toward establishing teacher preparation academies. Teacher apprenticeship programs, now an allowable apprenticeship program through the Department of Labor, follow a similar playbook. At a symbolic level, these efforts have been controversial as they imply that innovation takes place outside TPPs.[40] There is, however, clear evidence to the contrary. For instance, teacher residency programs have been established as a collaboration between school districts and university-based TPPs in many cities.[41] More practically, real concerns exist regarding the extent to which AC programs will induce more prospective teachers to seek out less comprehensive (and time-intensive) preparation outside a university-based TPP.

Though the field lacks rigorous evidence on the extent to which AC programs have increased teacher supply, the increase in the number of AC teachers suggests a demand for these entry pathways.[42] Our analysis of federal Title II data from 2011–12 indicated that 29,310 individuals completed an AC program compared with 34,776 in 2021–22. This represented 22% of all individuals completing a TPP in 2021–22, a 57% increase from 2011–12. This expansion was perhaps most vivid in the states of Florida and Texas, where there is widespread availability of alternative routes into teaching and as many as half of candidates did so outside a TPP in 2021–22.[43]

Even with this expansion, differences in state licensure requirements and the range of approved AC programs result in a wide variation in both the reach and design of AC programs. The best measured distinction is whether programs are based in institutions of higher education (IHE) or are independent programs. IHE-based programs provide candidates with a bachelor's degree the opportunity to earn their teaching license without earning a second bachelor's degree. Candidates in these programs will often work as the teacher of record while completing other licensure requirements (e.g., additional coursework and a licensure exam).[44] Non-IHE-based programs are most commonly associated with selective preparation programs, such as Teach For America and TNTP's Teaching Fellows Program, focused on recruiting academically talented individuals into teaching. Other mission-driven programs focus on recruiting students in a specific subject area, students of color, or students to work in a particular community.[45] This includes a growing number of Grow Your Own programs focused on recruiting and preparing community members and people of color to become teachers. Preparation in AC programs is also increasingly taking place online, with the Teachers of Tomorrow being the largest of such programs.[46]

There is not clear evidence on the ways that different AC programs fill teaching vacancies, though compared with traditionally prepared teachers, they target schools with greater difficulties in filling vacancies.[47] As schools with hiring difficulties also enroll a disproportionate share of the country's students of color and low-income students,[48] some have questioned whether the expansion of AC programs serves to maintain long-standing teacher quality gaps among schools serving more low-income students and students of color. Others point to the ways in which mission-driven AC programs are improving access to talented and racially diverse teachers in schools whose staffing needs have never been fully met by TPPs.[49]

Our reading of this evidence is that AC programs have addressed immediate and acute staffing needs in many schools. They have also helped to improve the racial/ethnic diversity of the teacher workforce, possibly because pre-service teachers of color have not been adequately supported in TPPs.[50] Yet we are hesitant to assert that they provide a clear remedy to teacher shortage. AC teachers turn over at higher rates than traditionally certified teachers.[51] As a result, these programs may improve teacher supply in the short term, but the overall stability in the teacher labor market, and thus shortages, may be unchanged. We elaborate on this evidence in the next chapter.

It may, however, be inappropriate to compare teachers from TPPs and AC programs and more realistic to compare alternatively certified and uncertified teachers.[52] Though a traditionally prepared first-year teacher may ultimately be a better hire than an alternatively prepared teacher, that may not be the hiring choice faced by school and district administrators, who may instead be faced with hiring an uncertified teacher or a long-term substitute.

Uncertified Teachers

The hiring of uncertified teachers and long-term substitutes has been described as a "dirty little secret" of the teacher workforce.[53] Unlike alternative-route teachers who receive most of their training while serving as the teacher of record, uncertified teachers have little to no training and often have not had to fulfill other requirements, such as demonstrating subject-matter expertise or passing licensure exams. The fraction of teachers who are uncertified virtually disappeared during the early 2000s as states worked to close loopholes for long-term substitutes and emergency certification in response to the "highly qualified teacher" clause of No Child Left Behind.[54] Since the mid-2010s, though, the number of uncertified teachers has again begun to creep up. Data from the Civil Rights Data Collection showed that 1.7% of public school teachers were uncertified during the 2013–14 school year.[55] By 2017–18, 3.1% of teachers were uncertified.[56] Similar to patterns for AC teachers, the fraction of uncertified teachers is nearly four times greater in higher-poverty schools compared with lower-poverty schools.[57]

The growth of uncertified teachers has shown no signs of subsisting in the wake of the COVID-19 pandemic. In some states, relying on uncertified teachers is not merely done to fill vacancies in schools but is in fact more widespread. For instance, 19.6% of newly hired teachers in Texas in the 2021–22 school year were uncertified, with an additional 1.9% teaching with an emergency certificate.[58] Though we return to evidence on their retention in the next chapter, it is fair to say that this group of teachers can be characterized as a short-term fix to teaching vacancies.

Reserve Pool

Though many newly prepared teachers do go directly from their preparation program into teaching, many postpone entry or never enter. Delayed entrants may be waiting on a preferred school or grade level before taking their first teaching job. There are also teachers who temporarily leave teaching with the intention of returning at some point, often referred to as re-entrants. These three groups of teachers, those who do not go into teaching, those who delay doing so, and those who leave and re-enter, have come to be referred to as the *reserve pool* of teachers. Their presence in a teacher labor market is critical for school staffing, though is sometimes overlooked.[59] Of growing concern in recent years is that the reserve pool is shrinking, resulting in a smaller pool of qualified teachers to recruit from in many districts.

Though measuring the reserve pool is challenging for researchers, evidence suggests that the teacher workforce was characterized by a small reserve pool in the first decade of the 2000s. By 2012, the combination of high levels of newly credentialed teachers and slowed hiring in the wake of the Great Recession resulted in a reserve pool of an estimated 120,000 teachers. Since then, the number of newly hired teachers has far outpaced newly prepared teachers—suggesting a growing reliance on the reserve pool for teacher staffing.

National data show that the prevalence of delayed entrants continues to grow. Forty-five percent of certified teachers in 2004 began their teaching career in the same year. By 2018, the share of delayed entrants decreased by 10 percentage points.[60] Other research following graduates from TPPs into the classroom showed that the rate at which teaching candidates are hired depends, in large part, on larger labor market conditions. Specifically, slowed hiring during the Great Recession left many teaching candidates unhired in the first years after graduating. Most concerning for teacher hiring is that many of these qualified teachers did not seek out classroom teaching in subsequent years.[61]

Re-entrants are an even more important source of teacher supply than are delayed entrants. Schools heavily depend on teachers who have teaching experience but did not teach in the previous school year to staff their schools. Federal data from 2004–2012 indicate that anywhere between 37% and 49% of new hires were re-entrants.[62] The reason why school and district leaders would hire re-entrants is clear: they already have classroom experience and the necessary credentials to teach. In contrast to new teachers who often require significant mentoring and support, re-entrants have an easier transition back into teaching. Unique features of the teaching profession make re-entry more common than other professions. A uniform salary schedule and limited professional repercussions for leaving teaching temporarily have been associated with high levels of re-entry among teachers.[63] Many female teachers have been shown to leave teaching temporarily to raise their young children and then return when their children reach school age.[64] Higher salaries at the time of exit have also been shown to increase the likelihood of returning to teach.[65]

This well-established pattern of re-entry has weakened of late, raising concerns about teacher shortages. More recent data on teacher re-entry indicate that only 19% of teachers who exit return to teaching.[66] This trend is concerning not just for a depleted teacher supply, but it suggests an increasing number of teachers who spent time in the classroom and no longer want to teach. There may be a growing dissatisfaction with features of teachers' work environments. In other words, the depleted reserve pool may be a harbinger for broader shifts in the work lives of teachers where retention is a growing challenge.

Switching Schools

We began this chapter with a somewhat idealized depiction of the teacher hiring process. In reality, teacher hiring is a year-round activity for many school and district leaders, particularly those facing teacher shortages.[67] The reason is that teacher turnover does not only happen between school years, which forces principals to fill vacancies that arise during the school year.[68] Educational leaders are known to seek out referrals to teachers who may be interested in moving to their school and thus market their school to prospective teachers.[69]

The on-cycle hiring process is shaped, in large part, by district deadlines and processes.[70] Typically, the first round of the hiring cycle is reserved for internal transfers. Teacher contracts often have provisions that favor current district teachers and often include additional seniority-based transfer protections. These provisions include restrictions on involuntary transfer to other schools in the district and/or a "leg up" in voluntarily transferring to another school in the district with vacancies.

Seniority preference rules have received significant research attention given how they might contribute to more experienced teachers transferring to schools serving more socio-culturally privileged students. This pattern would result in a larger number of vacancies being filled disproportionately by new teachers and in a larger share of novice teachers remaining in underserved schools For instance, data from the Civil Rights Data Collection indicate that 17.2% of teachers in schools with a high enrollment of students of color were in their first or second year of teaching, compared with 9.1% in schools with a lower enrollment of students of color.[71] Following a number of inconclusive and conflicting studies, more recent research suggests that these provisions do contribute to inequitable teacher sorting.[72] Thus, teachers' contract provisions contribute to staffing patterns that leave some schools with more vacancies than others, thereby exacerbating shortages.

Another key feature of the teacher hiring process that shapes teacher shortages is the degree to which the process is centralized. There is variation in the extent to which school staff members have a role in teacher hiring. In some districts—particularly large urban districts—seniority-based provisions inform a highly centralized process that determines where teachers work.[73] An increasing number of districts have moved toward more decentralized hiring processes, meaning that principals and sometimes other school staff take on a larger role in teacher hiring. In such districts, hiring responsibilities are shared by district and school leaders, with some tasks still filled by the district (e.g., advertising positions and screening for eligibility) and others conducted by school staff (e.g., interviews and teaching demonstrations).[74]

Though school-based teacher hiring is still marked by significant variation from district to district—and even for schools within the same district—it may serve to reduce teacher shortages. By interacting with principals and other school staff, applicants learn about the school and can judge how well they would fit into its culture. In school-based hiring, school leaders also exercise more preference in selecting the types of candidates they are looking for. This process could result in a better match between teachers and their schools, which might reduce teacher turnover.[75]

Other features of the hiring process appear to disadvantage schools with fewer resources that enroll more low-income students and students of color. Schools often have brief hiring windows in which they can interview applicants. Following any seniority-based teacher transfers, subsequent rounds of teacher hiring are open to teachers moving in from outside the district, student teachers, teachers who have temporarily dropped out of the workforce, and possibly other teachers from within the district.[76] Cross-state mobility has also been cited as an additional factor that leads to elevated teacher shortages in historically underserved schools.[77] Teachers have been shown to move to schools serving demographically similar students to the schools they attended and to schools close to where they grew up. For a teacher workforce that disproportionately graduated from suburban high schools, this sorting has been described as a "hometown disadvantage" for many schools.[78] These teacher sorting patterns are yet another factor in explaining how teacher shortages are often not a universal phenomenon but are more acute in historically underserved urban school districts.[79]

Teacher preferences for better working conditions also affect shortages. It is often the case that teachers do seek out schools enrolling students from particular demographic backgrounds but rather seek out schools for their reputed working conditions. In particular, teachers express a strong preference for and are shown to seek out schools with administrative and disciplinary support as well as higher salaries.[80] That teachers desire to work at schools with these conditions, conditions that are difficult for an outsider to observe without having familiarity with the school, suggests that teachers rely on their social networks in making labor market decisions.[81]

Finally, organizational features of the hiring process appear to pose greater challenges to schools enrolling more low-income students and students of color. In large districts, delayed timelines in hiring have been linked with diminished candidate pools and qualified candidates accepting offers at other schools.[82] This latter point intimates a clear downside for decentralized teacher hiring systems. School leaders report that they often find themselves in competition with one another for qualified teachers, particularly those in high-need subject areas.[83]

When principals are juggling the staffing of multiple positions at the same time—an occurrence much more common in underserved schools—conducting a timely hiring process is clearly difficult.

This discussion of teacher hiring helps drive home the central arguments of our book. Teacher shortages are not a universal problem faced by all schools. A nonnegligible share of schools have few vacancies and clear district processes by which candidates are recruited, screened, and hired. For other schools, including many enrolling large concentrations of students of color and students living in poverty, leaders need to fill a large number of vacancies, have fewer applicants, and struggle to fill all vacancies by the start of the school year. When vacancies are filled, the candidate is more likely to be a beginning teacher with support and development needs. In summary, numerous compounding challenges present obstacles to staffing underserved schools each year.

Conclusion

Teacher shortages are often understood as being caused by a short supply of new teachers entering the profession. Findings we presented early in the chapter, however, illustrated that only a small share of vacant teaching positions are filled by beginning teachers. More commonly, the new hires come from the reserve pool or switch from another school, so the reserve pool provides a critical supply of teachers in any given school year. This labor mobility in teaching brings its own challenges for school systems. There is constant uncertainty about how many teachers in the reserve pool will choose to enter or re-enter teaching. In addition, there is growing evidence that the reserve pool is shrinking, which is due in part to a dissatisfaction with teaching that makes entering or re-entering teaching less attractive—a troubling sign possibly reflecting a growing dissatisfaction with features of teachers' work environment. A smaller reserve pool constrains the number of qualified and experienced applicants vying for open positions, thus limiting the quality of newly hired teachers.

When teachers switch schools, the redistribution raises other challenges for school systems. Working within a single salary schedule, teachers tend not to be differentially compensated for working in different schools, even though some schools may have less favorable work environments. One way that more experienced teachers improve their working conditions is by switching to a school with a better work environment. The consequence is that many teachers work in schools with more challenging working conditions and with fewer veteran teachers to serve as mentors—a pattern that can contribute to a revolving door for new teachers, which we describe in the next chapter.

Even though many vacant teaching positions are filled by current teachers or those in the reserve pool, understanding the overall labor supply for teaching is still important. The total number of entrants and completers of teacher preparation declined over the 2010s, and fewer aspiring teachers graduated from university-based TPPs. Given that these programs helped to create a career model of teaching over the course of the twentieth century, the consequences of this decline are only beginning to be assessed. In the next chapter, we explore how the features of teachers' preparation not only shape their career retention but also affect a suite of other school conditions and policies.

CHAPTER 4

The Revolving Door Keeps Spinning

Describing Teacher Turnover

IMAGINE A TEACHER who has been teaching computer science for a couple of years at the high school she attended, but she has been wondering if it is time for her to switch jobs. She has deep roots in the community and loves teaching, but there are several things that have her questioning whether she wants to remain a teacher for the long haul. Her salary is not commensurate with her skill set, she has only a couple of free periods a week to prepare her lesson plans or meet with students, and her principal visits her classroom only sporadically and does not seem to appreciate what she is trying to accomplish with her students. On top of all that, the incoming superintendent has promised to launch a "rigorous" new curriculum, scripted to the minute every single day, which is being trumpeted as greatly improving student learning. For these reasons, she is considering leaving at the end of the school year or perhaps giving teaching another year before she tries a different job.

There are many reasons why teachers leave their school, whether to teach somewhere else or to leave the profession altogether. All the movement of teachers going from one school to another or exiting the profession, as well as that of new teachers starting their career, creates flux in the teacher labor market that has serious implications for student learning, access, and equity. If the one teacher qualified to teach a course leaves a school, students may find themselves unable to take the class they want. Teacher turnover negatively affects student achievement whenever a school cannot find a replacement or has to hire someone without the training or expertise needed.[1] What is more, the cost to replace a single teacher is a substantial amount when some districts may spend from $10,000 to $17,000 to replace a teacher who leaves.[2]

Complicating this issue further, teacher turnover is not uniform across schools and districts. Teachers tend to move away from schools that have fewer resources and more demanding working conditions and that serve larger shares of low-income students and students of color and toward better-resourced schools and districts. Moreover, highly effective teachers and fully credentialed teachers tend to prefer to work in more advantaged schools.[3] This type of movement (i.e., nonrandom sorting of teachers across schools) creates situations where some schools have difficulty attracting and retaining teachers while other schools have a surplus of high-quality teachers and applicants (what researchers refer to as *inequitable distributions of teacher effectiveness*). In fact, research finds that the most disadvantaged schools are the hardest to staff and are more likely to be staffed by teachers with below-average effectiveness or lacking certification.[4]

Since attrition is a key contributor to the overall number of teacher vacancies, scholars have devoted much time to studying what factors (sometimes known as *correlates*) are associated with teacher mobility. Due to the large literature in this area, we leverage our prior work that systematically examined the empirical literature on teacher turnover.[5] After examining more than 25,000 scholarly articles on this topic, we found three primary categories that influence whether teachers stay at or leave their current school—(1) personal factors, (2) school factors, and (3) external factors—which are summarized in figure 4.1.

Personal factors are the characteristics of the teachers themselves. These can be subdivided into teachers' background characteristics (e.g., age, gender, race/ethnicity) and their qualifications (e.g., teaching experience or content specialty such as special education). School factors

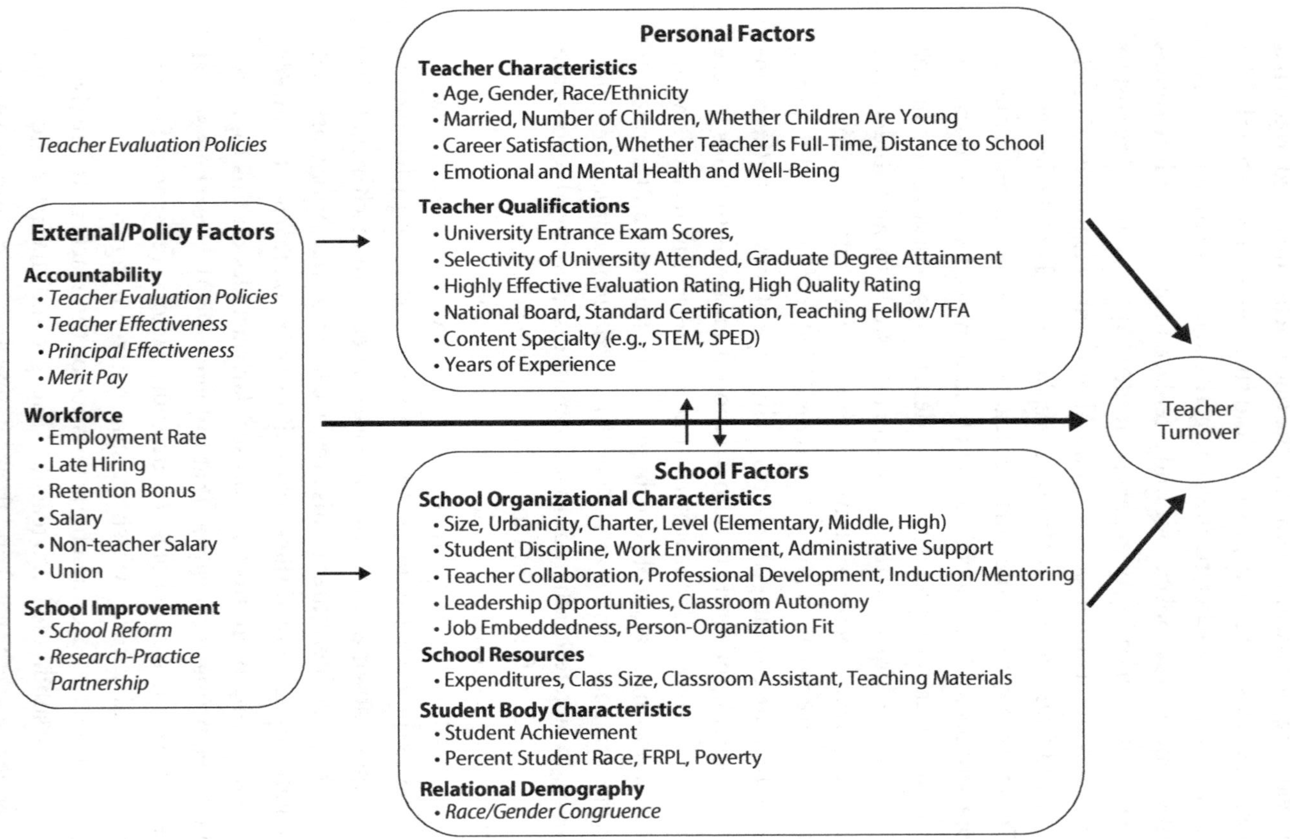

FIGURE 4.1 Conceptual framework for teacher turnover. FRPL = free or reduced-priced lunch; SPED = special education; STEM = science, technology, engineering, and mathematics; TFA = Teach For America

relate to teachers' work environments, with subcategories for school organization (e.g., school urbanicity, administrative support), school resources (e.g., class size, teaching materials), student body characteristics (e.g., student achievement, percentage of students with free or reduced-price lunch), and relational demography (e.g., race/gender match between teachers and administrators). External factors are conditions beyond a school's control that potentially affect teachers. These include the subcategories of accountability (e.g., teacher evaluation policies), workforce (e.g., employment rate or salary), and school improvement (e.g., school reform or research-practice partnership). Figure 4.1 illustrates how these factors interact with one another to influence teacher turnover.

In the sections that follow, we discuss how the factors in these categories are associated with teacher attrition. We provide both a narrative description of these relationships as well as a quantitative synthesis in tables 4.1, 4.2, and 4.3 (which feature findings from our prior meta-analysis on this topic). Some of these findings are commonsensical, but it is important to know that they are empirically verified across high-quality studies in the field. At the same time, we point out that many of the correlates of teacher attrition cannot be controlled by random assignment; thus, for most factors we discuss, whether they cause turnover cannot be determined with confidence. When the evidence is more rigorous, we note this in our interpretation of the findings. We also present findings that may not seem intuitive or have changed over time to illustrate how teacher turnover is not static and does, in many ways, reflect changes at the societal level.

Even though one of the overarching goals of this book is to describe the conditions that contribute to teacher retention and to propose how policies and practices can be leveraged to retain teachers, the focus of this chapter is on the factors that are linked to teacher turnover and the groups of teachers prone to leave teaching. For instance, early-career teachers, STEM teachers, and special education teachers are more at risk of turning over, sometimes moving to another school with better working conditions or pay and other times leaving the profession altogether. If we are to build school systems better at retaining teachers, these systems will need to reach groups of teachers that tend to leave at elevated rates. Because ending teacher shortages requires both systemic changes and targeted approaches, it is important to recognize when targeted interventions are necessary and for whom. Knowing this, we focus below on specific types of teachers more at risk of leaving the classroom, and when and where we can, we highlight conditions and factors that contribute to teacher retention.

Personal Factors Relating to Turnover

Teacher Background Characteristics

In the subcategory of background characteristics, we consider the variables of teachers' age, gender, and race/ethnicity and how these correlate with teacher turnover (table 4.1, panel A). To start, with respect to age, young teachers who leave the profession tend to do so within the first few years of teaching.[6] Conversely, older teachers are less likely to turn over than younger teachers.[7] This pattern is not surprising as young folks are testing the water to see if teaching is the right career for them, as many do in other fields who decide to switch careers early on.[8]

Teacher gender appears unrelated to average turnover rates, though this general pattern may overlook important changes over the last few decades and over the course of teachers' personal and professional lives. Older studies suggested that female teachers are more likely to leave teaching.[9] However, more recent studies indicate that this may have changed as female teachers are not more or less likely to leave than male teachers.[10] This shift may reflect broader economic changes and how women are navigating childbearing in their career.[11] To this point, married teachers are not more likely to leave teaching than non-married teachers.[12] Some research indicates that teachers with young kids to care for are also not more likely to leave teaching.[13] Other studies show that women teachers with young children exit teaching at higher rates, though often only temporarily until their children are of elementary school age.[14] In short, the pattern of how younger and older teachers, male and female teachers, and married teachers and teachers with children leave the profession has changed over time, possibly reflecting changes to economic conditions and social norms.

In terms of race/ethnicity, the most recent federal data show that, on average, teachers of color turn over at higher rates than white teachers (19% versus 15%).[15] After accounting for differences in the characteristics of schools where teachers of color and white teachers work, teachers of color turn over at *lower* rates than white teachers. This finding may be explained by sorting in the teacher labor market, whereby teachers of color are more likely to work in schools with more challenging working conditions, that is, schools where *all teachers* turn over at higher rates.[16] In addition, significant qualitative evidence has shown the personal and professional challenges faced by teachers of color, including exclusion from school decision-making and feeling disconnected from their colleagues.[17]

Next, we consider the extent to which full-time teaching status, proximity of the school to a teacher's hometown, commuting time, and job attitudes (i.e., job satisfaction, burnout, job fit) are related to teacher mobility. First, full-time teachers are, unsurprisingly, more likely to stay teaching compared with part-time teachers.[18] It makes intuitive sense that people who have full-time jobs are more likely to stay than are those who work part-time. Geographical proximity also seems to matter, whether in terms of teachers' proximity to where they grew up or their commuting time. In one of our studies, teachers who grew up in the district where they teach were found to be 25% less likely to turn over in their first year than teachers from outside the district.[19] As the commute time between where teachers live and where they teach decreases, the more likely they are to stay in their current job.[20]

Also, teachers who are more satisfied or less burned out with their teaching career are more likely to stay than those who are less satisfied, more burned out, or report worse fit with their school or job.[21] When teachers who have left are asked why, dissatisfaction with testing, accountability pressures, and other aspects of their job are the most cited.[22]

For these teacher characteristics and job attitudes, we cannot underscore enough that these factors are not determinative. In some ways,

TABLE 4.1 Personal factors as correlates of teacher turnover

		Main effect estimates					
Factor	No. of studies	Odds ratio	Logged odds ratio	Standard error	Lower bound	Upper bound	*p*
Panel A: Teacher Characteristics							
Age (continuous)	10	0.948	−0.054	0.030	−0.113	0.005	0.072
Age (>28)	9	0.698	−0.359	0.189	−0.729	0.011	0.057
Male	37	1.023	0.023	0.036	−0.047	0.093	0.523
Black	14	1.080	0.077	0.320	−0.551	0.704	0.811
Hispanic	11	0.473	−0.749	0.176	−1.095	−0.404	<0.001
Non-White	12	0.842	−0.172	0.087	−0.342	−0.002	0.048
Married	4	1.091	0.087	0.050	−0.012	0.186	0.084
Number of children	1†	0.379	−0.971	0.294	−1.548	−0.394	0.001
Young child	2	0.561	−0.578	0.154	−0.880	−0.275	<0.001
Career satisfaction	7	0.847	−0.167	0.056	−0.276	−0.057	0.003
Full-time teaching	7	0.616	−0.485	0.123	−0.725	−0.244	<0.001
Distance to school	1†	1.014	0.014	0.004	0.006	0.022	<0.001

Panel B: Teacher Qualifications

Ability (test scores)	5	1.118	0.112	0.069	-0.024	0.247	0.105
School selectivity	5	1.108	0.103	0.130	-0.152	0.358	0.429
Grad. (PhD v. none)	17	1.047	0.046	0.094	-0.138	0.230	0.623
Grad. (MA/PhD v. BA)	4	0.929	-0.073	0.151	-0.369	0.222	0.627
National Board	1	0.548	-0.602	0.453	-1.489	0.286	0.184
Teaching Fellow / TFA	2	1.017	0.017	1.009	-1.960	1.994	0.987
High quality rating	2	0.932	-0.070	0.354	-0.763	0.623	0.843
Internship	1†	0.459	-0.779	0.395	-1.553	-0.006	0.048
Standard certification	16	0.526	-0.643	0.227	-1.087	-0.199	0.005
Specialty (STEM)	12	1.087	0.083	0.052	-0.019	0.185	0.111
Specialty (special ed)	6	1.099	0.094	0.061	-0.025	0.214	0.121
Specialty (other)	2	1.353	0.302	0.463	-0.606	1.210	0.514
Experience (continuous)	10	0.996	-0.004	0.017	-0.037	0.030	0.834
Experience (<3)	13	1.542	0.433	0.097	0.243	0.623	<0.001

NOTE: Assumed correlations between multiple within-study outcomes is 0.5. † denotes a single study estimate, not meta-analytic results. TFA = Teach For America; STEM = science, technology, engineering, and math.

these descriptive findings reassure us that the teacher labor market is not so different from that of other professions and has been changing over time in ways that are commensurate with other societal changes. We highlight the differences for personal factors as they are often important first places for state and local educational leaders to look if sharp differences in turnover emerge according to demographic characteristics. For instance, if turnover is higher among female teachers or teachers of color, we hope this evidence offers some reason why these patterns exist as the basis for possible improvements. Similarly, districts and states looking to increase retention could think about ways to decrease teacher burnout, improve job fit, and increase job satisfaction. In chapter 6 we return to the ways in which efforts to improve retention increasingly need to be customized to the distinctive needs of teacher subpopulations.

Teacher Qualifications and Effectiveness

In this section, we examine the evidence on how teacher qualifications, broadly defined, are associated with teacher turnover (table 4.1, panel B). We summarize the research on teaching experience, academic ability (as measured by college entrance test scores or test scores on licensure exams), and advanced degree attainment. Beyond examining whether teachers have standard certification or in their specialty (e.g., STEM), we also look at teacher academic ability, selectivity of their undergraduate degree, having a graduate degree, National Board certification, and others. These factors matter because they have implications for individuals' and organizations' investment that may not translate to teacher retention.

To start, teachers with more teaching experience are much more likely to stay at any given time compared with teachers in their first three years of teaching.[23] This pattern is often summarized by the oft-mentioned statistic that half of teachers will quit their job in their first five years.[24] More recent research has questioned the veracity of this statistic but still points to extremely high levels of new teacher turnover. Our longitudinal study of new teacher turnover in North Carolina showed that 62% of new teachers had turned over at their first school by the end of their third year of teaching. This high turnover rate includes 33% of teachers who left teaching in the state in their first three years of teaching. Of particular concern for school and district administrators is the extremely high turnover rate in teachers' first year, with our analysis showing that one in three new teachers turned over in their first year. These findings strongly suggest the need to provide substantial supports and encouragement for teachers who are beginning their teaching career. If teachers survive, or better yet thrive, in their first three years of teaching, they are likely to stay for the long run. Still, even among new teachers, there is tremendous variation in turnover rates across entry pathways, schools, and districts.

Murnane and coauthors' seminal book on the teacher workforce from more than three decades ago summarized the emerging view that schools were not keeping their most academically talented teachers. Since then, research has accumulated evidence supporting the view that teachers with higher scores on college entrance and licensure exams are more likely to turn over, as was confirmed by our meta-analysis.[25] Similarly, teachers who attended more competitive colleges are more likely to leave teaching than those who attended less competitive colleges.[26] These findings likely reflect the fact that teachers with higher academic ability or who attended more selective colleges have more job opportunities outside teaching than do their counterparts.

In terms of having a graduate degree (master or doctoral), the findings are fairly mixed; some studies find that teachers with graduate degrees are more likely to stay relative to those with only undergraduate degrees, whereas some studies find the opposite.[27] Similarly, studies show mixed results for being highly qualified as defined by No Child Left Behind or by having internship experience.[28] There is a lack of consistent findings to show that being highly qualified or having internship experience prior to teaching would result in higher teacher retention. In other words, existing studies do not provide convincing evidence for correlations between graduate degrees, being highly qualified, or internship experience and teacher turnover.

Among teacher qualifications, certification status has arguably been of most interest to policymakers as having standard certification has come to indicate the completion of a comprehensive teacher preparation program. As states have a significant bearing on certification's requirements—to be discussed in chapter 5—this is one potent way in which state policymakers can shape both the supply of teachers and their retention. Studies consistently find that teachers with a regular or standard license to teach are much more likely to stay than are those without certification or with emergency/provisional license certification.[29]

Less clear is why regularly certified teachers turn over at lower rates. Some contend that teachers who have obtained standard licensure are more committed to their career than their counterparts who are either testing the water or have obtained emergency certification to teach for a short spell. For others, licensure sets a floor for teaching quality, and new teachers who enter the classroom after completing a comprehensive preparation begin teaching with a set of instructional skills and curricular resources that facilitate a smooth transition into teaching. As teachers who leave are most likely to leave in their first few years, having these skills coming in is likely a contributor to the lower turnover rates of teachers with a standard certification. Other benefits of a comprehensive university-based preparation that leads to a standard license are more understated. Pre-service teachers begin to develop their professional identity as a teacher, likely making it more difficult down the road to envision another career. These pre-service experiences also build teachers professional network, a network that can help them find a first teaching position where they are a good fit with the school culture.

Even among teachers with standard licenses, however, some types of teachers are more difficult to retain than others. Specifically, STEM teachers are often more likely to leave than non-STEM teachers.[30] This is even more pronounced for STEM teachers in high-needs schools.[31] This difficulty in retaining STEM teachers owes partly to the fact that they have more opportunities apart from teaching than do their peers. As STEM fields are growing and have constant demand for labor, STEM teachers are able to leave for better-paying jobs with greater benefits and less stress than the teaching profession. Due in part to this frequent turnover of STEM teachers, there has been a constant STEM teacher shortage in the United States over the last several years.[32] Prior research has shown that STEM teachers are particularly responsive to both changes in salary and working conditions. For instance, Ingersoll and May found that working conditions, such as the leadership of a principal, contributed to the retention of science and math teachers and that, for science teachers, a $10,000 increase was associated with a substantial reduction (15%) in the odds of teacher turnover.[13] In sum, while it is difficult to retain STEM teachers, particularly effective ones and those working in high-needs schools, we do have evidence of remedies that could be implemented to retain them.

Another type of teacher that is difficult to retain is special education teachers. Research has found that special education teachers are particularly difficult to retain and that there are many reasons for this, such as the heavy workload, poor working conditions, and low salary, which can drive them out of the teacher workforce.[33] Similar to STEM teachers, there is a persistent shortage of special education teachers.[34] Researchers increasingly emphasize that the outsized expectations placed on special educators often exceed their capacity and the level of support they receive. This view is supported by a growing awareness among researchers that all teachers face a variety of job demands but that some have developed better instructional resources to address these demands, whether that comes from a comprehensive pre-service preparation, high-quality professional development and coaching, or support from their principal or peers.

What is especially disconcerting is the dire need for more special education teachers of color.[35] This need stems in part from special education teachers of color being asked to take on additional responsibilities, such as translating for families or managing students of color who are not even in their class.[36]

A natural reaction that some commentators have to teacher turnover is to worry less when the least effective teachers are the ones turning over. Perhaps the teachers who are leaving are not strong instructors, and they either decide that teaching is not for them or are counseled to go by their administrators. Less effective teachers have generally been found to turn over at higher rates than more effective teachers, as measured by teacher value-added and teacher observation scores. The turnover of less effective teachers includes higher rates of exiting teaching as well as transferring to other schools.[37] Though the elevated attrition rates may be less detrimental when schools are able to find replacement teachers, this last finding suggests that less effective teachers are churning through public schools.

In sum, the relationship between teacher qualifications and turnover is complex and requires targeted decision-making. What is clear, though, is that certain types of teachers, namely, STEM and special education, are more likely to turn over. Due to the higher turnover rates and shortages for STEM and special education teachers, we revisit these two groups later in the chapter. In the next section, we turn to school factors that have been empirically examined with respect to teacher turnover.

School Factors Related to Teacher Turnover

School Organizational Characteristics

Much of the recent research on teacher retention has considered what school organizational characteristics may be leveraged to positively impact the teacher workforce (table 4.2, panel A). Below we consider both characteristics that describe the school environment in which teachers work and the teacher working conditions related to their turnover. The overarching finding from this body of research is that teachers are much more likely to turn over at schools with challenging working conditions. Said differently, teachers are more likely to stay in schools with supportive working conditions.

Recent studies tend to find that general features of the school such as its grade levels or size are not highly correlated with teacher mobility. For instance, school size seems to be unrelated to teacher turnover.[38] High school and middle school teachers may be slightly more likely to leave teaching than elementary school teachers, although some studies have found mixed results.[39]

That said, teacher turnover is elevated in some school contexts. Even though there has been a lot of discussion about teacher shortages in public school, it is not always recognized that the vast majority of public school teachers stay in their schools from year to year. In comparison, charter school teachers are more likely to leave their school or leave the teaching profession than are public school teachers.[40] This in part reflects the type of teachers who select to work in charter schools and the charter school environment itself.[41] Though teacher turnover does not appear to vary to a large degree by urbanicity,[42] schools located in remote rural areas experience high levels of turnover.

In terms of other conditions of the schools where teachers work, teachers are more likely to stay in schools with fewer student disciplinary problems, including schools with a lower level of threats to teachers or teacher victimization.[43] Similarly, teachers are also more likely to stay in schools with better facilities and in schools where teachers have stable teaching assignments, such as having teaching the subjects/courses from year to year.[44]

In terms of teacher autonomy and leadership, teachers with higher classroom autonomy are more likely to stay than are those without it, as they can exercise their professional discretion.[45] Some work finds, however, that teacher-reported high levels of teacher leadership and influence at a school are associated with more likelihood of leaving.[46] At the same time, some studies have shown that teachers who participate in a teacher leadership program or are given the opportunity to take on more responsibilities and leadership may be more likely to remain in the classroom.[47] In short, while greater teacher autonomy seems to be associated with less turnover, the literature is fairly mixed in explaining how teachers' participation in leadership contributes to retention.

On the other hand, the research on administrative support suggests that having it is critical for retaining teachers. Across more than a dozen studies, teachers are more likely to stay in schools with stronger administrative support than their counterparts in schools with weaker administrative support.[48] Administrative support can assume several different forms, including taking a proactive approach to support novice teachers, being committed to providing professional

TABLE 4.2 School factors as correlates of teacher turnover

		Main effect estimates					
Factor	No. of studies	Odds ratio	Logged odds ratio	Standard error	Lower bound	Upper bound	*p*
Panel A: School Organizational Characteristics							
School size	10	1.001	0.001	0.002	-0.003	0.004	0.792
Urban	9	1.059	0.058	0.090	-0.118	0.233	0.521
High school v. elem.	4	1.312	0.272	0.199	-0.119	0.662	0.172
Middle school v. elem.	4	1.505	0.409	0.144	0.126	0.691	0.005
Secondary v. elem.	7	1.462	0.380	0.165	0.057	0.702	0.021
Charter v. trad. public	2	1.983	0.685	0.167	0.358	1.011	<0.001
Private v. trad. public	2	1.584	0.460	0.428	-0.380	1.299	0.283
Student discipl. problem	4	1.186	0.170	0.105	-0.035	0.375	0.103
Better work environ.	5	0.557	-0.585	0.271	-1.116	-0.054	0.031
Administrative support	13	0.796	-0.229	0.061	-0.348	-0.110	<0.001
Teacher collaborations	5	0.888	-0.119	0.090	-0.295	0.057	0.186
Teacher leadership	4	1.022	0.022	0.099	-0.172	0.216	0.824
Professional develop.	3	0.838	-0.176	0.077	-0.327	-0.026	0.022
Induction/mentoring	11	0.767	-0.265	0.051	-0.365	-0.166	<0.001
Classroom autonomy	5	0.959	-0.041	0.078	-0.194	0.111	0.594

Panel B: School Resources							
Class size	6	1.018	0.018	0.013	−0.008	0.043	0.184
Classroom assistant	2	0.933	−0.069	0.104	−0.273	0.134	0.504
Teaching materials	2	0.845	−0.168	0.062	−0.290	−0.046	0.007
Panel C: Student Body Characteristics							
Student achievement	10	0.901	−0.105	0.020	−0.144	−0.065	<0.001
Percent Black	6	1.004	0.004	0.003	−0.002	0.010	0.161
Percent Hispanic	4	1.005	0.005	0.005	−0.004	0.015	0.290
Percent minority	13	1.003	0.003	0.004	−0.005	0.011	0.492
Percent FRPL	13	1.006	0.006	0.004	−0.002	0.013	0.153
Poverty	4	1.019	0.019	0.072	−0.122	0.161	0.791
Percent with enhanced support†	5	0.999	−0.001	0.009	−0.019	0.018	0.945
Panel D: Relational Demography							
Race/gender congruence	2	0.545	−0.607	0.786	−2.147	0.933	0.440

NOTE: Assumed correlations between multiple within-study outcomes is 0.5. † enhanced support includes an individualized education plan or limited English proficiency. FRPL = free or reduced-price lunch.

growth for teachers, furnishing consistent curricular support or being encouraging toward teachers, and helping to address student disciplinary issues.[49] In all, rigorous work has shown that better administrative support benefits teacher retention.[50]

Novice teachers who participate in teacher induction and/or mentoring are more likely to stay than those without these experiences.[51] Despite the preponderance of evidence supporting this conclusion, we must mention that two large-scale experimental studies of mentoring and induction showed no consistent evidence in favor of first-year teacher retention.[52] This null result may stem from the fact that new teachers seek out mentors regardless of whether they are formally assigned one, but it is important to make a caveat when interpreting this body of evidence. Some rigorous evidence suggests that the benefits of mentoring to retention are more pronounced for teachers who have mentors who work in the same school and also receive high-quality professional development.[53]

Overall, we have consistent evidence that many school organizational characteristics are highly associated with teacher retention. With the right approach and implementation, many of them could be leveraged to reduce turnover. Specifically, student disciplinary problems, administrative support, professional development and induction/mentoring for beginning teachers, and teacher autonomy may all be changed to improve teacher working conditions and increase teacher retention. We want to note that researchers have been able to measure only a small set of school working conditions, but given the wealth of evidence published at this point, they seem particularly impactful with respect to retaining teachers.

School Resources, Student Body Characteristics, and Relational Demography

Next, we examine how school resources, student body characteristics, and relational demography are related to teacher turnover. A substantial amount of scholarship has been devoted to examining how these important factors may influence how teachers decide their career path.

While we know a lot about how school resources are related to student achievement, the evidence is less clear on how school resources are related to teacher mobility. Indeed, the findings on this relationship are mixed.[54] Reducing class size or providing classroom assistants is not highly related to teacher turnover.[55] The only resource for which we have some consistent evidence in favor of retention is the sufficient provision of teaching materials to teachers.[56] In other words, making sure that teachers have sufficient teaching supplies contributes to the positive working conditions that may induce them to stay in the classroom; teachers are more likely to stay if they do not have to spend their time and meager salary buying materials just to be able to teach their students.

In terms of how student body characteristics are related to teacher turnover, we have substantially more evidence. Descriptive data show that turnover tends to be highest in lower-achieving schools, schools with more students living in poverty, and schools enrolling more historically underrepresented minorities. The most recent federal data indicate that, on average, 12% of teachers turn over annually from the schools with the lowest poverty compared with 22% from schools with the highest poverty.[57] We also have consistent evidence showing that teachers are less likely to leave schools with higher student achievement.[58] This holds true when we compare average student test scores with teacher turnover or when we compare high-performing schools and low-performing ones: teachers tend to stay in schools where students perform well. Stated differently, low-performing schools have a difficult time holding on to their teachers, which does not bode well for an equitable education system. Related to this point, teachers in high-minority schools are more likely to leave the profession than are those in low-minority schools.[59] These findings indicate that teachers leave low-performing schools at higher rates, a pattern attributed to the challenging working conditions in these schools serving more students who are traditionally disadvantaged. This type of churn is detrimental to students as well as schools.

The reasons for this pattern are complex and are important to unpack in some detail, as they speak to how broader inequities in the

American public school system contribute to an elevated turnover in schools serving more low-income students and students of color. Long-standing patterns of school segregation result in a growing subset of schools with concentrated poverty. In such schools, the lack of a robust social safety net is apparent in the lives of students. Many students living in poverty come to school with acute needs related to food insecurity and access to health care.[60] Though state and federal funding helps to address some student needs (e.g., through school meals), it is often insufficient. As an example, school psychologists on staff are in short supply in many school districts, which leaves schools ill equipped to address students' mental health, behavioral issues, and academic needs. As a result, students living in poverty often enter the classroom with unmet needs that can hinder their learning.

These systematic patterns are compounded by more granular features of the teacher labor market. First, teachers have been shown to have a strong preference for working close to where they grew up.[61] On its own, this sorting may be innocuous. Yet, when combined with lower average educational attainment for those living in higher-poverty districts, teachers' preference to work near where they grew up can result in shortages in higher-poverty districts. Moreover, when teachers move schools, they tend to move from lower-performing schools enrolling more poor students to higher-performing, more affluent schools. For instance, Feng and Sass found that when teachers moved within school districts, their new school had an average of 8% fewer students eligible for free or reduced-price lunch (52% versus 44%).[62] Such schools not only tend to have more teacher vacancies to be filled annually, but their vacancies are disproportionately filled by underprepared beginning teachers—teachers who, as we saw in the section on personal factors, turn over at comparatively higher rates.

A relatively recent line of inquiry in the literature of the teacher turnover is that of relational demography. This research finds that the demographics of the school do not alone affect teacher mobility; rather, the match between teachers, their students, and their administrators matters as well.[63] The idea behind relational demography is that similarity between a teacher and others at the school with respect to gender and race/ethnicity can affect their attitudes and behaviors.[64] Research suggests that there are positive outcomes for students of color when there is a student-teacher race match, with no detrimental effect to white students.[65] Is there evidence for teacher retention when there is teacher-principal demographic congruence? We do have some consistent, growing evidence in support of this. For instance, teachers are more likely to stay when they are of the same race as the principal, and to a lesser extent, teachers are also more likely to stay when they are of the same gender as the principal.[66] This is a promising area of inquiry in need of further study as it has implications for both teacher mobility and educational equity.

External and Policy Factors Related to Teacher Turnover

To this point in the chapter, we have focused on the personal and school factors most strongly associated with teacher turnover. Among education researchers, there is a greater understanding of how these types of factors predict teacher mobility compared with external policy factors that are often outside the control of teachers and school administrators. That said, there is a growing recognition that state and federal policies also shape teacher satisfaction, burnout, and retention. In this section, we discuss how accountability and compensation policies affect teacher turnover, emphasizing the areas in which research findings have not always aligned with public perception.

Accountability

Beginning with the passage of No Child Left Behind (NCLB) in 2001, the federal government has taken a much more active role in educational governance. Accountability policies, either for schools or individual teachers, have been the primary policy tool used by the federal government. When discussing accountability policies, we acknowledge that they include a mix of policies directly aimed at teachers (e.g., NCLB's highly qualified teacher clause) and general accountability policies aimed at improving schools that may affect teachers' work in both intended or unintended ways. There was concern that these federal policies would reshape teachers' work lives in ways that would drive them out of the profession. Media accounts of NCLB and RTTT (Race to the Top) often claimed that they made teaching less fulfilling. Yet rigorous evaluations of NCLB and RTTT have found that these federal initiatives have had small to minimal effects on many of the factors driving teacher mobility, such as autonomy and satisfaction, and turnover itself.[67] Specifically, Sun and colleagues found that there was a slight increase in teacher attrition under NCLB in the early years but a slight decrease in later years, yet these results were not statistically significant at the conventional threshold. We are aware of only one other study that provided some suggestive evidence that Black teachers were slightly more likely to stay under NCLB's subgroup accountability.[68]

RTTT was also a driver of expanded teacher evaluation reform. While there are some concerns that teacher evaluation may have negative effects on teacher retention, this has not affirmed by empirical research (table 4.3, panel A). In fact, contrary to these concerns, rigorous research has provided evidence that teachers who receive high-stakes evaluations are not more likely to leave teaching than are those who are not evaluated, though this pattern varies by the measured quality of the teacher.[69] Surprisingly, teachers, on average, are more likely to stay when they are evaluated.[70] Moreover, teachers who receive a substantial increase to their accountability score (i.e., a *positive shock*) are more likely to stay, while teachers who receive a substantial decrease (i.e., a *negative shock*) are more likely to leave.[71] In short, the evidence does not suggest that teacher evaluation necessarily makes teachers want to leave. On the contrary, teachers can learn what they do well and what they can improve, and that possibility for growth and improvement may lead to an increase in self-efficacy and a decrease in turnover.

Overall, the existing evidence suggests that accountability practices do not systematically or automatically increase teacher turnover. That said, there may be other unintended negative consequences for evaluation measures,[72] including those related to other antecedents of teacher turnover (e.g., perceived autonomy).

TABLE 4.3 External/policy factors as correlates of teacher turnover

		Main effect estimates					
Factor	No. of studies	Odds ratio	Logged odds ratio	Standard error	Lower bound	Upper bound	p
Panel A: Accountability							
Teacher evaluation	5	0.947	-0.054	0.027	-0.106	-0.002	0.041
Teacher eff. score	7	0.964	-0.037	0.021	-0.078	0.004	0.079
Principal eff. score	3	0.710	-0.342	0.108	-0.553	-0.131	0.001
Merit pay	3	0.784	-0.243	0.099	-0.436	-0.049	0.014
Merit pay (lin. prob.)	10	*	-0.016	0.007	-0.029	-0.003	0.016
Panel B: Workforce							
Employment rate	1†	0.969	-0.032	0.014	-0.059	-0.005	0.022
Late hiring	1†	1.781	0.577	0.124	0.334	0.820	<0.001
Retention bonus	1†	0.990	-0.010	0.060	-0.128	0.108	0.868
Non-teacher salary	2	6.305	1.841	2.789	-3.625	7.307	0.509
Salary	18	0.977	-0.024	0.007	-0.038	-0.009	0.001
Union	3	0.745	-0.294	0.173	-0.634	0.046	0.090

NOTE: Assumed correlations between multiple within-study outcomes is 0.5. * denotes reporting linear probability model estimates, not odds ratios. † denotes single study estimate, not meta-analytic results. eff. = effectiveness.

Teacher Salaries, Pensions, and Job Protections

The reasons why teachers decide to leave or stay in their jobs can often be traced to general findings from studies on why employees quit.[73] These reasons include the job opportunities available both inside and outside education, as well as policies at the school district or state level that might make a teacher more likely to stay or go (table 4.3, panel B). For example, some of these factors are how many jobs are available, how much teachers get paid compared with other jobs, whether schools hire teachers late in the year, if there are bonuses for staying, the job security of having tenure, and other job benefits (e.g., insurance or a pension). In particular, the overall number of jobs available and the presence of other job options play a big role in whether someone decides to leave their current job.[74]

One workforce factor well studied in education is teacher salary. Across 30 studies over decades of research, the evidence indicates that increases in salary are associated with higher teacher retention.[75] Yet this association may be explained by other factors that co-occur in school districts with salary increases. When salary is measured as an increase per $1,000, its relationship with teacher turnover is small but still positive, but the relationship between salary and retention is more modest when high salary is compared with low salary.[76] For instance, several studies that examined high salary versus low salary have found that the influence on teacher retention was modest and positive.[77] Overall, we note that increases in salary are associated with increases in teacher retention, but the size of the salary increase is rather important. We should not expect substantial and meaningful changes in teacher retention when salary increases by a small amount. Additional employment opportunities within school systems (such as tutoring, coaching, and teacher leadership roles) can provide teachers with an opportunity to earn additional income as an extension to their primary instructional role, and this is also related to higher retention.[78]

Moreover, retention bonuses—additional money given to teachers if they stay in certain schools or hard-to-staff subject (such as STEM or special education)—can reduce teacher attrition, with rigorous evidence supporting the efficacy of these financial incentives.[79] However, these effects may dissipate as salary incentives are reduced or removed.[80] On the flip side, competition from external opportunities, such as competing STEM jobs, presents a challenge to teacher recruitment and retention. The availability of higher-paying jobs outside teaching can make it harder to recruit and retain teachers.[81]

The design of teacher pensions may also shape the longevity of teachers' careers. Before reviewing the empirical evidence on pensions, let us take a slight detour to describe their design. The defined-benefit (DB) pension plan provides teachers with guaranteed lifetime benefits that are based on a predetermined formula that consists of the number of years of service, the final average salary (typically over the last three to five years of service), and a benefit multiplier (typically from 1% to 2.5%).[82] For example, a teacher who taught for 30 years with a final average salary of $60,000 over the last five years and a multiplier of 2.0% would then receive a guaranteed pension of $36,000 a year ($60,000 times 30 times 0.02) and without social security benefits, as teachers in these DB plans do not contribute directly to social security. While this annual income is not high, it is a stable and modest source of income that is guaranteed for the lifetime of the teacher. The DB plan promotes and rewards longevity, and there is no investment risk for the individual teacher, as the employer, being the state or the district, assumes all responsibility for the investment that pays out these benefits. In short, teachers receive lower base salaries in exchange for secured and guaranteed higher retirement benefits under the traditional DB system.

With the current design of DB systems, researchers have outlined three ways they have implications for teacher turnover. First, there is a broad set of economic arguments for shifting away from DB systems, primarily related to their long-term financial sustainability. The main reasons for budgetary shortfalls with pensions include lower-than-expected investment returns (particularly in risky investments and during recessions), a low level of governmental contributions to the system over time, and longer life expectancies for pensioners.[83] Most teacher pension systems are severely underfunded, which is to say that the states running them do not have sufficient assets to cover the benefits. Teacher pensions are often funded by investment in risky assets that can fluctuate and underperform relative to expectations, particularly during recessions.[84] When investments do not meet expectations, states then incur debt to pay for benefits, and these debts come with interest that has to be repaid each year; if not paid in full each year, the debt carries over. In 2016, the national shortfall for DB plans was around $500 billion, and for every 10 dollars that states contributed to teacher pension plans, 7 went toward paying past debt, and only 3 went toward actual benefits for teachers.[85] Another way of characterizing this shortfall is to say that over one-third of all retirement contributions made by teachers and their employers is spent on repaying pension debt and not on paying teachers' retirement benefits.[86] As a result, the chief concern is that future teachers will continue to pay more yet their contributions will never keep up with the growing debt of the pension plans.

Second, there is a long "vesting" period, which is the minimum number of years a teacher must work before they are eligible to receive pension benefits, and until a teacher is vested, they do not qualify for the employer-funded portion of the pension (meaning that the only benefit an unvested teacher receives is their own contribution). This vesting period is typically 5 to 10 years.[87] So, unless a teacher has taught in the same state for the requisite length of time, when they leave, they forfeit contributions from the state. As teacher turnover is high in the first five years, whether they leave the profession or teach in another state, most teachers receive little to no retirement benefits under the DB system. In fact, only 28% of teachers remain in teaching for 20 or more years, and only one in five remains in teaching for 25 or 30 years.[88] Stated differently, DB pensions do not appear to incentivize many beginning teachers to remain in the profession, and as a result, a majority of teachers do not receive full benefits under the DB system. That said, pensions do appear to promote retention among veteran teachers nearing retirement.

Third, there is a lack of portability with the DB plan: if a teacher continues to teach but does so in a different state, her previous service does not count in the new school system. Their "service" time starts over at zero in the new state. This reset may deter teachers who move across state lines from continuing to teach.

Despite these concerns, there has been hesitance to cut teacher pensions for fear of how it could hurt teacher morale and retention. Recent evidence from a policy shift in Texas that cut pension annuities and early retirement benefits suggests that this fear may be overblown.[89] Even when teachers received a less generous pension, discouraging early retirement actually decreased teacher turnover in the years after the policy was adopted. Given the important role of pensions in the development of a career model of teaching, we see this as an important area of future research to fully assess unintended consequences from pension reform.

Another consistent finding is the relationship between union membership and teacher retention. Teachers are significantly more likely to stay when they are members of a union.[90] It could be that teachers' unions improve conditions of teachers' work—including compensation and school factors—that are related to higher retention levels. At the school level, the grievance process provides teachers a means to redress workplace issues; non-unionized teachers may lack such procedures and instead leave their school. That said, this association between union membership and retention may simply reflect differences in who becomes a teacher in states with unions or who joins a union in right-to-work states. Lacking historical evidence on how teacher unionization directly impacted turnover, the strongest evidence of the relationship between teacher unionization and turnover comes from recent state-level efforts to weaken public employee unions. Laws such as Wisconsin's Act 10, a 2011 law that weakened teacher unions, can significantly increase teacher turnover.[91]

Relatedly, several states have made changes to tenure laws with mixed results on teacher turnover. Tenure extension reform in New York made teachers whose tenure was delayed by the extension leave their schools, and they were replaced by more effective teachers.[92] Others have found that the elimination of teacher tenure in Louisiana increased teacher turnover.[93] In short, how tenure reforms influence teacher turnover will need further examination to provide policymakers with a more reliable set of policy levers.

What the research does not currently provide is specific guidance on how compensation, collective bargaining, and tenure policies should be designed in the interest of retaining teachers. For instance, pensions may have promoted a career model of teaching in the past, yet their fiscal challenges today suggest that future teacher retirees may not benefit to the same degree if they have to pay higher amounts or their pension plan becomes insolvent.

Who Is Most at Risk of Turning Over?

In the previous sections, we discussed the various teacher, school, and external factors that are related to teacher turnover. It is also important to recognize that some specific types of teachers, and teachers with overlapping characteristics, are most at risk of leaving. This warrants special consideration and further discussion of new and early-career teachers, STEM teachers, and special education teachers. In this section, we briefly discuss each of these groups, what we know about their rate of turnover, and how they fit into the larger picture.

Early-career teachers, those who are in their first five years of teaching, are particularly at risk of leaving.[94] In fact, brand-new teachers are especially likely to leave their teaching career soon after they begin it. When we examine all teachers, at any level, we find that, on average, about 85% of teachers stay in their current school every school year, which means that about 15% of teachers leave their current school each year.[95] Half of this turnover consists of teachers switching from one school to another, and the other half is teachers leaving the profession. In comparison, only about 75% of new teachers stay in their current school from year to year.[14] Prior to the COVID-19 pandemic, about 11% of new teachers left the teaching profession every year, and 14% of new teachers switched schools every year. During the pandemic, early-career teachers were even more likely to leave than before.[96] In short, new and early-career teachers are substantially more likely to leave their current school compared with more experienced teachers.

The challenges that new teachers face are often compounded by the conditions of the schools in which they work. New teachers are much more likely to start their career in economically disadvantaged schools and/or majority-minority schools where working conditions and teacher turnover are higher than in more affluent or majority-white schools. In 2012 more than half of new teachers began their careers in these traditionally disadvantaged schools, which was more than did so in 1988. Early-career teachers are also more likely than veteran teachers to leave their job during the school year.[97] Stated differently, new teachers tend to begin teaching in underserved school settings where they are less likely to receive supports and guidance, and consequently, they are much more likely than experienced teachers to seek a job elsewhere, in part due to poor working conditions and burnout.[98] Early-career teacher turnover, both during the school year and at year's end, disrupts learning environments to the detriment of student learning.

Another group that deserves special consideration is STEM teachers. As noted previously, STEM teachers are more likely to leave teaching than non-STEM teachers, which is even more prevalent at high-need schools. STEM teachers in traditionally disadvantaged schools are more likely to leave the profession and are more likely to switch schools.[99] As STEM teachers have more opportunities outside teaching, they can more easily leave their teaching career behind. At the same time, the STEM teacher production has dropped precipitously in the last decade (figure 4.2). While the number of science and math teachers nearly doubled from 1980s to the early 2010s,[100] enrollment and completion in STEM teacher training have dropped since then. Since 2010, the number of STEM candidates, those who have completed courses in a teacher preparation program and taken in-state certification exams, has dropped from around 31,700 to about 21,800, a staggering 31% decrease. During this time, STEM teacher shortages were reported by most states every year.[101] An Economic Policy Institute report suggests that teacher shortage, including in STEM fields, is large and growing.[102] Moreover, schools and districts report difficulty in filling STEM positions three to four times more frequently than they do for other positions.[103] In short, we need more STEM teachers,

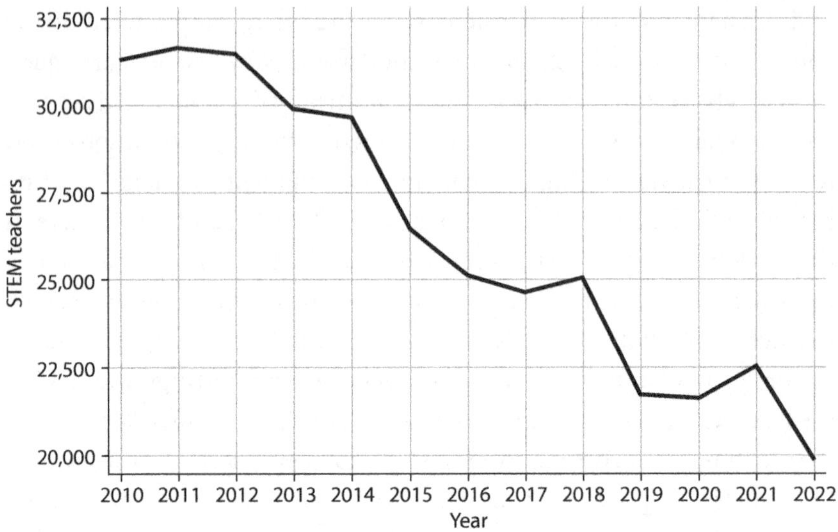

FIGURE 4.2 STEM teacher production over time. *Source* of data: Authors' calculation using Title II data

and we need to do all we can to incentivize potential STEM teachers to join the profession.

Special education teachers are also in constant demand in many school districts. While STEM and special education teachers' preparation and job opportunities are different from each other, there are some similarities. Special education teachers tend to leave the profession more than other teachers do in part because of poor working conditions and a great workload.[104] Similar to STEM teachers, the output of new special education teachers has lagged over the past decade. The number of special education teachers currently does not meet the demand nationally, a demand driven by a substantial rise in the number of identified special education students.[105] There is an insufficient production of special education teachers and a high turnover rate for special education teachers.[106] In other words, both the front and back ends of the pipeline for special education teachers, the recruitment and retention of these teachers, are at fault for not meeting the need. Unlike STEM teachers who may been drawn away from teaching by other job opportunities with higher earnings, special educator teachers require a significant amount of training and expertise for which they are often not well compensated.

This picture is even more dire when we consider the needs of students of color and special education teachers of color. The most recent work suggests that current policy efforts to recruit and retain special education teachers of color are not enough to address the growing problems associated with the whiteness of the special education teacher workforce.[107] Based on the current number of new special education teachers of color, the percentage of these who will enter the workforce as soon as they gain their credentials, and the percentage of these teachers who are retained every year, there are no realistic scenarios in which there will be a sufficient number of special education teachers of color to serve the growing number of special education students of color over the next several years. As shortages of special education teachers threaten our schools' abilities to provide needed services to special education students, particularly for students of color, we need to consider a host of policy changes to meet current and future demands.

Conclusion

As teacher turnover is a key contributor to teacher shortages in the United States, we have discussed how various factors are associated with teacher turnover. In particular, we categorized these factors into three main categories: (1) personal factors, (2) school factors, and (3) external factors. Personal factors are the characteristics of teachers; school factors are the characteristics of the teachers' work environments; and external factors are conditions beyond schools' immediate control that potentially affect teacher retention.

In each of these categories, we discussed how specific factors are related to teacher turnover. While there are many factors related to turnover, some are more relevant for policy and practice. Specifically, there are lots of data showing that early-career teachers, STEM teachers, and special education teachers, as well as teachers working in traditionally disadvantaged schools, are particularly at risk of leaving the profession.

One of the key takeaways from this chapter is that we should do everything we can to retain these teachers so that our students are well served. Some of the practices we can do to retain teachers should happen at the school level, while others should occur at the district and state level. Toward this end, in the next two chapters, we reframe the narrative of teacher retention to more intentionally create schools and environments where teachers will want to stay.

CHAPTER 5

Policies to Increase Teacher Recruitment

RECRUITING MORE TEACHERS into the profession, while it sounds straightforward enough, is more challenging than we would like. Teaching has historically been characterized as a semi-profession with a meager salary.[1] In recent years, salaries have stagnated, teachers report being less satisfied, and teaching has been viewed as less prestigious.[2] Additionally, the hyper-politicization of education through partisan politics has put teaching and teachers under the microscope, opening teachers to intense and unwarranted criticism.[3] As such, we have seen an unprecedented drop in teacher enrollment programs, and many schools and districts struggle to hire qualified teachers to teach.[4]

Interconnected with these contemporary challenges are the many steps someone needs to take to arrive, from having an interest in a teaching career to conducting their first day of class. Though a pipeline is commonly used as a metaphor to describe the process of attracting, preparing, licensing, and hiring new teachers, we believe a funnel is a metaphor more apt. Regardless of how many people are interested in becoming teachers, only a fraction will ever end up actually teaching.[5] As people move down the funnel, fewer and fewer complete the steps to becoming a teacher, whether entering a teacher preparation program, graduating, completing all licensure requirements, or finding a teaching position.

In response, policymakers have taken steps to change the incentive structures to becoming a teacher by reducing the costs (i.e., financial incentives) or standards (e.g., lower scores on licensure exams; alternative entry pathways into teaching). We believe these types of policies—which we review in this chapter—can make it easier to become a teacher *on the margin.* Teacher recruitment policies likely make it easier for more people to take the steps to becoming a teacher. These strategies alone, though, will not end teacher shortages unless accompanied by more comprehensive changes to teacher compensation and working conditions. To return to our funnel metaphor, we envision a widening of the funnel's mouth that is only made possible when teaching is viewed as a more attractive career for many more people. This view is not to discount the efficacy of this suite of teacher recruitment strategies but to place them in a broader context of what can reasonably be expected by their adoption.

There are three main categories of recruitment policies: (1) financial incentives, (2) requirements for a full license, and (3) alternative certification for a provisional license. Financial incentives are exactly what they sound like: policies that appeal to an interest in money, whether by reducing the costs of becoming a teacher or by increasing teacher salary. The second category is licensure requirements, which concern how teachers can become fully licensed as a teacher in their state, usually by completing a state-approved teacher preparation program at a college or university, plus meeting other requirements (e.g., holding a bachelor's degree; passing pedagogy and/or content exams). The third category consists of alternative pathways to the teaching profession for a provisional license (e.g., programs like Teach For America or Grow Your Own). This category is related to regular licensure but is different enough to warrant its own grouping. We note that teacher residencies have traditionally been an alternative pathway into teaching, but recently many traditional university-based teacher preparation programs have established their own teacher residency programs, blurring the line between full licensure from a traditional preparation program and provisional licensure from alternative certification.

Overall, many of these initiatives aim to increase the general number of teachers across a wide spectrum, while some target specific kinds of teachers (e.g., STEM or special education) or aim to diversify the teaching profession. Below, we discuss each of these categories, the different types of strategies under each, and the empirical evidence for how effective these strategies have been. Then we turn our attention to policies targeted to recruiting certain types of candidates into teaching or recruiting teachers for certain types of schools (e.g., economically disadvantaged schools, majority-minority schools, geographically isolated schools) and to district practices that could improve recruitment (e.g., limiting late hiring; updating current job postings).

We place an emphasis on scalable policies, including those with the strongest track record of recruiting more teachers where such evidence exists. In particular, we discuss medium-to-large financial incentives that bring more teachers into teaching, the trade-offs of different considerations of licensure and preparation requirements, and new alternative pathways that are increasing the number of teachers and diversifying the teacher workforce. We believe this evidence-based approach is appropriate as it can guide educational leaders and policymakers toward policies with the greatest likelihood of success.

The overall effectiveness of these approaches to recruitment must be balanced against other factors. The decentralized public education system in the United States has often made it difficult to enact systemic teacher-centered policies that enlarge the pool of prospective teachers by making teaching a more attractive career, as opposed to making it easier to become a teacher for those who are already interested in a teaching career. Though the policies we discuss in this chapter may address discrete aspects of the pipeline into teaching, we caution that they must be adopted as part of a more cohesive and coordinated system. To this point, while there are scalable policies for increasing teacher recruitment, they are, in our opinion, unlikely to end teacher shortages in and of themselves. Even as we present evidence of the effectiveness of some of these policies, we believe that more substantial, and arguably more drastic, changes must be made to end teacher shortages. We revisit this point in chapter 7.

Financial Incentives to Recruit Teachers

Inadequate pay is often cited as one of the most significant barriers to recruiting more teachers in the United States. Yet teaching is often viewed as a safe career, as we have always needed teachers, in good or bad economic times. It is widely recognized that though teacher pay is low compared with other occupations requiring a similar education, salary is not a primary reason why people become teachers in the first place.[6]

From a research standpoint, detecting what is believed to be a small relationship between increased teacher salaries and the supply of new teachers is complicated by the difficulty in identifying who should actually be counted as part of the pool of newly available teachers. This is largely due to an inability to know exactly how many teacher candidates are prepared in any given geographic region with specific expertise.[7] Consider three hypothetical graduates who just completed their teacher preparation program. One is moving back home on the other side of the state to find a job. Another graduate is dual-certified in special and elementary education and is open to jobs in either area. The last decided to hold off on looking for her first teaching position until she decided whether teaching was what she truly wanted to do. If a state policymaker was looking at program-level data, then three new teaching candidates were produced in the state. Yet, from the perspective of a local school district, only one of these teachers belongs to the current labor supply, and whether this candidate will fill a vacancy in general elementary or special education is uncertain. Lacking clear data sources from which to measure teacher supply has made it difficult for researchers to study how financial incentives shape who goes into teaching.

For studies of teacher scholarships, there is always the counterfactual scenario of what would have happened if a prospective teacher had not gotten the scholarship that subsidized her teacher education. That is, did receiving the scholarship incentivize her to become a teacher when she would not have otherwise? Research suggests that many preservice teachers who received a scholarship expected to become teachers regardless of whether they received the scholarship.[8] For these teachers, the scholarship may have eased their path into teaching and perhaps reduced the amount in student loans they borrowed, but it may not have decided their career path.

Even where there is unclear evidence of a causal relationship between financial incentives and new teacher supply, we still think it important to discuss the ways in which state and federal policymakers have used financial incentives to recruit more people into teaching and to review their efficacy, when data are available. In general, there are three main financial policy levers that have been adopted: overall salary increases, teacher scholarships, and loan forgiveness.

Of the few studies that connect salary increases and teacher supply, evidence suggests that across-the-board salary increases can improve a district's ability to attract new teachers. One study from Texas showed that increasing the base salary in a district increased the share of teachers, with the largest effect for early-career teachers.[9] In the case of the Quality Teacher and Education Act of 2008 implemented in San Francisco Unified School District, additional funds were provided for across-the-board salary increases, retention bonuses, bonuses for teaching in hard-to-fill subjects or hard-to-staff schools, and a number of other initiatives. Researchers found that the salary increase improved the district's ability to attract teachers, in terms of both the size and the quality of the applicant pool.[10]

If beginning teacher salaries were higher, it would likely not only help to increase the supply of teachers but also to make teacher scholarships and loan forgiveness less necessary. Amid the continued presence of low teacher salaries, at least 14 states have enacted legislation to provide scholarships, grants, and loan forgiveness to potential candidates. As two representative state-level examples, aspiring teachers in Arkansas can apply for a $3,000 tuition reimbursement grant through the Teacher Opportunity Program; in South Carolina, the Teaching Fellows Program, established in 1999, forgave up to $24,000 in debt over four years while recipients worked toward initial teacher certification.[11]

Despite the substantial amount of money awarded by programs such as these, there are only a few programs of teacher scholarships and loan forgiveness that have been rigorously evaluated. One is North Carolina's Teaching Fellows Program, established in 1986, that provided scholarships of $6,500 per year for four years to attend a North Carolina university and teach for four years in North Carolina public schools.[12] This merit-based scholarship attracted teacher candidates with better academic qualifications, produced teachers who taught lower-performing students and were able to raise those students' academic achievement more so than traditionally prepared teachers, and stayed in public schools at higher rates than teachers who had entered through other pathways. In other words, this scholarship was able not only to recruit more academically capable teacher candidates but also to retain them at higher rates.

Additionally, qualitative evidence suggests that another program influenced some candidates' decision to become a STEM educator. The Woodrow Wilson Fellowship program in New Jersey, which provides a one-year $30,000 scholarship to high-achieving candidates in STEM fields to teach in high-needs schools for three years, has had some measure of success: recipients are substantially more likely to teach in high-needs schools and are also more likely to persist in teaching.[13] Similarly, the Governor's Teaching Fellowship in California provides a $20,000 scholarship to select groups of teachers and successfully recruits teachers for low-performing schools, and these teachers are more likely to stay than other teachers.[14]

There are also federally funded programs aimed at increasing the supply of new teachers. The Personnel Development Program of the Office of Special Education Personnel (US Department of Education) provides grants to institutions of higher education to train special education teachers. The National Science Foundation's Noyce Teacher Scholarship distributes funding to STEM teacher candidates at college and university preparation programs in exchange for a commitment to teach in high-needs schools.

Each of these programs tends to provide a rather generous scholarship for aspiring teachers. Some descriptive and survey data suggest that scholarships influence potential candidates' decision to complete a teacher certification program.[15] However, another study found that recipients of Noyce Scholarship would have likely become teachers without it.[16] No rigorous evidence indicates whether these programs improve overall teacher supply.

The federal government's Teacher Education Assistance for College and Higher Education (TEACH) grant, which provided $4,000 a year for people planning to become teachers who commit to teaching in high-needs subject areas in high-poverty schools for a specific period of time, has produced minimal evidence of effectiveness. The most credible evidence that exists suggests that the TEACH grant had no impact on the production of undergraduate education degrees or in specific fields such as STEM or special education.[17] As with other teacher scholarships, TEACH grants likely reduced the financial barriers to becoming a teacher, including the amount of student loans a teacher-to-be had to take out, but likely did not have a marked effect in growing the supply of teachers.

Further evidence supporting a negligible effect for these programs is that the small amounts of money provided by some of them appear to be insufficient to change people's decisions and behaviors. For instance, a study examining Arkansas's Teacher Opportunity Program found that the amount was too low to attract teachers, and recipients of the Oklahoma Future Scholarships, which provided from $1,000 to $1,500 to teachers, said they would have gone into teaching science regardless of the scholarship.[18]

Loan forgiveness programs seem like a less promising solution to addressing teacher supply, though their efficacy may depend on how these programs are designed. The largest-scale effort at loan forgiveness for teachers is through the Teacher Loan Forgiveness program, which canceled between $5,000 and $17,500 in student loans for teachers who had worked for at least five years in high-needs districts. One study found that this program did not appear to attract teachers to higher-poverty schools nor to retain those who had moved to these schools. When probing why, the authors' findings suggest that prospective teachers may value loan forgiveness, but the complex design and administrative barriers with this particular program likely limited any behavioral response.[19] In contrast, California's Assumption Program of Loans for Education provided loan forgiveness of between $11,000 and $19,000. The program was shown to impact new teachers' decisions to work in low-performing schools where students were eligible for student debt cancellation.[20] In survey studies, teachers have reported that loan forgiveness would shape their decision to become a teacher.[21] Whether this same behavioral response would also be seen in those who are still considering becoming a teacher is less certain.

Summary of Financial Incentives Used for Recruitment

The evidence, taken as a whole, suggests that financial incentives may be able to attract potential teachers to the profession and into the classroom.[22] For instance, the evidence from the North Carolina Teaching Fellows Program, the Quality Teacher and Education Act in San Francisco, and the Woodrow Wilson Fellowship indicates that financial incentives, in the form of scholarships and teacher scholarships, can recruit candidates into the profession. Loan forgiveness may be beneficial, but it appears to depend on the amount of debt to be forgiven and how easy this process is for teachers to undertake.

There are several caveats to consider here. First, as we noted, there is limited rigorous evidence measuring the outcomes of many financial incentive programs. Second, the amount of the incentives is unlikely to have any consequential effect when it is small. It seems that potential candidates are not swayed to join the profession for a few hundred or a few thousand dollars; the amount has to be larger for it to have an effect on recruitment. Even for programs that offer larger teacher scholarships or forgive substantial amounts of teachers' student loans, we urge policymakers to exercise a degree of circumspection when estimating their benefit to growing teacher supply. That is not to say that scholarships and loans do not reduce financial barriers to becoming a teacher;

such a benefit may be particularly enticing for historically underrepresented groups within teaching. These incentives are likely to ease the way for individuals who were already considering a career in teaching. Most important to teacher supply, though, are base levels of teacher salaries, a point we return to in detail in chapter 7.

Licensure and Preparation Requirements in Teacher Recruitment

The second category of strategies for teacher recruitment is licensure and preparation requirements. In this section, we first describe the policies for teacher licensure and preparation requirements; then we discuss the evidence of their effectiveness. Licensure and preparation requirements are the technical aspects of how states determine who can be fully licensed as a teacher in the state, which usually includes completion of all programmatic requirements at a state-approved college or university teacher preparation program along with various other requirements they must meet (e.g., holding a bachelor's degree; passing pedagogy and/or content exams).

As we discussed in chapter 1, these criteria for qualification were formalized over the twentieth century in efforts to improve the competence of teachers and reduce churn in the teacher workforce. These requirements have served as a barrier that makes becoming a teacher more difficult for some groups than for others. Because licensure requirements, by definition, limit who can become a teacher, during shortages, some states have lowered teacher preparation and licensure requirements in efforts to fill ongoing vacancies. For instance, Assembly Bill 7 in Nevada allowed licensed teachers without the appropriate endorsements (for instance, a licensed social studies teacher who would instead teach physics) to teach in low-performing schools if they were hired due to a teacher shortage.[23] Arizona's Senate Bill 1042, a controversial bill at the time, allowed school districts, not the state board of education, to determine whether an applicant is eligible to teach;[24] the main concerns were that the legislation would lead to decreasing teaching standards as well as diminishing the status of the profession, which, ultimately, would hurt children because their teacher might be less effective.

By the 2022–23 school year, two years after the onset of the COVID-19 pandemic, when teacher vacancies reached approximately 55,000 nationwide, states took substantial actions to try to expand their teacher workforce rapidly to meet growing demand. Alaska's Senate Bill 20 allowed new license types, expanded requirements for initial licensure, and made it easier to transfer licenses from out of state. In Arizona, with about 2,890 vacant positions in the 2022–23 school year, the state changed the licensure requirement so that applicants without a bachelor's degree could teach.[25] In 2023, Kentucky's Senate Bill 49 declared a state of emergency for the teacher workforce, expanded alternative pathways to certification, and allowed teachers with emergency teaching certification in the 2022–23 school year to be eligible to renew for another year.[26] Changes like these almost always include lowering standards (such as the need to hold a bachelor's degree or to meet a minimum in test scores), widening the eligibility for alternative pathways into teaching and allowing for more provisional and emergency licensing and making them renewable.

While there are many factors important to the recruitment of teachers with respect to licensure requirements, there are notable trade-offs, in our opinion, that scholars and policymakers must consider: how having licensure exams can limit the potential pool of teacher candidates (including diverse candidates), how setting cutoff points on qualifying exams relates to future teacher effectiveness on the job, and alternatives to licensure exams. We next discuss what these licensure requirements are and the trade-offs to consider.

The core requirements for teachers are these: having a bachelor's degree in teacher education, having a minimum grade point average, passing required exams, gaining student teaching experience, and meeting state standards for knowledge of pedagogy and subject content. Some of these requirements have been examined by researchers (e.g., licensure exams), while others have not been examined (e.g., number of student teaching hours). The question for recruitment policy is how changing these requirements would affect the supply and quality of certified teachers.

On the one hand, if higher standards for teacher licensure result in having more effective teachers who are capable of increasing student learning, then we should aim to maintain higher standards. However, if higher standards are not highly correlated with teacher effectiveness, then maintaining them would not accomplish much of anything beyond erecting roadblocks to some interested candidates and keeping more people out of the profession. Increasing the cutoff points on licensure exams would exclude a portion of ineffective teachers, yes; at the same time, it would might also exclude a comparatively larger portion of teachers who would prove to be effective in the classroom.[27] Moreover, we also have to consider that licensure exams disproportionately prevent Black and Hispanic candidates from obtaining a license to teach, particularly given the mixed evidence that links licensure exams with eventual teaching effectiveness.[28] The best evidence on licensure requirements does not concern the overall supply of teachers but rather the types of people who become teachers. Thus, we focus on this evidence base when giving our recommendations for how to design teacher licensure requirements in ways to increase teacher recruitment.

In terms of the effects of licensure exams—specifically, written exams such as the Praxis tests used to determine licensure status—there is limited but growing evidence showing that more stringent cutoff scores can reduce the number of effective teachers who could otherwise join the workforce.[29] For instance, increasing the cutoff scores on licensure exams for elementary teachers would exclude less than 1% of very ineffective teachers, but it would also exclude 7% of effective teachers.[30] Other studies tend to reach a similar conclusion or find that teacher licensure test scores are unrelated to teacher effectiveness, though some evidence suggests the opposite.[31] The relation may also vary depending on whether a candidate fails a basic skills test (Praxis I) or a subject-matter test (Praxis II). One recent study shows that failing Praxis I deters those would be less effective teachers, but failing Praxis II would disproportionately deter relatively effective potential teachers.[32]

On the whole, using higher cutoff scores on licensure exams risks doing more harm than good as it excludes people who would eventually become effective teachers. Based on this existing evidence, we expect that ongoing efforts to reduce standards for entry into teaching will increase the supply of teachers without substantially sacrificing teacher quality, but it remains to be seen where the cutoffs should be set to balance the trade-off between increasing supply and decreasing quality. Some individuals with less demonstrable content knowledge may require additional mentoring and induction when they enter the classroom. We worry, though, that reducing standards may be viewed as an easy way for state policymakers to improve teacher supply, whereas, in reality, such a change appears to affect only a small subset of teachers on the margin of passing their licensure exam, a point we develop further when reviewing the empirical evidence on changing licensure requirements.

The COVID-19 pandemic brought a wave of changes to teacher licensure requirements that has helped researchers better understand how various requirements affect teacher recruitment. In 2020, Massachusetts implemented an emergency teaching license whereby applicants needed only a bachelor's degree to qualify, bypassing the Massachusetts Tests for Educator Licensure requirements required for a provisional license. The result of this emergency license increased the supply of teachers in two different ways.[33] First, it enabled entry for candidates who wanted to become teachers but could not meet the traditional licensure requirements (via the exams), and second, it increased the pool of people who would be interested in becoming a teacher. Emergency-licensed teachers were more ethnoracially diverse than their peers with a traditional license. They were also no more likely to leave teaching than provisionally licensed teachers, except in the case of emergency-licensed teachers who had not previously worked in public schools or engaged in the teacher pipeline, suggesting that greater flexibility in teacher licensing may be beneficial for teacher supply. Again, whether this type of policy change helps recruit career-minded teachers with the requisite skills and content knowledge to thrive in the classroom hinges on the provision of developmental supports in their first years in the classroom and their having means to comprehensive preparation, even if that occurs on the job.[34]

Since traditional licensure exams may not clearly differentiate between effective and ineffective teachers, educators and policymakers have considered other approaches. Since 2014, the educative Teacher Performance Assessment (edTPA), a performance-based semester-long project to assess prospective teachers' readiness to teach, has gained momentum across the United States. By 2018, edTPA has become mandatory for at least eight states.[35] If edTPA can clearly differentiate between candidates who are ready to teach and would be effective in the classroom from those who are not, then it may be a better screening tool for states to use in licensure decisions. However, if it does not clearly differentiate effective and ineffective teachers, then it may essentially act as an additional barrier that would deter prospective candidates from joining the profession on account of the time and monetary investment required.

Some scholars have argued that performance-based assessment better reflects the skills needed for teaching than written exams do, yet there is substantial evidence showing that edTPA may reduce the supply of teachers due to the testing and miscellaneous fees, time commitment, and mental stress, as well as a disconnect between different pedagogical approaches and that of Pearson/SCALE used by edTPA.[36] These impacts may be particularly detrimental to the supply of teachers of color. Preliminary evidence from Washington state showed mixed findings for edTPA as a predictor of teacher effectiveness, and Hispanic candidates were over three times more likely to fail than white candidates.[37]

Recently, using nationally representative data in a rigorous quasi-experimental design, researchers found that edTPA actually reduced the teacher supply (specifically, prospective teachers in undergraduate programs), particularly for less-selective and minority-concentrated universities, and on top of that, they found no evidence that edTPA increased student test scores.[38] Stated otherwise, the most current and rigorous evidence on this growing licensure assessment strongly suggests that it is acting as a barrier that keeps out potential candidates, particularly those who do not attend the highly selective institutions and minority candidates, and it does not clearly predict teacher effectiveness or increase student achievement. These findings reflect prior serious concerns about the scoring design, reliability of assessments, and the impacts of edTPA on licensure.[39] This also reflects the broader point we hope to get across about licensing: though teaching licensing helps ensure that potential teachers meet some threshold minimums, these requirements can limit who comes into teaching in undesirable ways.

Summary of Licensure and Preparation Requirements

Taken altogether, the existing evidence suggests that scholars and policymakers need more investigation to determine the efficacy and fairness of licensure exams. In particular, scholars and policymakers need to (1) examine the extent to which licensure exams would unnecessarily exclude a more diverse teacher workforce, particularly one that reflects the demographics of the students they serve; (2) determine the cutoff points where substantially more ineffective teachers are kept out of the profession than effective teachers are excluded for failing the test; and (3) consider allowing test takers who come close to the threshold score some alternatives to passing in lieu of retaking the test, such as writing an essay, taking a licensure exam from another state, or demonstrating subject-matter knowledge through an educator preparation program or coursework. There are trade-offs for each one of these possibilities, but there may be sweet spots where these alternatives to licensure exams would enable highly interested candidates to join the profession, allow more effective teachers into the classroom (or at least minimize the exclusion of effective teachers), and diversify the teacher workforce. To this point, there are alternative pathways to recruiting teachers into the profession, which we discuss next.

Alternative Pathways into the Profession

There are several alternative pathways for teachers to obtain provisional licenses to enter the teaching profession that could be altered or leveraged to increase teacher recruitment. Commonly we think about alternative certification programs (ACPs), but there are also teacher residency programs (TRPs), Grow Your Own (GYO) programs, and teaching apprenticeship programs.[40] We note that teacher residencies have traditionally been an alternative pathway into teaching, but recently many traditional teacher preparation programs have established their own TRPs, blurring the line about how to categorize these programs. Below we discuss each of these different pathways, how they are related to each other, and what we know about how they are used or could be used to recruit teachers into the profession.

Alternative Certification Programs

ACPs allow potential candidates with a bachelor's degree to serve as the teacher of record and complete their licensure requirements while teaching.[41] ACPs have grown substantially since the 1990s, in conjunction with the expansion and adoption of Teach For America (TFA), and by the early 2020s, ACPs could be found in every state, with about a quarter of the teacher workforce being alternatively certified.[42] In fact, due to the severity of the teacher shortages in some states, ACPs have provided a lot more teachers than a quarter. Though ACPs vary in size, scope, and recruitment strategy, they appear to be effective in recruiting potential candidates who did not go through a traditional preparation program, many of whom are teachers of color. About half of teachers who entered the profession through an ACP indicated they would not have become a teacher otherwise, and about a third of candidates are people of color in contrast with the 10% or 11% of the current teacher workforce.[43]

For instance, by 2008, more than half of newly certified teachers in the state of Mississippi came through an alternative route.[44] In response, the College of Education at Mississippi State University and the Mississippi Department of Education developed the Learning and Educating through Alternative Programs to spur recruitment. The initiative awarded scholarships of up to $5,000 for candidates who would teach in at-risk school districts for at least three years. After an intensive, multiprong marketing and recruiting campaign, the program ended up exceeding its goal, providing more than 150 certified teachers, many of whom were STEM teachers.

Probably the most well-known alternative pathway into teaching is through TFA, a nonprofit organization that recruits college graduates—most of whom do not have a background in education—from selective universities around the United States to teach in low-income rural and urban schools for two years. TFA members are provided with an intense summer training prior to joining the classroom in the fall. While there is substantial debate over whether TFA is good or bad for public education, thousands of TFA members have served millions of students since 1990. Still, this represents less than half of 1% of teachers in the United States.[45] Moreover, there is mixed evidence for how effective TFA teachers are relative to other brand-new teachers. Studies employing more rigorous methods tend to find TFA teachers perform worse relative to certified teachers, with the exception of math TFA teachers.[46] To be sure, TFA supplies teachers in hard-to-staff subjects in schools that would probably employ worse-prepared teachers or long-term substitutes, but there are questions about the detrimental impact on school systems and communities that rely on inflows of new teachers who mostly stay only a short while.

The New York City Teaching Fellows, an ACP that was influenced by Teach For America, was created to replace uncertified teachers with alternatively certified teachers who had stronger academic credentials.[47] The candidates, like TFA members, had higher exam scores and grade point averages and came from more or very selective institutions. In two years, the program was able to recruit more than 600 math teachers with a strong academic background and had high one-year retention rates for Black and Hispanic teachers (90%), though this dropped to 64% and 52%, respectively, for the three-year retention rate.

A RAND evaluation of the TEACh (Teacher Effectiveness and Certification) program, an alternative teacher preparation program in collaboration with TNTP (formerly The New Teacher Project), found that TEACh was able to attract and recruit teachers of color and teachers in hard-to-staff subjects as identified by the district (e.g., STEM or special education), deliver consistent teacher preparation, and produce high-quality teachers whose performance was comparable to many traditionally certified teachers in the first year.[48]

Related to this point, one of the many reasons why potential candidates go through an ACP, in addition to the quicker preparation, is that it is substantially cheaper than traditional university-based programs in many cases and that the ACP can cater more to their needs. For instance, Black men interested in special education programs indicated that funding was a key reason for enrolling in an ACP, that they agreed with the program's mission, and that they felt connected to other Black men who found success in the program.[49]

In sum, ACPs, by providing quicker preparation pathways, often at reduced cost, have generally been able to attract and recruit candidates for teaching that traditional preparation programs did not. Moreover, these candidates are more likely to be people of color. Next, we discuss other alternative pathways that are related to ACPs but are distinctly different.

Teacher Residency Programs

Even with ACPs and traditional university-based programs, many districts and states still struggle to meet the demands for teachers. One of the steps that policymakers have taken to address this challenge is through the creation of TRPs. Though much of the research on TRPs has come from stand-alone residency programs, we point out that a growing number of university-based preparation programs have moved to a residency model for their clinical teaching. TRPs are designed to recruit and prepare potential candidates, particularly for underserved schools, and they have grown substantially in the past several years.[50] TRPs offer candidates enhanced training and are often designed to recruit teachers of color.[51] Some of the defining features of TRPs include (1) collaborative partnerships among school districts, teacher education programs, and/or community; (2) a year or more of classroom teaching with a mentor teacher; (3) coursework taught by a local educational agency or teacher preparation program at the same time; (4) a graduate-level program leading to a teaching certificate and/or master's degree; (5) strategic recruitment and selection of residents; (6) ongoing mentoring and induction support, with some optional post-residency support; and (7) financial incentives and job opportunities in exchange for residents' committed service in underserved schools.[52] In many ways, TRPs aim to take a different approach to training by requiring more and longer training compared with ACPs that try to reduce barriers into the profession.

The evidence on TRPs suggests that there may be several advantages to this prolonged and more intense pathway.[53] The yearlong training, also known as the clinical teaching period, allows the candidates to experiment with strategies and practices of teaching with the help of their mentor teacher.[54] Since residents teach and take classes at the same time, they are afforded more opportunities to connect practice to theory, applying the concepts they learn to their own classroom, all in real time. Moreover, TRPs often aim to recruit teachers of color, many of whom have direct connections to the schools and community in which they work and serve. There is also preliminary evidence that residents are effective teachers.[55]

As an example, some of the earliest TRPs were urban teacher residency programs in Boston that were created to meet teacher shortages.[56] In particular, the urban TRPs aimed to have more STEM teachers, special education teachers, and teachers of color. In 2007–8, the newly established TRPs were able to attract more than 650 applicants and accepted 137 residents between the two programs. Many of these residents were STEM teachers and special education teachers, and the majority were teachers of color. Moreover, both programs had better than 90% three-year retention rates after the residents joined the workforce (that is, more than 90% were still teaching after three years). Keep in mind that, nationally, about 30%–50% of teachers leave the profession within the first five years of teaching. In comparison, the retention rates of these two programs were much higher.

TRPs that focus on specific types of teachers, such as special education teachers, have also found some success in recruiting and retaining prospective teachers. A special education TRP in southern California admitted nearly 125 residents between 2010 and 2015, and 121 completed the program.[57] Moreover, the vast majority of these 121 special education residents were hired in the first year, and 75% remained in teaching even after six years of having entered the workforce and after their three-year service obligation ended. Additionally, more than half of the residents were people of color. Overall, this special education TRP more than met its goal of recruiting special educators, had a large number of teachers of color, and had very high retention rates.

Similarly, TRPs that focus on Black educators also have successful track records of recruiting and retaining Black candidates. Specifically, the National Council for Teacher Residencies' Black Educators Initiative developed materials that highlight people of color, recruited staff who had similar cultural experiences with their prospective candidates, and provided close communication with them, along with stipends, scholarships, and emergency funds allowing Black residents to continue in the program despite potential difficulties.[58] Moreover, the program matched Black residents with effective teachers and created affinity groups for residents to share and process their experiences as well as helped them find jobs and then supported them through their first few years as teachers. As a result, the program was successful in recruiting and retaining Black candidates. What else did the program do to be successful? To recruit candidates, program administrators leveraged alumni networks of high schools and local organizations. The residents were also drawn to the social justice messages that were prominently displayed on the program's websites.[59] In many ways, these recent residency programs built on many of the core principles that were advocated by scholars in the early days of residency programs.[60]

Evidence from a qualitative study suggests that participants in TRPs spend a lot of time in school, feel confident about teaching, are more prepared to teach, and would recommend the program to others.[61] These findings corroborate those of a national study that examined residents and graduates from TRPs, largely indicating that TRPs seem to be successful in recruiting, preparing, and retaining participants.[62] Related to this point, as some high-needs districts have a limited ability to attract quality applicants,[63] TRPs could work with these districts to recruit quality applicants. Due to the initial successes of TRPs, many states are investing substantial amounts of money and effort to leverage TRPs to address teacher shortages.[64]

Grow Your Own Programs

In recent years, an alternative licensure initiative related to TRPs, GYO programs, has expanded tremendously across the United States. GYOs are similar to TRPs in some ways but different in others, and some GYOs are also TRPs and vice versa.[65] Broadly speaking, GYOs are designed to recruit teacher candidates locally to enter the profession, in part to increase the local teacher supply (and address issues of how localized the teacher labor market is) and also to attract candidates who are more reflective of the racial/ethnic and cultural diversity of the students they would serve.[66] For instance, the Urban Teacher Academy Program, a GYO in Florida, prepares high school students for careers in urban education, and graduates are guaranteed a job in the district.[67] Moreover, some GYOs are intended to meet demand for specific types of teachers, such as STEM and special education teachers.[68] Due to the potential of GYOs to increase the teacher supply and diversify the teacher workforce simultaneously, several states (e.g., Tennessee and Texas) and the US Department of Education have invested millions of dollars into these programs. Scholars have often recommended GYOs along with TRPs as ways to attract, recruit, and retain teachers, especially teachers of color.[69]

GYOs belong to a broad category that describes many different types of teacher pipelines with different aims, participants, and program features. Taking a nationwide perspective on GYOs, their stated objectives, and program features, researchers have found that there are about 100 GYO programs across 20 states and are growing in number over time.[70] GYOs can aim to increase the teacher supply, increase teacher diversity, reduce teacher shortages, improve teacher effectiveness, and improve teacher retention. However, there seems to be substantial misalignment between the stated purposes of some GYOs and the program features they have. For instance, less than half of GYOs have program features that are explicitly connected to increasing diversity or boosting teacher retention. In short, while there is a growing interest in GYOs, these initiatives are in the beginning stages, and we need evidence on how effective they are in meeting their main purposes of increasing the teacher supply and diversifying the teacher workforce.

Summary of Alternative Pathways into Teaching

Overall, the evidence suggests that alternative pathways into teaching can recruit more candidates and often candidates from more diverse backgrounds. Alternative certification programs provide quicker preparation at reduced costs compared with traditional programs of teacher preparation, are relatively effective in recruiting candidates who did not enroll in a traditional program, and succeed in attracting many candidates of color. Early evidence on TRPs suggests they are successful at recruiting and preparing teacher candidates, but it is unclear what magnitude of change they can bring about. Similarly, GYOs have been touted as effective teacher pipelines, particularly for isolated communities and communities in need of teachers of color, but we have limited evidence on how effective they really are.

Pipeline Policies for Recruiting Teachers

In the previous sections, we discussed the different categories of recruitment policies and strategies. However, we can also think about these strategies from another perspective. Instead of what type of policies to use in recruiting teachers, we can think about where in the teacher supply pipeline we can implement policies, programs, and initiatives to recruit more teacher candidates into the profession. Through this lens of "when" instead of "how," there are three main points of entry into the profession that we can potentially influence: before college, during college, or after college. The majority of the policies and initiatives that we discussed previously aim to increase teachers during or after college. As such, we want to review what has been done to recruit teacher candidates into the profession before they enter college. In other words, we focus on programs aimed at high school students. There are two main ways to increase the number of candidates interested in the teaching profession before they attend college: (1) loans and grants/scholarships to reduce postsecondary costs and (2) GYO pipeline programs.

The first approach to increasing candidates before college provides offering loans, grants, or scholarships to interested high school students who agree to enroll in a teacher preparation program at a traditional university. For instance, the South and North Carolina Teaching Fellows Program recruits high school seniors into the teaching profession and awards up to $6,000 ($6,500 in North Carolina) in annual scholarships for four years.[71] The Teacher of Science and Math program provides scholarships to high school seniors to become teachers.[72] Though many teaching candidates who receive these financial supports apparently do become teachers, the existing literature is not clear about whether these individuals would still have entered teaching without the scholarships. Thus, it is unclear whether these initiatives help to attract candidates to the profession.

The second approach is through GYO programs. These programs aim to increase the number of high school students interested in teaching through training courses, extracurricular programs, or hands-on experiences with children. The main idea here is that these candidates will be more interested in entering the profession and return to teach in their local communities, given that most teachers work less than 50 miles from where they grew up.[73] These GYOs that aim to encourage high school students to become teachers have grown substantially in the past decade, with about three out of five GYOs having this specific aim.[74] There is currently little evidence, however, examining the effects and efficacy of these programs. It is unclear how much they increase the number of teachers.

In many ways, the pre-college portion of the pipeline is where we have the least evidence, in part because the programs tend to be small in scale and many are too recent to have been formally evaluated. Moreover, that aspiring teachers need to complete so many steps as they move toward classroom teaching, we worry that the ultimate impact of these programs may be somewhat muted unless widely adopted across US high schools. We develop what this expansion might look like in chapter 7, with a helpful comparison of the Junior Reserve Officers' Training Corps.

Diversifying the Teacher Workforce and Attracting Teachers in Shortage Areas

Diversity in the teacher workforce is lacking in two principal ways. First, traditional teacher training programs have not been able to produce enough teachers in some geographic areas and in some subjects. Second, the teacher workforce is overwhelmingly white and female. In this section, we discuss recruitment strategies designed to diversify the teacher workforce demographically (for more male teachers, teachers of color, and teachers from rural areas) and in specialty (for more teachers of STEM, special education, and bilingual education).

Diversifying the Teacher Workforce Demographically

The good news here is that we have evidence that there are multiple ways to recruit candidates from various racial/ethnic backgrounds and candidates from rural areas. In terms of recruiting teachers from different racial/ethnic backgrounds, there are a variety of models and examples to follow. For instance, there are the Minority Access to Teacher Education in South Carolina, a school-university partnership in New York, or the Abriendo Caminos / Opening Pathways GYO program in Nevada, or the Call Me Mister program to recruit Black males into teaching.[75] Some recruitment programs are effective at attracting diversity along multiple dimensions. For instance, the Generation Schools Network in Colorado is able to attract applicants from rural areas as well as minority applicants.[76] Math Immersion programs in multiple states are able to attract male, Black, and Hispanic teachers.[77] The New York City Teaching Fellows program attracts both Black and Hispanic "community-insiders," those who have roots in their community in which they teach.[78] TRPs and GYOs in particular seem to have a good track record of attracting and recruiting minority applicants.[79] We are, however, cautious in interpreting these success stories, as they are small in scale and, for the most part, have not been rigorously studied. It is thus unclear the extent to which they can increase supply on a large scale.

These programs and initiatives have pointed to measures that may contribute to success: (a) promoting open and frequent communications to establish trust and rapport; (b) providing experiences to ease entry into college and/or the program; (c) having reliable leadership at the institution; (d) creating and leveraging early outreach programs; (e) establishing a mission statement and philosophy that are meaningful to the targeted participants; (f) providing culturally relevant perspectives and experiences, including affinity groups; and (g) offering grants and stipends for candidates from disadvantaged backgrounds.[80]

To increase the pool of teachers of color will require more than simply increasing salary (in small to moderate amounts) to attract those who could pursue other better-paying careers.[81] A comprehensive recruitment strategy would need to attract pre-college students, community college students, and those who serve within the community. For instance, partnerships with school districts are necessary for recruiting employed paraprofessionals. Cross-institutional agreements that clarify which community college courses will transfer to four-year colleges are crucial for accessing the considerable pool of students of color in two-year colleges. Collaborating with community-based organizations, such as churches, civic groups, and service agencies in communities of color, is also beneficial for identifying potential recruits interested in teaching and committed to returning to their communities as educators. Historically Black college colleges and universities and minority-serving institutions are another underutilized source of racially minoritized teachers, particularly when affordability is no longer a primary issue.

Research into growing the number of teachers for rural districts suggests that financial incentives and alternative certification, including transitioning paraprofessionals into teachers, in rural settings may be effective in attracting candidates, though, again, much of this research is not rigorous and should be viewed with some caution.[82] For instance, the Generation Schools Network through the Colorado Rural Education Collaborative nearly doubled the number of students enrolled in the program. Principals from Minnesota's public schools regularly use alternative licensure as a recruiting tool in rural areas.[83] As noted earlier, the LEAP initiative in Mississippi had success in recruiting teachers for poor rural school districts.[84]

From research on teacher recruitment in non-rural areas, there are several takeaways that may apply to recruiting teachers in rural settings:[85]

- Rural schools and districts should establish a long-term enduring relationship with nearby educator preparation programs.
- Exposing teacher candidates to rural teaching opportunities is an important step in recruiting them to rural locales.
- Support and funding should be a community endeavor that involves state legislatures, boards of education, and institutions of higher education.
- Recruitment has to be strategic, sustained, and rooted in the community.

There are also advertisement strategies that can be used to recruit teachers:[86]

- ads highlighting non-materialistic and student-centered incentives such as classroom autonomy and the ability to develop close relationships with students;
- ads identifying advantages of rural teaching and living that are not solely economic incentives;
- ads highlighting the positive aspects of the job yet are also candid about the challenges;
- ads specific to schools or subject areas;
- ads clearly visible on district and school websites and sustained over time;
- ads using employee perspective, quotes, and word-of-mouth;

- ads emphasizing how rural schools are rooted in the community; and
- ads providing accurate, contain credible information coming from reliable sources.

In sum, the research on recruitment indicates that there are specific strategies that should be leveraged in order to recruit teachers to rural areas. We note that most of these strategies are non-financial strategies that would require minimal monetary investment to implement.

Attracting Teachers to Subject Areas with Shortages

While shortage areas for teachers vary by district and state, we focus here on STEM and special education teachers since they are most commonly needed in most districts and states. Much of the literature on teacher recruitment for STEM and special education suggests that financial incentives, either as grants/scholarships or salary/bonus, seem to work to some extent. For instance, science and math teacher education recruitment programs, like the Noyce Scholarship of the National Science Foundation, which provide scholarships in exchange for a commitment to teach at high-needs schools, are able to recruit some candidates into the profession. Similarly, the Teacher of Science and Math program that provides scholarships to high school seniors, pre-college students, and professionals looking to change careers can recruit STEM teachers. There is some descriptive and qualitative work suggesting that these programs can recruit candidates.[87] For instance, a loan forgiveness program in North Carolina may have shaped some candidates' career goals toward STEM education, but it is unclear how much it would influence people who are not already interested or would have joined the profession anyway.[88] For special educators, a $10,000 salary bonus in 2020 was able to reduce the proportion of vacant special education teaching positions by 32% and underqualification by 35%,[89] but this is the only rigorous study we are aware of that has examined how financial incentives affect the special education teacher workforce.

In short, there are some challenges to consider in how grants and loan forgiveness may attract and recruit more people into the profession.

First, these programs tend to be small in scale (some Noyce programs fund a handful of Noyce Scholars each year). Second, we know of no large-scale rigorous analysis of how effective these programs are at recruiting candidates, and we also know of no studies that conduct a cost-to-benefit analysis of these programs (which would examine how much it costs to recruit a single STEM teacher with a large grant like the Noyce and what benefits that would provide to school districts). This does not mean that providing financial incentives to recruit STEM teachers is a bad idea, but it does mean that we need more evidence for their effectiveness, and we also have to consider how financial incentives may not be able to solve STEM teacher shortage by themselves.

At the moment, there is evidence that ACPs, TRPs, and GYOs seem able to recruit candidates for STEM and special education. For instance, as previously mentioned, the Generation Schools Network in Colorado was able to attract math teachers and alleviate some math teacher shortage.[90] A special education residency program was able to recruit more than 120 special education teachers over a five-year period.[91] An alternative route program that focused on social justice elements and supports for Black men successfully recruited and retained many Black male special educators, a rare group of special educators.[92] Many teacher residencies and alternative certification programs also succeed in recruiting STEM and/or special education candidates.[93] Yet whether these are individual success stories or could be scaled up is uncertain. In summary, changing licensure requirements and allowing alternative ways for candidates to show their expertise may increase the supply of STEM and special education teachers, but there is a continued need to gather additional evidence in support of this strategy.[94]

Conclusion

The journey from initial interest in teaching to stepping into the classroom is a long and complex one. Only a fraction of candidates makes it through each stage: entering preparation programs, graduating, meeting licensure requirements, and securing a teaching position. This narrowing of the pipeline is not accidental; it reflects measures in place to ensure that beginning teachers have achieved important milestones and met certain standards designed to ensure that teachers are sufficiently prepared when they enter the classroom. At the same time, structural barriers can discourage prospective teachers along the way, a concern particularly among aspiring teachers of color and teachers in shortage areas.

In response, policymakers have introduced recruitment strategies aimed at lowering entry barriers through financial incentives, reduced licensure requirements, and alternative pathways of entry into a teaching career. Our review of the evidence suggests that these policies can make it easier for individuals to become teachers. Yet we worry that they are ultimately insufficient in making a serious dent in teacher shortages. As an example, though financial incentives can be used to recruit teachers, they are not necessarily the only way to attract more people into the profession. Other factors, such as candidates' confidence in their ability to teach and their getting encouragement from family and friends or the community, also contribute to outcomes,[95] and some of these factors are not easily malleable (e.g., confidence or family encouragement). To this point, while financial incentives could attract many to teaching, small financial incentives alone will not attract enough people into the profession or into schools that need them.[96]

A critical appraisal of these policies is particularly important when considering their role in attracting and recruiting potential candidates for high-shortage areas like STEM and special education and for racially diverse candidates. Alternative certification, teacher residency, and Grow Your Own programs all have potential for growing a more diverse pool of teachers, although whether these efforts can be scaled sufficiently remains unclear. More concerning is that even when such programs recruit and prepare candidates toward meeting local staffing needs, many of these teachers will face the same challenging conditions that drive off other teachers. For recruitment initiatives to reduce shortages will require making teaching a more attractive career option to a broader population, and this necessitates systemic reforms to teaching itself, which we elaborate on in the next two chapters.

CHAPTER 6

Policies to Increase Teacher Retention

AS WE DISCUSSED IN CHAPTER 3, teacher turnover is one of the key contributors to teacher shortages in the United States and elsewhere. Over the past three decades, before and after the COVID-19 pandemic, about 16% of teachers left the classroom every year.[1] Approximately half of these teachers leave their school to teach at another school, while the other half leave the teaching profession altogether. Nationally, this means that more than 250,000 teachers will leave their current school annually, and a similar number will leave the profession. While this 16% annual turnover rate has been consistent for decades, it should not be seen as a natural part of schooling. As this constant movement has substantial monetary and non-monetary costs to students, schools, and districts,[2] school leaders and policymakers have spent a great deal of time and effort to retain teachers in the classroom. Broadly speaking, the resulting initiatives can be organized into three general buckets: (1) financial incentives, (2) preparation and support, and (3) working conditions. We view system-level improvements in each area as critical for strengthening a career model of teaching where teachers feel adequately compensated for their labor and supported to carry out what can be an incredibly taxing job.

Similar to financial incentives to recruit teachers, there are many financial incentives that can be implemented to retain teachers (e.g., bonuses, salary increases). Though improved compensation is an important starting point, it must be accompanied by systems that help to support the work of teachers. The second category, preparation, support, and professional development, is about providing pre-service and in-service teachers with experiences, training, and ongoing guidance, such as high-quality mentoring and induction or instructional coaching, to help them become better teachers, feel successful, and remain in the classroom. The last category is the school conditions in which teachers work. This expansive category ranges from the number of courses assigned to teachers to the administrative support they receive. For each of these categories, we discuss where their respective policies have been implemented and the extent to which they have been evaluated and found effective. Then we examine whether these policies have been used to target the retention of specific types of teachers (e.g., STEM, special education). More importantly, these are the types of teacher-centered policies that will make teaching more attractive and build conditions for schools in which teachers want to stay.

When recommending policies to increase teacher retention, we prioritize rigorous studies when available and note the areas with this strong evidence base. We see the evidence presented in this chapter as providing an important foundation for the steps that school and district leaders can take to increase teacher retention. Much of this evidence focuses on strategies targeted toward teachers or schools facing shortages. As a result, these strategies can help to address specific groups of teachers but are less likely to foster the broader conditions that we believe are needed to reinvigorate a career model of teaching poised to end shortages. The purpose of this chapter is to prioritize policies with more rigorous evidence before sketching our more aspirational vision for ending teacher shortages in the next chapter.

Financial Incentives to Retain Teachers

Given the many types of financial incentives we have to recruit teachers, it only makes sense that we also have many financial incentives that can work to retain teachers. Specifically, there are bonus programs and salary increases that districts and states have at their disposal that could be implemented to retain more teachers. We conclude this section by discussing teacher pensions. In each area, we pay careful attention to when these policies have been successful and to important considerations for policymakers to take into account.

Bonus Programs

Financial incentives, including bonuses, salary increases, and other pecuniary benefits, are usually the first thing the public, school leaders, and policymakers think of that could be used to incentivize teachers to stay in the classroom. To this point, financial incentives have been used frequently to try to influence teachers' decision to stay, and, generally, these bonus programs have been found to be effective in retaining teachers to varying degrees of success. For instance, an $1,800 bonus was provided for math, science, and special education teachers working in low-performing or high-poverty schools in North Carolina if they stayed in their school. This relatively small bonus decreased attrition rates by 15%–18%, and it had the biggest effects for teachers having between 10 and 19 years of experience.[3] A similar retention bonus program in Florida was found to decrease turnover by nearly a third.[4] Math and science teachers who received an additional $21,000 over six years in Georgia were less likely to leave.[5]

To be clear, bonus programs do not necessarily have a constant effect on all types of teachers. For instance, in one rigorous analysis of teacher retention bonuses, Springer and colleagues found that a $5,000 retention bonus for effective teachers had no effect for the general population of teachers but had a consistent positive effect for teachers in tested subjects and grades.[6] More importantly, they found that, for every teacher retained by the bonus, their students would learn substantially more than if the teacher were replaced by someone else and that the bonus program would pay for itself through tax revenue from estimated eventual student earnings, even if only 10% of the teachers receiving the bonus stayed in the program. There have also been initiatives, such as the IMPACT teacher evaluation program in Washington, DC, where performance-based bonuses did not seem to effectively retain teachers.[7] However, a systematic review and meta-analysis of these performance-based program, also known as "merit pay programs," found that, on average, merit pay programs increase teacher retention.[8] In particular, meta-analytic results that quantitatively synthesize all available studies examining merit pay found that such programs decreased teacher attrition by 1.6 percentage points, or about 10% of the probability of switching to another school or leaving the profession.

Moreover, merit pay programs have positive effects on student learning by potentially changing the composition of teachers by retaining effective teachers. Though not all studies are rigorously designed, they tend to show a positive relationship between merit pay programs and teacher retention, particularly for more effective teachers.[9] For instance, Missouri teachers in a performance-based career ladder program (bonus pay of $1,500–$3,000) were less likely to move to a different district and less likely to leave teaching,[10] and similarly, Texas teachers in a merit pay program (performance incentives from $2,500 to $3,000) were less likely to turn over.

Another type of financial program incentivizes teachers to stay in or move to traditionally disadvantaged schools, such as resource-constrained schools that serve greater proportions of low-income or minoritized students. Studies examining this type of incentive found that a medium-to-large incentive (e.g., $20,000 over two years) can result in effective teachers moving to high-needs schools and increasing their retention.[11] It should be noted, however, that some of these programs did encounter implementation problems such as incorrectly rewarding some teachers (or not rewarding others) as well as being opaque in terms of the criteria for obtaining the bonus.[12]

In fact, these financial incentive programs may be more effective than we recognize. The efficacy of these programs may be understated if teachers question whether the incentives will be available in the long run. If teachers (and districts) are reassured that these programs have a long-term future, they may be more inclined to move to and stay in traditionally disadvantaged schools. To this point, some of the key considerations that policymakers should keep in mind for implementation include these:

- Clearly identify the goals of the financial incentives, and design the program to meet stated goals (e.g., weighing the benefits of across-the-board raise versus targeting specific teachers or teachers in shortage areas).
- Clearly communicate program goals to teachers and administrative leaders.
- Implement the program as stated (i.e., implementation fidelity).
- Ensure long-term sustainability of the program.
- Consider unintended consequences and adverse effects (e.g., raising starting teacher pay to attract and retain new teachers versus concerns about wage compression, which may result in turnover for more experienced teachers or create morale issues if only some teachers get bonuses).

Overall, there is reasonable evidence showing that bonus incentives, particularly for effective teachers or in shortage areas, can improve teacher retention, particularly when implemented well.

Salary Increases

While there are fewer studies leveraging rigorous quantitative approaches that have examined the relationship between a base salary increase and teacher retention, the results do indicate a positive correlation. For instance, a study examining Florida data found that by increasing salary in a low-income district to make it comparable with a more affluent district could increase retention of early-career teachers by about one percentage point.[13] Another study found that a 10% increase in salary was associated with a 14% decrease in teacher turnover.[14] Using detailed longitudinal data from Texas, one of the few causal studies on the topic found that increasing teacher pay reduced teacher turnover.[15] While these effects are smaller than retention bonuses, salary increases tend to be smaller than retention bonuses and are more diffuse by affecting more teachers, both of which may explain their diminished effects.

In examining nearly 30 studies establishing the association between salary increase and teacher retention, Nguyen and colleagues found that increases in salary were generally associated with improved teacher retention.[16] When salary is measured as an increase per $1,000, its relationship with teacher retention is rather small but generally positive.[17] When we compare high salary to low salary, the relationship is stronger.[18] It should be noted that when salary increases are only temporary or in a small amount, then the effects are small (and not practically meaningful) and may dissipate entirely when the incentives are no longer present.[19]

Recently, some states have implemented substantial increases to teacher base salary (e.g., Arkansas), but there is only limited evidence on how this will influence teacher retention. The preliminary evidence for increases in teacher base salaries points to a positive, though modest, relationship. In their rigorous study, Zamarro and colleagues found suggestive evidence showing that raising the minimum salary from $36,000 to $50,000 in Arkansas had modest effects on teacher retention.[20] Future work will need to carefully examine the trade-offs between targeted incentives and across-the-board raises in terms of teacher recruitment and retention as well as other considerations beyond teacher recruitment and retention (e.g., mitigating district poverty rates, particularly for rural and high-poverty districts; the cost of living in high-cost cities and regions). However, we see substantial increases to teacher base salary as a very promising path to significantly improve teacher recruitment and retention, which we discuss in more detail in the next chapter.

Pensions and Retirement Benefits

Rigorously designed studies suggest that the model for teacher pensions and retirement benefits could be changed to advance some of the other goals we have outlined in more financially viable ways. Existing evidence suggests that many teachers do not value defined-benefit (DB) pension benefits and would prefer higher salaries.[21] Additionally, teachers are much more responsive to salary changes than to equally sized pension changes.[22] Using a life-cycle model of consumption and retirement, it is estimated that more than 10% of retirement-eligible teachers would have been retained in Wisconsin if the state had cut pensions rather than salaries.[23] In other words, if we shift from DB pension plans to alternative models and raise teacher salary, then teachers, on the whole, would respond positively to these changes. Having a higher starting salary would raise the prestige and societal status of teaching and do more to recruit and retain teachers than would maintaining pensions or even raising them by an equivalent amount. Moreover, since these alternative models do not make total teacher compensation severely back-loaded (in the traditional DB plan, benefits accrue rapidly near retirement), the higher salary would also likely attract more talented candidates and improve teacher quality.[24]

In terms of how the pension system influences teacher retention, the evidence strongly suggests that increases in the pension system do not seem to have a strong relationship with employee retention until the end of teachers' careers. Increases in pension benefits, even the generous increase of 60% in pension wealth that occurred in St. Louis public schools in 1999, do not meaningfully improve teacher retention and are not cost-effective, particularly given the cost of the enhancement to future unfunded liabilities.[25] Moreover, when given a choice, the majority of teachers prefer the hybrid plan over the traditional pension plan.[26] Recent evidence also suggests that teachers who transferred out of DB plans into hybrid plans are less likely to turn over than teachers who stay in the traditional pension plan.[27] Moreover, teachers opting into the hybrid plan tend to be more effective than teachers who stay in the DB plan.[28] Relatedly, substantial salary increases would likely reduce the probability of older teachers retiring while increases in pension benefits would likely increase the probability of retirement.[29] Recently, simulation evidence suggests that switching from a pension plan to a defined-contribution, or DC, plan, would lengthen the teaching career of older teachers by about two years.[30] Similarly, an increase to a pension plan serves only to accelerate teacher retirement and to reduce teacher quality while an increase to DC plans has the opposite effects.[31]

Despite the historical evidence that pensions have been a hallmark of the career model of teaching, we see them as an important area for revision. There are alternative cost-neutral models, including a DC plan, where both teachers and the employers (state or district) contribute a set amount, usually with the state matching the teacher contribution; cash balance (CB) plans, a type of DB plan that provides a guaranteed rate of return; and hybrid plans that include a mix of pension and DC elements.[32] Other levers include extending social security coverage to include teachers, as most teachers are not eligible for both social security benefits and pension plans and to make current pension plans more portable. We see these changes as important, particularly if it paves the way for direct financial compensation during teachers' careers, which is likely to improve retention to a greater degree.

Preparation and Support to Retain Teachers

In this section, we discuss how teacher preparation (certification and training) as well as induction, mentoring programs, and professional development (i.e., in-service activities and training to enrich teacher pedagogy and keep them up-to-date with recent research) are related to teacher retention.

Teacher Preparation

To start, we have a large amount of evidence showing that teachers who are prepared by traditional university preparation programs or have standard certification are more likely to stay in teaching.[33] Much of the academic literature finds that teachers with regular or standard certification are much less likely to leave the profession than those who do not.[34] Another way of thinking about this is that teachers who have regular preparation are substantially more likely to stay in teaching relative to teachers who have "lateral entry," where they come in through alternative certification pathways or provisional licensure.[35] Yet it is important to emphasize that since teachers select into different pathways, it is difficult to determine definitively whether the preparation program themselves cause these patterns or else some underlying differences between the teacher candidates influence who selects one entry pathway over another.

By increasing access, these alternative entry mechanisms allow more candidates to become teachers and attract a more diverse pool of applicants. However, there is a trade-off between recruitment and retention for traditional teacher preparation programs and alternative pathways into teaching, as those opting for this lateral entry are less likely to stay in the teaching profession. This could be because candidates who are more inclined to stay in teaching are also more likely to seek out traditional programs than those who may test the waters to see if teaching is the right profession for them (and thus seek out alternative pathways that are not as time consuming or expensive). Moreover, teachers who have comprehensive preparation are likely better positioned to handle the demands of teaching as they have substantially more coursework related to the theory and practice of teaching as well as having experienced teaching during a field experience or student teaching. For instance, teacher candidates who completed more weeks of student teaching planned to stay in teaching longer.[36] Teachers who did not have student teaching were substantially more likely to leave teaching than those who had student teaching.[37] We further note that it is not only having student teaching experience that matters but also the quality of the student teaching experience.[38]

While the type of program and its specific characteristics are related to how long pre-service teachers remain in teaching, there is also evidence showing that where student teachers are placed when they are learning to teach (i.e., field placement) also matters. On one hand, if student teachers are placed in harder-to-staff or traditionally disadvantaged schools, they may be better equipped to learn and work in difficult working environments later. For instance, these student teachers may have more opportunities to learn how to manage a classroom than student teachers in schools where there are few classroom behavioral issues. Alternatively, easier-to-staff schools may provide a more supportive setting and better professional development for student teachers. Easier-to-staff schools can attract and retain teachers better (by dint of being easier-to-staff), suggesting they have or can provide positive working conditions. Empirical research finds more support for the second hypothesis. Specifically, student teaching in an easier-to-staff school has positive effects on teacher retention, as well as positive effects on student achievement.[39] This finding remains true even if the student teacher ends up teaching in the hardest-to-staff schools. It suggests that placing student teachers in a positive working environment to start their learning would bolster their teaching ability as well as induce them to stay in teaching longer.

Other studies suggest that there may be important features of teacher preparation, though we emphasize that they have not been rigorously tested. One example is mission-driven cohort-based programs. For example, pre-service teachers in the Multicultural Urban Secondary English program at the University of California, Berkeley, found that the cohort model was particularly important for teachers-in-training. The cohort provided a space for these pre-service teachers from different backgrounds and experiences to support each other, during and after the program.[40] Freedman and Appleman also found that several factors contribute to teacher retention, particularly for high-poverty urban schools.[41] Specifically, a sense of mission, the development and/or reinforcement of hard work and persistence by the teacher education program, synergy between theory and practice for teaching, and ongoing support from other teachers in the same program all contribute to teacher retention.[42] Teacher residency, apprenticeship, and Grow Your Own programs are all recent attempts to adopt these program features in different ways; with the possible exception of residencies, however, it is too soon to say to what degree teachers from these program are likely to have an extended career in teaching.

To summarize, the overwhelming majority of teachers still enter teaching through traditional university-based preparation programs, which has been shown to predict a longer career in teaching. We believe that such programs should continue to be fostered and supported as the backbone of a high-quality, stable teacher workforce. At the same time, the current landscape of teacher preparation reflects a growing recognition that the "to and through" model of teacher preparation in university-based preparation programs fails to encompass the diverse set of ways that people now become teachers. We applaud the policy and programmatic shifts that encourage greater experimentation but emphasize that alternative entry pathways must still include the comprehensive supports that ensure teachers will bring the needed content and pedagogical knowledge to their first teaching job. When new teachers lack such preparation, we worry that the demands of teaching make it too easy for many teachers to call it quits when they do not feel successful in their first teaching job.

Teacher Mentoring, Induction, and Professional Development

Working teachers need help from others to succeed. As obvious as it may sound, this is critical for us to remember. In this section, we adopt a "life course" perspective to teachers' career development that emphasizes a range of supports to help them hone their craft throughout their career.[43] For early-career teachers, this includes mentoring and comprehensive induction programs. For veteran teachers, this includes professional development and instructional coaching.

To start, we discuss how mentoring and induction programs can provide fertile ground for teachers to thrive and thus to remain in teaching for a long time. A large amount of evidence suggests that teachers who participate in mentoring or induction programs are substantially less likely to leave the profession than those who do not.[44] Similar to apprentice models, these mentoring and induction programs can provide the hands-on experience and support that acclimate teachers to the profession and bridge any gaps that may exist in their training. Over and over, studies find that mentors and induction programs are associated with substantial increases in teacher retention.[45] For instance, rigorous studies of national data have shown that first-year teachers who participate in induction programs are much more likely to stay in the same classroom than those who do not.[46] Other descriptive studies have found that an induction and mentoring program reduced teacher attrition by more than 25% in just two years.[47] Regarding mentoring programs, the effect of having a mentor who has experience working in the same school is even better.[48]

We note, however, that it is not absolutely clear what level of support and mentoring is necessary to help teachers be successful and to stay in the profession. Experimental evidence examining high-dosage compared to low-dosage mentoring showed no relationship with teacher retention.[49] A more recent experimental study examining a case of intensive, instructionally focused coaching to teachers also found no difference for teacher retention.[50] In both of these studies, the control group included teachers who received mentoring usually provided by the district instead of more intense and targeted interventions, suggesting that the most important factor may be whether a teacher has a mentor. It is also possible that the mentors who provided the supports in the treated conditions had less knowledge of the specific school context than did the school-based mentors, so they were unable to provide context-specific guidance.

Synthesizing the literature on mentoring programs, scholars have recommended that induction and mentoring programs include mentoring with observation, authentic collaboration, and reduced teaching load or fewer different courses or course preps.[51] Moreover, best practices include matching mentors and mentees by field/subject area or grade level in elementary school, providing stipends/salary bonuses for mentors, administrative supports for mentoring, having common planning time to enable mentors and mentees to interact frequently, and providing ongoing training.[52] Yet these specific features have not been rigorously tested, and thus the optimal design of mentoring programs is an area of ongoing research.

For more experienced teachers, professional development and instructional coaching may continue to help them develop throughout the course of their careers. To start, a seminal meta-analysis examining 60 causal studies found that instructional coaching can increase student learning.[53] While this is robust evidence about the effect of instructional coaching on teacher instruction and, subsequently, on student learning, there is less evidence on how instructional coaching may affect teacher retention. In general, however, prior work has established that professional development is correlated with job satisfaction and a sense of success, leading to higher retention.[54] Moreover, teachers who report having strong in-service professional development are more likely to stay.[55] That said, these studies were not designed to determine whether instructional coaching or professional development affects retention.

Even if it has not been rigorously tested, researchers have offered recommendations for reaching teachers who do not have regular access to professional development, such as rural teachers or teachers with few colleagues in their school or the district (i.e., STEM and special education teachers) due to a lack of "critical" mass. In other words, in rural and professional isolation settings, it is important for schools and districts to provide professional development when and where they can.[56] This should include pooling nearby district resources to provide professional development, sending teachers to urban areas where professional development is more abundant, and accessing online professional development or virtual learning communities.

In sum, the evidence on teacher mentoring, induction, and professional development seems to strongly suggest that these efforts provide fertile grounds for teachers to grow and to improve their instructional skills. Early-career teachers who have access to high-quality mentoring or induction programs not only improve their effectiveness as instructors but are also more likely to stay in the profession. Instructional coaching and professional development can invigorate more established teachers and push them to further hone their craft, which may be linked with an increased likelihood they will stay in teaching. From the moment teachers first set foot in the classroom until the last year of their teaching, they should be provided with opportunities to improve, increasing their effectiveness in teaching and increasing their commitment to the profession.

Improving Working Conditions to Retain Teachers

A consistent finding in teacher retention research is that teachers' working conditions matter. Seminal work by Susan Moore Johnson and others has illustrated how teacher working conditions are critical to teacher retention. For instance, based on longitudinal interview data from 50 new teachers, Johnson and Birkeland find that teachers who are provided with collegial interactions and opportunities for growth and are assigned appropriate classes to teach, adequate resources, and schoolwide structures to support student learning are more likely to stay in their schools than those who are not.[57] Schools that have positive working conditions for teachers have teachers who are happy and well supported, and consequently, they are much more likely to remain in the same school.[58] Teachers in Arizona public schools who rated their working conditions, including use of time, school facilities, and school leadership, as more satisfactory were more likely to stay.[59] A more rigorous study from New York City indicated that improvements in school scholarship, school safety, and teacher relationships were all associated with improved retention.[60] These three domains consistently emerge as important working conditions associated with teacher retention. Others include the physical work environment, teaching assignments, and teacher autonomy.

What is more, across dozens of studies, teachers were found to be more likely to stay in schools with stronger administrative support.[61] One of our nationally representative studies shows that when teachers report higher levels of administrative support, they are much more likely to stay in their current school. Better administrative support can consist of administrators encouraging faculty on a regular basis; consulting with faculty on decisions that affect the school, their work, or students; or procuring additional resources and equipment for the school.[62]

A key way that principals appear to positively shape teacher working conditions is in terms of maintaining a safe and orderly working environment. Teachers are also more likely to stay in the same school when there are fewer student disciplinary issues or lower teacher victimization.[63] Given the increase in threats and violence directed at teachers, policymakers are working on developing and implementing national research, practice, and policies to address this problem, and administrators are critical to these initiatives.[64] In sum, principals can create work environments that are supportive of teachers and enable them to feel that their work is meaningful, which then increases the likelihood teachers will stay in their school.

In all of this work, it is difficult to understate the role of the administration, particularly the principals, in engendering positive working conditions for teachers. A large body of literature has shown that principals have the responsibility and power to shape teacher working conditions and can take different approaches to supporting and retaining teachers.[65] For instance, principals who are aware of challenges that affect new teachers, those who take a proactive approach to support new teachers, and those who are committed to professional growth for themselves and their teachers retain teachers at higher rates than those who do not.[66] Moreover, effective principals who communicate regularly to the faculty, recognize faculty for their accomplishments inside and outside school, and enforce school rules equitably are also better able to retain teachers at higher rates.[67] To this point, teacher perceptions of administration and administrative support have a substantial role in teacher decisions to stay or leave their school, with some work showing that they may have the biggest influence on teacher decisions to stay in or leave their school.[68]

Comparable to administrative support, teachers are also more likely to stay when they report higher levels of teacher collaboration or cohesion at their school—though this finding tends to come from correlational studies.[69] Teachers are also more likely to stay in teaching when they participate in cross-school collaboration.[70] An interesting finding is that, when teachers report high levels of teacher cooperation, they are less likely to leave their school for another one.[71] In other words, when teachers feel that the faculty is cooperative and works well among themselves, they are much more likely to remain in the same school since they enjoy the working environment.

Schools with better facilities and physical workspace experience less teacher attrition, though, again, these studies tend to not be rigorously designed.[72] Simply put, schools are where teachers spend a major portion of their waking hours, so the work environment matters for teachers as much as it does for everyone else. In particular, many schools have poor indoor-air quality, faulty heating or cooling, or harsh classroom lighting with minimal natural light, all of which affects teacher satisfaction as well as their mental health. Research in this area suggests that teachers strongly prefer to work and stay in schools with better facilities.[73]

Teachers who have stable teaching assignments, such as having the same subjects/courses from year to year, are also more likely to stay,[74] as having stable teaching assignments greatly reduces the amount of time it takes for teachers to prepare for classes. Teachers who report positive working conditions are consistently more likely to stay than those who report otherwise.[75] We note that even something as seemingly small as having adequate teaching materials matters for teacher retention.[76]

Given the highly localized nature of teacher labor markets, there are also local policies that shape the organizational conditions conducive to whether a teacher stays or leaves, including the degree to which teachers have control over instructional decisions (e.g., pacing guides, common assessments), are involved in school and district decision-making, and have robust school support systems to help them successfully work with students with a diversity of academic and behavioral needs. For instance, teachers with more classroom autonomy are more likely to be retained in the same school than those with less autonomy.[77]

What is very clear to us from our own research and from that of other scholars is that teacher working conditions matter greatly for teacher retention. In particular, administrative support and engagement are especially compelling as administrators are able to customize their supports in ways that benefit individual teachers. For instance, some teachers may think having more curricular materials would help their instruction and reduce workload, while other teachers may find this reduces their autonomy, and administrators are able to accommodate these differences. While we see this area as promising, we do note that most of these studies on teacher working conditions are observational and that no strong research record exists on stipulating how to foster these working conditions without unintended consequences or adding an undue amount of work for administrators. As such, we advocate for interventions to improve teacher working conditions while minimizing potential harms.

Retention for Early-Career Educators, Teachers of Color, and Teachers in Hard-to-Staff Settings

As the human resources model becomes more embedded in school systems, it has become apparent that customized approaches to teacher retention are needed. This includes careful attention to policy approaches aimed at early-career teachers, teachers of color, teachers in hard-to-staff subjects (e.g., STEM teachers, special education teachers) and teachers in schools most likely to face hiring difficulties (e.g., higher-poverty schools), as these teachers are most vulnerable and are most likely to turn over. Thus, similar to our discussion on teacher recruitment policies, we pay careful attention to policy approaches aimed at early-career teachers, teachers of color, and teachers in hard-to-staff subjects and in hard-to-staff schools. Though we find it important to focus on these subpopulations of teachers who turn over at higher rates (in the case of early-career teachers), are underrepresented within the teacher workforce (in the case of teachers of color), or face the most acute shortages, we note that the evidence base informing this section is not as rigorous as that reported elsewhere in this chapter.

We start with early-career teachers, that is, teachers in their first five years of teaching. We focus on this specific group because they are the most likely group of teachers to leave.[78] While all of the discussion above holds true for early-career teachers as well as more experienced teachers, there are some additional considerations that we should take into account, given that 40%–50% of early-career teachers leave the profession by year five. Some of the key factors that influence early-career teachers' retention include collegiality and support, student engagement and behavior management, working conditions and teaching resources, professional learning/development, workload, and isolation/belonging.[79] If early-career teachers are not supported and do not feel they belong in teaching or are not well suited to the school, then they are much more likely to leave the school and the profession altogether.[80] Both qualitative and quantitative evidence suggests that these issues are particularly influential for early-career teachers, and international evidence also suggests that these factors play similar roles for teachers in various countries.[81] As noted in the previous section, principals in particular should be intentional with how they support early-career teachers because the principals can create work environments that are supportive and appealing to early-career teachers.

While there is definitely a need for more teachers of color in education, this is not necessarily because these teachers are quitting at higher rates than other teachers, particularly once we take into account the poor working conditions where they often start their teaching career.[82] A systematic review examining teacher attrition and retention has shown that teachers of color are not more likely to leave teaching than white teachers.[83] In fact, across some studies, Hispanic teachers are actually more likely to stay in teaching than white teachers.[84] One of the primary reasons why prior studies observed minority teachers leaving at higher rates is simply that many minority teachers begin their career in hard-to-staff schools or schools with challenging working conditions.[85] It is largely the working conditions and lack of support that drive these teachers out of the classroom. In many ways, similar to early-career teachers, minoritized teachers need to be supported, have good working conditions, and feel that they belong in order to stay where they are; however, because of labor market segmentation, these supports may be in short supply for many of these teachers.[86]

At this point, it may not surprise the reader to learn that many of the policies and practices that would create positive working conditions for early-career teachers and minoritized teachers would apply to all teachers working in high-needs schools that serve a high proportion of economically disadvantaged students and racially minoritized students or students in rural settings. Some factors, however, are even more salient for these high-needs schools. For instance, making a difference to students and the community, being a part of the community, and feeling valued by the school and community are particularly important for retaining teachers in high-needs settings.[87] The high-quality preparation and ongoing support of teacher residency programs and Grow Your Own programs may improve teacher retention in high-needs schools.[88]

There are additional challenges facing rural schools. Due to geographic constraint in rural settings, rural schools tend to offer lower salaries, limited resources and amenities, and reduced professional development opportunities for teachers. In addition to issues mentioned above for all teachers, an exploratory analysis of the key reasons why rural teachers leave includes the location of the school or district, low salary, and job assignments or teaching load.[89] As such, some of the ways we can improve rural teacher retention include raising salaries, increasing resources to teachers, strategic recruitment, and providing more professional development,[90] some of which may require districts to pool their resources while the state or federal government supplements with additional monies. Districts should be creative in offering support and professional development such as facilitating group outings for new teachers or providing weekly group meetings with administrators. There are also leadership and administrative policies that can help with rural teacher retention. Specifically, rural schools and districts should provide structural supports for teacher development and opportunities for authentic relationships to be built.[91]

Rural teachers appreciate regular interactions and check-in from administration as these can deepen relationships and prevent isolation.[92] In particular, administrators can help teachers, especially novice teachers, to build positive peer relationships and figure out school culture as well as look for opportunities to validate and celebrate teachers' successes inside and outside the classroom. The connections to the community and personal and professional ties are critical for rural teacher retention.[93] Teacher candidates who develop relationships with the communities where they conducted their student teaching are more likely to work and stay there.[94] In short, opportunity for real growth as a teacher and a sense of belonging are paramount for rural teacher retention.

Last but not least, we discuss teacher retention in hard-to-staff subjects, particularly STEM and special education. While salary plays an important role in STEM and special education teacher retention (as well as their recruitment), professional development and working conditions are critical to their retention.[95] As an example, STEM teachers welcome getting guidance from other STEM teachers in teaching specific content or running certain labs or experiments, particularly hands-on work that get students excited about learning. For special education teachers, they need continual training and support, particularly since they are called to care for more students with a wide range of disabilities and have an ever-increasing caseload size.

In sum, there are good reasons to pay special care to the retention of early-career teachers, teachers of color, and teachers in hard-to-staff settings such as geographically isolated schools or in the areas of STEM and special education. These teachers often are at much higher risk of leaving their school or leaving the profession altogether, so we absolutely need to do more to ensure they have the supports they need to succeed.

Conclusion

Retaining more teachers is the most critical way to maintain a robust workforce of teachers for public education. We cannot and should not spend millions of dollars to train and recruit teachers, only to lose them a year or two into the start of their career. We need to do everything we can to keep effective teachers in the classroom. We discussed three main ways to increase teacher retention: (1) financial incentives, (2) preparation and support, and (3) working conditions.

In terms of financial incentives, we see the intrinsic appeal of across-the-board salary increases on grounds of fairness—a norm that has for so long been part of the ethos of teaching. As we elaborate in the next chapter, it also has the benefit of being able to clearly market to people considering teaching or reentering teaching. While higher salaries would likely increase teacher retention, such an approach is not feasible in many districts. We worry that financial constraints faced by many school districts would result in salary increases that are too small to make a dent in turnover. This is not to say that teachers should not receive raises to keep up with inflation and be competitive with other occupations. If the goal is to improve retention, we worry that small across-the-board salary increases will not consistently achieve this policy goal. When financially possible, policymakers should commit to large increases in teacher salaries.

To supplement salary increases, a good amount of evidence shows that bonus incentives can increase teacher retention. We have seen bonus initiatives to increase retention implemented in North Carolina, Florida, Georgia, Missouri, Texas, and many other states and districts. Merit pay or performance pay programs, though requiring substantial investments and sparking controversy with some teachers and communities, have been shown to have positive effects on student achievement as well as on teacher retention. Medium-to-large financial incentives for teachers to stay in or move to traditionally disadvantaged schools have also been able to shift effective teachers to high-needs schools and increase their retention. While there are substantial challenges, such as transparency for receiving the award, proper implementation, and the political will to push for these programs, these financial incentives for teachers can make a meaningful difference.

In addition to financial incentives, we should also think about how we prepare and support teachers in the first place. While teachers who obtain their license from traditional preparation programs are more likely to stay in teaching, alternative pathways are better able to recruit more diverse candidates. While scholars figure out what components of traditional preparation programs are most important for training effective teachers who are more likely to stay in the profession and then adapt them to alternative pathways, we should experiment with different pathways to teaching, not only to meet current demands and address existing teacher shortages but also to determine how we can diversify the pool of teachers and retain effective teachers. We hope this evidence is helpful in pushing back on efforts to fast-track more teachers into the profession with minimal preparation and support.

Along this same line, we have robust evidence that high-quality mentoring and induction programs can improve teacher quality as well as increase their retention. High-quality mentoring and induction programs should be available to all teachers who are beginning their careers. And to help teachers to continue to grow, districts and states should provide high-quality professional development to experienced teachers. When we are able to provide targeted professional development and coaching to teachers, they will become better teachers (as they figure out what they need to improve) and will want to stay as they become better year after year.

Last but definitely not least, we have a preponderance of evidence showing that working conditions matter a great deal for teachers. There is no version of a teacher retention effort where teacher working conditions should not play a central role. Over and over, the evidence indicates that teachers are more likely to stay in schools with more positive working conditions. And there is not just one way to improve working conditions. There are many ways to improve working conditions, from the physical work environment to teaching assignments to administrative support and teacher cooperation. In many ways, teacher working conditions are the most direct and cost-effective way to improve teacher retention. Administrators, particularly principals, can play an influential role in making these improvements, and many of these factors are arguably within their control. Yes, states and districts should absolutely provide additional money and resources so that schools and principals can experiment with what may work best for improving working conditions in their own circumstance.

Importantly, these strategies cannot be adopted in isolation from one another. Two critical insights from chapter 1 were that (1) the structures of teachers' jobs were amenable to policy change and that (2) efforts to improve teachers' material conditions and expertise complemented one another. We envision similar efforts in the present, with increased teacher compensation corresponding with improved teacher training and support, whether in the form of mentoring for new teachers or working conditions that are more conducive to successful teaching.

Financial incentives, preparation and support, and positive working conditions are particularly important for increasing the retention for early-career teachers, minoritized teachers, teachers in hard-to-staff subjects (STEM, special education), and teachers working in traditionally disadvantaged schools. Given the variation in teacher shortages across these and other groups of teachers, focusing on reducing turnover where it is highest is perhaps the most important strategy for reducing shortages. Consider a back-of-the-envelope calculation where we have about 3.0 to 3.5 million public school teachers: if the number of teachers who leave high-poverty schools was similar to the number of teachers leaving low-poverty schools (17% versus 14% respectively), we would have 45,000 to 52,000 more teachers every year.[96] Similarly, if we increase the national annual teacher retention rate from 84%–85% to 88%–89% (about four percentage points), we would have 120,000 to 140,000 more teachers in the workforce each year. In either case, this would substantially reduce teacher shortages in the schools with the most pervasive challenges in recruiting and retaining teachers.

If there is one thing to take away from this chapter, it is that we have proven ways to increase teacher retention. This is not a case where we have to experiment with lots of different things to figure out what may work. By and large, we know what works. Knowing, of course, does not make it easy to do, but it does make it possible.

CHAPTER 7

An Aspirational Model for Ending Teacher Shortages

OUR DESCRIPTION OF TEACHER shortages underscores their complexity. There is not a singular *teacher shortage* but rather shortages of various groups of teachers (e.g., teachers of color, special education teachers) that affect different schools in different ways (e.g., rural schools, higher-poverty schools). Shortages are characterized not only in terms of unfilled positions but also in terms of hiring of underqualified teachers. The causes of these different shortages are distinct, resulting from high levels of annual teacher turnover in some districts and an inadequate supply of new teachers and a small reserve pool of teachers in other districts—often in combination.

Despite their complexity and persistence, we do not view teacher shortages as insoluble. We believe that steps can be taken to reduce the levels of teacher shortages. The historical record affirms this point. If you told a school principal at the onset of the twentieth century that less than one in six teachers will leave their school each year, they would stare in disbelief. As we documented in chapter 1, concrete steps were taken throughout the twentieth century that improved the conditions of teaching materially, but also in terms of teachers' training and support. Many of these same approaches can be extended into the present.

In this chapter, we put forward a series of recommendations that try to envision a future without teacher shortages.

To develop this framework, we extend arguments made in the last two chapters about the role of financial incentives, preparation and support, and working conditions to develop the conditions that would make teaching a more sustainable profession. In our views, addressing teacher shortages requires a mix of deep systemic changes in how teachers are valued in their school and the community as well as targeted approaches aimed at recruiting and retaining specific types of teachers. For instance, districts struggling with recruiting and retaining enough special education teachers should not adopt policies directed toward all teachers (e.g., across-the-board salary increases) and expect it to address the special education teacher shortage area. There will be a need for targeted policy interventions. At the same time, teachers turn over at high rates, and teacher shortages are worsening in many districts and most states, which suggests that more systemic shifts in working conditions are needed that would help to increase overall teacher recruitment and retention. A one-size-fits-all solution would not be able to address a complex challenge of diverse and varied teacher shortages. Developing an aspirational case for reducing teacher shortages requires lowering the standard of evidence for the recommendations we provide. Unlike the last two chapters, which prioritized rigorous evidence when developing ways to reduce teacher shortages, this chapter builds on the previous two chapters while centering system-level changes and targeted strategies and that will reinvigorate a career model of teaching poised to end shortages.

We begin with the critical role of salary increases in building a teacher-centered system but emphasize that salary increases alone will not be sufficient to end teacher shortages. We then discuss innovative ways that systems can be developed that center the work of teachers. This includes new approaches to recruiting and preparing teachers, attending to career models of teaching, and thinking about new ways that teachers can have greater control over the broader policy conditions that shape their work. Upon this broad-based foundation that would affect all teachers, we then put forward the need for targeted responses that can address key challenges related to teacher recruitment and retention. In each of these sections, we advance an aspirational vision of what schools would look like that do a better job of centering teachers' work. We supplement this with some practical considerations in an effort to help educational leaders and policymakers enact the vision we put forward.

Start with Salary Increases, but Don't End There

As we hope is clear by now, we view shortages as a mix of persistent, large-scale problems that affect the teaching field as a whole and smaller-scale challenges affecting some teachers or schools more strongly. The first step in this process is to increase teacher salaries. A couple of recent policies are characteristic of recent attempts to increase teacher pay. The "Pay Teachers Act" would establish $60,000 as a federal minimum wage for teachers. Other state-level approaches have been framed similarly, such as New Jersey's "50K The First Day," negotiated by the state teachers' union, which set a $50,000 salary floor for new teachers. The key question for these policies is the degree to which starting salaries are high enough to incentivize more people to enter the teaching profession. Higher salaries are impactful not only because of teachers' improved material conditions but because they are interconnected with larger questions of societal status. Increasing salaries symbolizes to current and prospective teachers that teaching matters and is worthy of much higher compensation.

An additional benefit of transparent teacher policies is that they are easily marketable through public service campaigns. One of the historical benefits of the introduction of a uniform teacher pay schedule was its transparency. At a period in which prospective teachers severely underestimate how much teachers earn, establishing and promoting a higher salary floor can assure that teachers are not underpaid given their educational attainment and expertise and that there is widespread public awareness of this fact.

Significant increases to teacher salaries would stand to increase the overall supply of teachers, including attracting more teachers in some difficult-to-fill positions. In particular, math and science teachers appear to be most sensitive to salary levels, given that they likely have opportunities to earn more money outside of teaching. Moreover, higher salaries would also contribute to lower turnover rates, particularly if wages remain competitive with other occupations outside of education.

Practical Considerations in the Design of Teacher Salaries

Though our purpose is not to offer overly prescriptive recommendations, we share a few practical considerations when working to increase teacher salaries. First, salaries are undoubtedly subjected to budgetary constraints. As teachers are public employees, this includes voter backlash to setting salaries too high for local political and economic conditions. Political considerations must also consider the varied financial interests of teachers. Prioritizing salary increases for beginning teacher salaries risks introducing wage compression, which could have a demoralizing effect on veteran teachers and risk exacerbating their turnover.[1] Though there is an argument to be made to differentially raise beginning salaries, it should not be done at the expense of other steps in the pay schedule. Another strategy for increasing salaries is to reallocate a larger fraction of employee's retirement or health benefits toward salaries, a point we touched on in the previous chapter when discussing teacher pensions. New teachers often have a stronger preference toward this approach than veteran teachers.

Another key consideration is how teacher salaries fit into states' school funding formulas. We worry that teacher salaries tend not to be prioritized to the degree that they should, and in many states, there are no statewide salaries or even statewide minimums. Competing priorities often crowd out teacher salary increases. Short-term increases in school funding may do little to increase teacher salaries as districts need to be able to commit to future salary levels. School-funding formulas often allocate funding based on student enrollments rather than the resources needed to reach certain academic standards. With such a funding model, efforts to increase salaries at the state level are supplemented by local school districts, which often have a range of financial commitments that must be met. As an example, in the 2020s, Florida politicians set a goal of $50,000 for beginning teacher salary, though many small, rural districts did not have the local tax base to reach this goal.

Other strategies for increasing teacher salaries would change teachers' working conditions in more demonstrable ways. If school districts were to increase student-teacher ratios, a district would require fewer teachers and thus could pay teachers more.[2] This approach, however, comes at the expense of teaching larger classes, and teachers generally have a stated preference for small class sizes.[3] In addition, many states cap class sizes, which could make this approach difficult for districts to implement unless accompanied by additional policy intervention at the state level.

Another approach to increasing teacher salaries is to reduce district leadership positions and instead fund school-based teacher leadership positions. This approach must be weighed against reduced support services on which teachers depend. For instance, a special education teacher may be pulled from their school-based role to serve as a behavioral specialist in the district. To the extent they are able to support teachers in managing classroom behavior by "pushing in" to classrooms, their impact could be far-reaching, if it helps teachers positively address student behavioral issues. There are broader equity issues to shifting district staff to classroom teaching positions, as district staff are often in support of vulnerable students (e.g., homeless students or foster-family students), and limiting district staff who carry out these educational programs may disproportionately affect students placed at risk by society and its institutions.

Finally, we push back on efforts to use base teacher salaries as a bargaining tool to restrict other teacher work protections (e.g., removing an experience-based salary schedule; limiting due process in employment decisions). In reviewing the history of teacher compensation and teacher shortages, we emphasized how it was not simply the gradual increase in teacher salaries throughout the twentieth century that helped to reduce teacher turnover. The design of teacher compensation systems also empowered teachers in important ways. A single salary schedule increased teacher autonomy by eliminating administrative control over setting teacher salaries. Similarly, due process in employment decisions ensured that administrators show a "just cause" as the basis for termination and that elimination of such protection would challenge a career model of teaching. We worry that the benefit of higher salaries for recruitment and retention do not make up for these other job protections that help to make teaching a stable career.

We share these high-level considerations in an effort to articulate some of the competing priorities that could be made more explicit in setting teacher salaries. If we have one overarching recommendation, it is to involve teachers from a variety of backgrounds in identifying the preferred approach to setting salaries. This may require efforts to improve teachers' understanding of how schools are funded in their state, including how the design of school funding formulas shape teacher salaries. Though educational leaders and policymakers may understand the various constraints and possibilities shaping teacher salaries, supporting teachers in being able to advocate for their own material interests will further advance these efforts.

Build Systems, but Ones That Genuinely Center Teachers

When we speak about systems, we are referring to the structures that help to support the work of teachers, whether this is the schools in which they work, their school district, unions or professional organizations, their preparation program, or organizations that provide professional development for teachers or support them in advocacy efforts. This section includes new approaches to recruiting and preparing teachers, attending to career models of teaching, and thinking about new ways teachers can have greater control over the broader policy conditions that shape their work. This section is deeply informed by the work of Darling-Hammond and colleagues, who used international case studies to elucidate ways in which systems could be created that empower educators.[4]

Envisioning a Broad Multi-Pronged Public Service Campaign for Teaching

We concur with the broader argument made by Darling-Hammond and colleagues that teacher recruitment and preparation efforts hinge on high levels of interest in becoming a teacher, which are likely tied to perceptions of how much teachers are valued and compensated. While public service campaigns may play a role in shaping public opinion regarding the status of teachers, our general view is that salaries are a leading indicator of societal status. From a policy standpoint, increasing teacher pay is probably the most efficient way to shape public views of the value Americans place on teachers. When there is widespread interest in a teaching career, recruitment challenges tend to be more limited in scope.

Regardless of whether salaries increase in ways consistent with what we recommend at the start of this chapter, there are numerous ways in which teacher recruitment efforts could be broadened. We categorize these efforts under the umbrella of changing the narrative about what it means to be a teacher. We preface our recommendations with an acknowledgment that there is limited evidence on the ways in which public discourse shapes interest in teaching. Still, given that public perceptions of teaching are likely quite important in shaping interest in teaching, we suggest a couple areas of more active development.

We suggest ways for students, families, and other community members to share their positive experiences with their own teachers. Most people can think of how the actions of their teachers, both small and large, have shaped their social and academic development in ways that contributed to their lifelong trajectory. Too many of these stories remain untold. New media is well positioned for telling these stories. A school district could use their social media feed to highlight the work of their teachers and elicit stories from students or parents that attest to their impact. Teachers' unions and other national educational organizations could elicit and share stories about their best teacher (i.e., #bestteacherever). Longer stories could be shared on podcasts dedicated to the topic.

Increasing the number of accurate portrayals of teachers in television shows and movies may also help create a more positive narrative about what it means to be a teacher.[5] Unfortunately, most media accounts tend to be negative. While the documentary-style comedy *Abbott Elementary* may come closer to capturing the ups and downs of teaching than other recent depictions, most seem to omit the intrinsic satisfaction that can come from working with children and youth over the course of a school year or over the lifetime of a career. Some teachers have suggested the need for actual documentaries that portray teachers' work.

Media engagement may help to celebrate the work of teachers. Probably the best example of this at present is the Teacher of the Year program, where recipients at the local all the way up to the national level are celebrated for this accolade. Honorees of state-level Teachers of the Year make numerous media appearances as well as a trip to the White House. As ambassadors for the teaching profession, these individuals can help promote a positive image of what it means to be a public school teacher.

The viability of public service campaigns likely hinges on demonstrable improvements in teachers' working conditions. In a period when many teachers do not recommend that their own children or students become teachers, successfully marketing the teaching profession is clearly intertwined with our broader recommendations to improve the conditions of teaching. Unless such conditions are improved, it would be difficult to market the teaching profession authentically.

Teacher recruitment efforts could also be more systematized. As a helpful corollary, compare the infrastructure dedicated to military recruitment compared to that for teachers. Junior Reserve Officers' Training Corps (JROTC) programs are found in an estimated one out of every five high schools. While there are similar programs for future educators, their support and membership are dwarfed by that of JROTC. Similarly, the military has a finely tuned advertising campaign with decades behind it at this point.[6] Moreover, recruiters play an active role in the military in ways not seen in the decentralized education system. Though there is little research that attests to their efficacy, having media outreach, middle and high school teacher pipeline programs, targeted advertising, and more active recruitment would likely all help with teacher recruitment efforts.

For those who enter teacher preparation programs, comprehensive supports are critical for developing the skills, attitudes, and dispositions to be ready to assume their role as a classroom teacher. This includes taking courses combined simultaneously with rich clinical experiences that often first consists of observing practicing teachers and, over the course of a program, transitioning to student teaching where the pre-service teacher is responsible for all aspects of teaching (i.e., planning, instruction, grading, etc.). A growing number of programs have begun to experiment with compensating pre-service teachers during their clinical experiences. The foremost example is teacher residency programs, where teachers are compensated during a longer clinical experience under the supervision of a master teacher. Though there is too little evidence to demonstrate that financial supports will increase the supply of well-prepared teachers, covering more of the cost undoubtedly lessens barriers into teaching, particularly for aspiring teachers from lower-income families.

In a system that prioritizes teachers, their professional preparation does not stop once they become the instructor of record. Well-designed structured mentoring programs should bridge university-based preparation with the emergent and varied demands that come with classroom teaching. These programs can facilitate what is often a rocky transition into teaching, which is a key juncture at which many teachers leave.

Developing a Career Model of Teaching

Career models of teaching emphasize the importance of ongoing professional development opportunities to support teachers in refining their instructional practice and content knowledge and, for those that take on new responsibilities, training that is relevant to their role (e.g., mentor training, leadership training). We define teacher development more broadly than the term is typically used in order to emphasize any practice that helps to improve teachers' professional practice, broadly construed. By centering teachers in this work, we can begin with the question of what developmental supports are actually helpful in teachers' ongoing professional development.

This shift in thinking about teacher development has some important implications that separate our model from contemporary approaches to teachers' professional development. Centering the professional learning needs of teachers requires individualizing professional development. Identifying where teachers hope to develop can come from a couple different places, including professional portfolios where teachers can self-report their own growth areas, teacher evaluations conducted by administrators or peer teachers, and feedback from instructional coaches. Though growth areas for a critical mass of teachers may warrant collective professional development sessions, other professional development may need to be more self-directed than is currently the norm. At present, instructional coaching is the most effective means of personalizing professional support for teachers given that coaches can work shoulder-to-shoulder with teachers over an extended period.

Though developing their instructional practices is likely to constitute the growth area for most teachers, they may benefit from professional development in new areas should they take on additional responsibilities in their school. For instance, teachers who are serving as mentors may benefit from training on how to build and sustain mentoring relationships and how best to share critical feedback. Such training would have the added benefit of shaping a positive mentoring experience for mentees.

Teacher learning is also a highly social act, with teachers honing their instructional practice in collaboration with their peers. A growing number of models have been recommended to provide teachers with collective opportunities to learn from each other (e.g., collaborative planning; professional learning communities; lesson study; instructional rounds). Though educational researchers do not have evidence that any one model of teacher professional learning is more or less effective at improving teacher retention, previous chapters discussed the positive association between teacher collaboration and teacher retention. We suspect that this pattern relates not only to teachers' continuous improvement—and the perceived success with their students that accompanies this personal development—but also the enhanced connections with their peers.

School-based teacher development models are not the only way to further develop teachers' skills and abilities. Both within the United States and abroad, educators have experimented with networked learning communities. Networked learning opportunities provide a couple of unique benefits. First, they pool expertise beyond a single school. Second, for teachers in smaller schools or those who teach specialized subjects, these cross-school connections can provide professional connections and support for teachers who would otherwise be working in isolation, which could promote teacher retention in the process.

That the most relevant and useful teacher development approach for any given teacher will likely be idiosyncratic suggests the need for a high degree of personalization. Doing so probably requires a delicate balance between district- and school-based priorities. Our overarching recommendation is that resources for teacher development be allocated primarily at the school level. Teachers, in collaboration with administrators and teacher leaders in their school, can prioritize the types of development opportunities that will be most beneficial individually and collectively. For instance, teachers at one school may prioritize dedicated time for classroom observation and instructional rounds. At another, teachers may prefer the release time and funding to attend specialized professional development or participate in a statewide networked learning community. Finding ways to balance job-embedded teacher development and cross-school learning is likely most beneficial for helping teachers' individual development and fostering rich collegiality within schools, while also creating a shared professional identity. Such approaches may require allowing for more time in a teacher's workday to engage in authentic development activities.

A final way in which teachers can develop their practice is through performance review. In this chapter of aspirational propositions, we prefer to talk about performance review in contrast to teacher evaluation, which was discussed in chapter 4. Unlike evaluation, performance review speaks broadly about the ways teacher performance is monitored in line with teacher professional standards, teachers' individual learning goals, and school goals. Teacher evaluation systems are often described as developmental, though this lofty goal does not seem to occur in practice. Performance review systems that are intentionally designed to support teacher development prioritize formative review from teacher colleagues, instructional coaches, or master teachers rather than from administrators. These reviews can monitor teachers' success in meeting different professional standards, with administrators only involved when there are larger performance concerns. There are powerful models of how including peer review as part of performance evaluation has improved teacher retention.[7]

Performance reviews can include creative uses of growth plans, where teachers have the opportunities to outline their areas of strength, how they supported their students' growth, how they contributed to the school community and teaching profession, and what areas they want the support to continue to develop. These development areas can then be the focus of individual and collective professional development efforts. Importantly, these efforts are part of the goal of creating a fruitful teaching career where teachers have the opportunity to continue to mold their role and contributions to students, their school, and the profession as a whole.

Efforts to support teacher development are done primarily to improve teachers' instructional practice. Teachers who feel more successful are more committed to the teaching profession and more likely to make teaching their career. A career model of teaching not only emphasizes the ways that teachers can hone their instructional practice but also how they can take on new roles and responsibilities while keeping a foot in the classroom. Though the metaphor of a "career ladder" is often used to describe the ways in which school systems can create leadership roles for teachers, we prefer the metaphor of a "career lattice" to emphasize the new roles that teachers can take on without implying the hierarchy inherent to a ladder.[8]

A criticism of the organization of the teaching profession in the United States is that too few school systems have established structured opportunities for teachers to take on compensated roles within schools while maintaining their instructional role. Moving into school-based administration or taking on district administrative roles is often one of the few available ways to take on new responsibilities and increase one's salary.[9] We suggest a need to further institutionalize how teachers are eligible for these opportunities. States could develop more gradation in teacher licenses (e.g., probationary, proficient, professional, and master teacher licenses). Districts could then develop processes by which teachers progress across licensure bands, with teachers in higher bands eligible for compensated roles within a school—as mentors, instructional coaches, or department chairs—and others roles for a district, such as a curriculum developer or professional development facilitator.

New Avenues for Teachers to Control Their Work

To genuinely center teachers requires attending to the tension around the appropriate level of control over teachers' work. Our concern is that the growing controls over teachers' work—more standardized curricula, pacing guides, frequent student testing, performance standards, teacher evaluations—have brought fewer intrinsic rewards and may have contributed to lower levels of commitment to teaching.[10] Historically, school administrators coordinated the school-based activities that shape teachers' work, such as course scheduling and student assignments, allocation of instructional resources, and setting school policies. Over time, educational leaders and policymakers have exerted greater external control over what takes place in the classroom. Many of these efforts have been well-meaning and focused on benefiting students, particularly students historically and currently marginalized by the educational system. Setting academic standards is designed to ensure that all students are exposed to the same rich academic content. Establishing pacing guides and asking teachers to turn in lesson plans ensures that students who switch schools are not missing out on important material. A question is the degree to which such measures limit teachers' autonomy and self-direction in the classroom in ways that make teaching less enjoyable.

We see a critical challenge for school systems in finding ways to provide teachers with the instructional resources they need to succeed without usurping their authority in the classroom.[11] Negotiating the appropriate balance is by no means straightforward as there may be some areas of teachers' instructional practice where it is appropriate for teachers to have less autonomy than others (e.g., direct instruction to teach phonics). The most important way to address this challenge is to involve teachers in decision-making that affects their classroom to a much greater degree.

The primary way most teachers have participated in decision-making has been through their union or teachers' organization. Unions provide a tangible means for teachers to shape education policies from the school to the federal level. At the local level, unions and teacher organizations are led by teachers, who advocate for policies that improve the contracts under which teachers work. Union proponents emphasize how this participatory role of unions enables teachers to share their knowledge about the inner workings of schools, an exchange that stands to benefit not only teachers but also students.[12] While most teachers have a positive view of how teachers' unions impact schools, at least 20% of teachers do not view unions as making a positive contribution.[13] This could because some groups of teachers' concerns are not well addressed by unions or because, in some states, unions have limits on recruiting and collective bargaining for teachers.

Besides unions, the field does not have a great track record of genuine teacher involvement in decision-making. The teacher's role, as it has developed in the United States, is primarily concerned with classroom instruction, with administrators and policymakers making decisions for all that take place outside teachers' classrooms. When efforts have been made to increase teacher participation in decision-making bodies, Ingersoll claims the results tend to be so much window dressing, where decision-making power is not meaningful shared with teachers.[14] Examples of this would be the inclusion of Teachers of the

Year on state or national decision-making bodies or the School Ambassador Fellowship of the US Department of Education. Though some teachers likely have opportunities to share their expertise, questions remain about the degree to which their involvement significantly shifts education policy priorities.

If teachers are to be involved in state and federal governance, there will likely need to be more opportunities for teachers to develop the knowledge and skills relevant to making significant decisions about outside factors that shape their classroom. This aspirational goal is reflected in the Teacher Leader Model Standards,[15] which include a standard on "Advocating for Student Learning and the Profession." Expanding the role of teachers in decision-making bodies would normalize their involvement and expedite their onboarding. We see promising developments in this area with the Teach Plus Policy Fellowships or Educators for Excellence. These efforts clearly increase teacher agency; however, as with some of our other recommendations in this chapter, there is not a strong research base to suggest these efforts are linked to demonstrable improvements in teachers' working conditions.

Though there are clear advantages to increasing teacher involvement at the state and national levels, increased decision-making capacity will likely be most beneficial at the local level, whether within school districts or individual schools. Critically, many teachers already have decision-making roles through planning committees, open meetings, and teacher leadership roles, but more greater experimentation would be beneficial. One example is Albert Shanker's initial vision for charter schools, which were envisioned as empowering teachers to develop innovative approaches to schooling in collaboration with peers. Another would be collaborative decision-making models with schools and districts. Such an approach would include site-based decision-making or school improvement teams with norms that affirm inclusive voice and participation by teachers. On such teams, leadership roles could be distributed to teachers to ensure they have genuine ownership over school improvement efforts, particularly those related to decisions that impact teaching-learning processes in classrooms.

Practical Considerations in the Development of Teacher-Centered Systems

The goal of this section was to sketch the system-level supports that center the work of teachers. This vision affirms the need to further invest in teachers, including their preparation and development.[16] We highlight here a few practical considerations for education leaders and policymakers who are working to develop such a system, much of which stems from unique features of the public education system in the United States.

First, the United States' decentralized education system raises unique challenges for teacher preparation and development. Pre-service teachers are trained in a teacher preparation program to meet state standards, but their preparation may be poorly connected with the policies and procedures of the school district where they begin their teaching career. New teachers' mentoring experiences can be highly fractured: they may receive instructional guidance from a formal mentor, grade or subject-area colleagues, a school administrator, the central office staff overseeing their induction program, or, for alternatively certified teachers, program-assigned mentors. Teachers' professional development experiences are by no means seamless, with teachers engaged in a mix of continuing education courses to maintain their license, self-directed learning, school- or district-based in-service trainings, peer collaboration, and, for some teachers, more intensive instructional coaching. A concern for such a system is that there is no means by which teachers' can align their development with their broader professional goals.

These are complex coordination challenges, each with its own layered solutions. For instance, deepening partnerships between local school districts and teacher preparation programs will better ensure that teachers' preparation aligns with district needs. Grow Your Own and teacher residency programs are additional place-based approaches to teacher preparation. For new teachers, minimizing the number of mentors while increasing the time they can spend with their primary mentor seems useful, as does coordinating the mentor-mentee pair with the principal to ensure consistent support. Teaching portfolios are one tool that could be used for teachers to document their professional learning and explain how it connects with their areas of growth in the classroom and their broader professional goals. Portfolios could be linked to state teaching standards or the National Board for Professional Teaching Standards.

An additional concern for school and district staff who invest in teacher development is the high degree of mobility across schools and districts. Administrators, particularly those working in schools and districts with high rates of turnover, may be reluctant to invest the time and resources to support teachers' professional development. Given the central role that principals play in teachers' decision to stay or leave, we would urge principals to be more intentional about the instructional support they offer teachers, particularly those who are new to teaching.

A final concern stemming from the decentralized education system relates to the large education sector that exists outside traditional school district operations. Unlike other countries where current teachers play a large role in teacher development,[17] many former teachers in the United States transition to employment with curriculum developers, test developers, textbook companies, educational technology firms, professional development providers, educational advocacy organizations, educational researchers, and university instructors. Though these various groups may help support the critical infrastructure around teachers' work, it is notable that these roles are not filled by current teachers and that there are "pull" factors, whether higher compensation, better work-life balance, or overall job satisfaction, which draw former teachers into these roles.

In this section, we also pushed back on the model whereby teachers are the object of reform rather than participants in the education policy processes relevant to their work.[18] We advocate for an expansion of teacher involvement in decision-making, from the school to the federal level. One challenge with this recommendation, however, is that the current models for increasing teacher agency are filtered through existing decision-making bodies, bodies from which teachers are often excluded or belong to in only a symbolic role. Though teachers have an intrinsic understanding of the ways in which out-of-school factors shape their students' opportunities to learn in the classroom, they often do not have the social position or communicative repertoire to make themselves heard on their own terms.[19] Two concrete examples to increase teacher involvement would be to establish head teachers, a model where a teacher cycles into a leadership role for a few years before cycling back into the classroom, or a dedicated teacher advisory position on the school board. Similarly, at the federal level, teachers with National Board Certification or National Teachers of the Year could play a role in the decision-making process on bipartisan committees and legislative sessions.

When teachers are trained and given opportunities to engage more formally in education policymaking, such as with National Teachers of the Year, their trajectory is often not back into the classroom but into other advocacy roles. Moreover, when only a small segment of teachers have opportunities to engage in these levels of policymaking, serious questions remain as to whether these roles are in fact representative of teachers, writ large. Others have raised the critique that teachers' work is so complex and context-dependent that any efforts to involve teachers in higher levels of decision-making will intrinsically overlook the diversity of teacher experiences.[20] These challenges suggest to us that efforts to involve teachers in policy decision-making need to be expanded and made more substantive in nature. The alternative is a vision of teacher professionalism that advocates foremost for teachers having discretion and flexibility that is less encumbered by external reforms.

Moving from System-Level Changes to Targeted Responses

In the sections above, we discussed system-level changes that will aid teacher recruitment and retention toward ending teacher shortages. At the same time, we recognize the localized nature of the teacher labor market and the need for targeted policies to reduce teacher shortages, reduce teacher turnover, and increase teacher recruitment. In these next sections, we lay out our vision for targeted responses to ensure a robust teacher workforce at the local level.

Targeted Responses to Reducing Teacher Shortages

Targeted responses include any policy focused on a specific group of teachers (e.g., teachers of color, beginning teachers, special education teachers) or teachers working in particular school settings (e.g., rural schools, high-poverty schools). Unlike previous spots in this book where we discussed teacher recruitment before turnover, here we center efforts to reduce turnover given that recruitment depends to a large degree on conditions within teaching itself.

Targeted Responses to Increasing Teacher Retention

A first step to creating targeted policy responses is for education leaders and policymakers to examine the nature of teacher shortages. We provide a few practical considerations when examining data related to teacher recruitment and retention. While one reaction to teacher shortages is often to first examine how many (or how few) qualified teachers are applying to vacancies, we recommend instead first examining teacher turnover, including how turnover rates vary for different teachers and schools. This includes early-career teachers, STEM teachers, and special education teachers as well as teachers working in higher-poverty schools and historically underperforming schools.

For school district and state leaders, having some understanding of whether teachers are leaving teaching outright or moving schools can inform broader efforts of human capital management. For instance, in one district, beginning teachers might get their foot in the door by first working in a higher-poverty school, only to transfer to a more affluent school a few years into their career. In another, a large number of beginning teachers also begin their career in higher-poverty schools but leave teaching after a year or two. Though both districts might want to take steps to improve mentoring and induction programs, improve school working conditions, or supplement teacher pay, leaders in the second district will likely need to use data from exit surveys to assess why so many beginning teachers are leaving and then respond accordingly (e.g., by raising beginning teacher salaries).

Once educational leaders have identified the different ways in which teacher turnover affects some schools or groups of teachers more than others, there are a number of policy and programmatic responses at their disposal. One evidence-based approach to improving the retention of these teachers is the use of retention bonuses. For instance, a special education teacher who remains in their school from one year to the next would be eligible to receive a $5,000 bonus the following school year. If adopted, bonus programs must be clearly communicated to teachers and sustained if they are to have their desired effect.

The predominant strategy for increasing new teacher retention is mentoring and induction programs. New teachers' relationships with their mentors are critical to their successful transition into teaching. Mentors, whether formally assigned by the school or district or informally found by teachers, fill a variety of roles of new teachers. They help new teachers adjust to the social life of their school, manage the stress of the job, and develop strategies for classroom management, planning, and instruction. Despite these diverse ways in which mentors can support new teachers, research suggests that structured mentoring programs are most beneficial for teachers' organizational commitment when focused on developing subject-specific teaching knowledge and teaching practice (classroom observations, coteaching). Moreover, given the importance of frequent mentor-mentee interactions (e.g., weekly or biweekly), school leaders appear to play an important role in creating sufficient time for mentoring activities to occur. Recruiting mentors in the same subject area also appears to be important, as does training and compensating mentor teachers.[21] With mentoring as a cornerstone of induction programs, other supports can also assist with the transition into teaching, including learning about district policies and procedures, professional development, and reflection opportunities with other new teachers.

Given that new teachers tend to leave teaching at high rates, much of the discussion over increasing teacher retention has been on induction programs. An area for much greater emphasis is on broader ways that school principals positively impact the school conditions shaping teachers' work. Research we reviewed in chapter 4 indicates that when teachers feel supported by their principal, they are much less likely to turn over. The specific supports teachers require can be quite varied depending on their job demands. The diverse set of ways in which teachers depend on their principal underscores both the importance of principals in helping teachers feel supported and also how challenging it can be to accomplish this lofty goal in practice. Researchers have characterized principal support through a number of attributes, including that teachers believe their principal (1) respects their professional practice and trusts their professional expertise; (2) has an open line of communication with teachers, whether through being approachable, keeping teachers in the loop about school happenings, or eliciting teacher opinions in school decision-making; (3) backs them up on disciplinary issues; (4) provides the needed classroom resources for teachers to be successful; (5) provides opportunities for improving teacher practice, whether through coaching from the principal or opportunities for peer collaboration; and (6) cultivates a supportive work environment where teachers feel that they are valued.[22]

Respect for teachers' professional practice appears to be the basis for building trusting relationships between teachers and principals. This includes valuing teachers as the experts over their instructional practice and trusting their judgment over instructional decisions. When teachers feel like they trust their principal, it facilitates open communication, whereby teachers voluntarily bring challenges in the classroom to their principal. In doing so, problems can be addressed proactively, whether they pertain to instruction, student discipline, conflict with a parent or colleague, or some other aspect of teachers' work. Upon this basis, principals can provide the resources to help teachers address these varied job demands. Support may extend beyond curricular and technology resources to arranging the school schedule to allow for teacher collaboration. Though many of these leadership skills focus on helping individual teachers, they also contribute to a nurturing school environment.[23]

Importantly, though some leadership skills appear to be most important for teacher retention (e.g., principals' respect for teachers' instructional expertise; open communication; discipline; resource allocation), teachers report varying levels of importance regarding the leadership skills they most value, which underscores the diversity of ways teachers come to rely on the support from their principal. The challenge for principals lies in the provision of resources to address teachers' individual job demands.[24] In addition, though researchers have developed a compelling portrait of what a supportive school environment looks like, there is limited evidence showing that principals will be supported enough to develop these conditions.[25] Principals themselves are often stuck between balancing district pressure and parents' demands while also buffering their teachers from these outside pressures. Principal turnover also appears to exacerbate teacher turnover.[26] Regardless of these challenges, the preceding discussion should make it clear that the most important way to customize supports for teachers is through their school-based administrators. A mix of financial incentives and targeted district supports (e.g., mentoring and coaching) can be layered on these supports to assist teachers who are most at risk of leaving.

Targeted Responses for Increasing Teacher Recruitment

For school and district leaders, the process for examining teacher recruitment is similar to that for teacher turnover and will focus on the schools and subject areas with the most vacancies. As vacancy data will often align closely with patterns of elevated teacher turnover, the first step is to check whether this is the case. Examining human resources data can show how many applicants are applying to open positions, which can be supplemented by anecdotal information from principals or other hiring officials to understand whether applicants were in fact qualified.

Perhaps the most important factor to examine when looking at applicant data is where new applicants are coming from. This will likely be a mix of re-entrants, who had previously taught in the district or elsewhere, with beginning teachers. In many districts, new teachers will primarily come from university-based teacher preparation programs, with applicants having completed student teaching in the district. Increasingly, this will also include applicants who entered teaching through pathways offering an array of pre-service preparation, ranging from fast-track alternative route programs, where teachers will have had little pre-service preparation, to residency, apprenticeship, and Grow Your Own programs, where teachers had previous teaching or work experience in the district. Understanding where applicants are coming from is important not only for assessing the depth of the pool of incoming teachers but also for understanding the types of induction supports that will be needed. Partnerships with teacher preparation programs can help to further understand the pool of incoming teachers. This can include sharing data on current and anticipated staffing needs. Pre-service teachers' clinical experiences in the district can also help to prepare teachers for the district context.

School District Policies For school districts, the primary targeted policy tool is to use different financial incentives. This might include recruitment bonuses for teachers in hard-to-staff subject areas. Districts facing severe staffing shortages might assume a larger role in teacher recruitment through Grow Your Own programs.

State leaders have a larger policy role in shaping the supply of new teachers. We recommend that state leaders begin with data on the teacher preparation pipeline, their entry into schools and classrooms, and their retention rates. Whether through data dashboards or publicly available templates for examining teacher shortages, state education policymakers can examine where more support is needed in the teacher pipeline so that more aspiring teachers have access to a teaching career. This could include examining cohorts of enrollees in teacher preparation programs to see how many students graduate from an accredited program, pass licensure tests, become certified, and become a teacher. These data could help in identifying whether there are particular junctures in the preparation pipeline where teachers-to-be are most likely to exit.

When disaggregated for subpopulations of teachers, it could uncover the degree to which certain junctures are more detrimental to some groups of aspiring teachers (e.g., licensure exams disproportionately affect aspiring teachers of color; math and science teachers enter traditional preparation programs at low rates), which could be subject to targeted financial or programmatic supports. One example of such a dashboard is North Carolina's Educator Preparation Program Dashboard, which includes program-level data on enrollment, completion, feelings of preparedness, licensure exam passage rates, and retention in teaching after three years, among others. Importantly, these data can be disaggregated by subject area, gender, and race/ethnicity to help paint a nuanced picture of teacher supply.

As it is not just new teachers who fill vacancies, we also suggest that state policymakers leverage data on the reserve pool of teachers. Though rigorous evidence does not exist for how to re-engage these teachers, it could include actively monitoring and reaching out to active holders of teaching licenses. Targeted marketing campaigns could highlight recruitment bonuses or other benefits of returning to the classroom.

Practical Considerations in the Design of Targeted Responses

Conceptualizing teacher shortages as a multifaceted problem raises unique practical challenges to enacting successful policy responses. To begin, the success of targeted interventions in addressing teacher recruitment and retention requires an accurate understanding of what problems a district or state is trying to address. Imagine a scenario where a state's department of education wants to enact retention bonuses for teachers in state-identified shortage areas, which includes math, science, special education, and English as a second language. By conceiving of shortages in terms of subject area, differences in shortages across school urbanicity/rurality would be overlooked, as would considerations about the racial/ethnic diversity of the teacher workforce. As a result, if retaining science teachers in rural schools was most challenging, this policy would provide no additional resources for those science teachers working in a rural locale. As this example implies, the first challenge in creating targeted policy responses to teacher shortages is in developing a common understanding of the problem that one aims to address.

Developing this common understanding can raise its own problems when trying to address teacher shortages. Unlike broad increases in teacher salaries as suggested earlier in this chapter, it could be that the localized nature of teacher shortages precludes statewide policy responses. As a result, targeted responses to addressing shortages are needed. This approach could introduce collective action problems that make it challenging to develop support for an initiative from different groups of teachers (and administrators) that would stand to benefit most from targeted approaches. For instance, in a state where it is challenging to fill vacancies in rural schools, superintendents in these districts might need to advocate for a statewide recruiting bonus for teachers working in rural districts. Such an approach may prove challenging in some states where superintendents in the state's cities may still experience teacher shortages, though perhaps not of the same magnitude.

There are other implementation challenges that educational leaders and policymakers should be mindful of when considering using targeted approaches to addressing teacher shortages. When financial incentives are introduced, the chief concern is that teachers will respond in ways that are detrimental to the overall stability of the teacher workforce. For instance, chronically underperforming schools that receive targeted interventions to improve student achievement will sometimes provide recruitment bonuses for highly effective teachers. While such a policy can induce churn within a school district if teachers are moving schools at higher rates, when bonuses lapse—say, when the school loses funding upon no longer being identified as needing major improvement—teachers may move to a new school where the bonuses are present.

On more symbolic grounds, any shift away from the single-salary schedule challenges norms of equality and fairness that were a key accomplishment from teacher organizing efforts in the twentieth century. By moving away from a system where all teachers' work is equally valued, an alternative, market-based compensation system risks the perception that some teachers' work is more valued than others. Such a system could return to a compensation system of more than a century ago, when pay was stratified by school level, urbanicity, gender, and race/ethnicity. One potential solution is to have a high minimum salary with the same salary schedules for all teachers but then incentivize the recruitment and retention of teachers in hard-to-staff schools and subjects through recruitment and retention bonuses. Another approach might be to allocate state funds for teacher incentives based on district need (i.e., districts with the most acute shortages).

All of that said, we do not view any of these challenges as insurmountable. Overcoming them must be part of building coherent systems that genuinely center teachers in decision-making and leadership.

Conclusion

In this chapter, we put forward a set of affirmative strategies designed to create schools where teachers will want to stay. Though salaries are a first and important step in this process, they must be accompanied by other systemic approaches that center teachers and their work. This includes new approaches to recruiting and preparing teachers, attending to career models of teaching, and thinking about new ways teachers can have greater control over the broader policy conditions that shape their work. To end teacher shortages, these strategies will need to be implemented more coherently than they have in the past. This will include an alignment of efforts to support teachers from the federal level down to the school level, all with a shared goal of fostering supportive working conditions where teachers remain committed and others want to become teachers. This will be the type of system that helps make teaching a more sustainable profession.

Ending teacher shortages will also require targeted approaches focused specifically on the teachers and school contexts with the greatest shortages. Shortages are not a universal problem, and thus the solutions we recommend—even those that are more aspirational—need to be targeted. This includes much careful work to understand the nature of teacher shortages at the local level. Policy responses can then be directed accordingly, whether this is toward particular groups of teachers (e.g., new teachers or STEM teachers), teachers in acute shortage areas (e.g., special education teachers of color), or schools with high levels of teacher turnover or difficulty filling vacancies.

We close by returning to our driving question: Is there a future in which teacher shortages are not a normal part of schooling in the United States? Yes, but it would require concerted effort across our decentralized education system. Enacting the bold vision we have put forward will require moving beyond piecemeal efforts to increase recruit teachers and retain them toward the development of teacher-centered systems oriented around making teaching a more appealing and sustainable profession.

Conclusion

Promoting the Conditions for a Sustainable Teacher Workforce

TEACHING IS HARD. Teachers have to know what they are teaching and how they can teach it to a diverse group of students of varying abilities. Take, for instance, teachers of high school math. They have to know mathematics from arithmetic to calculus. In addition to this content knowledge, they have to be able to convey the often abstract ideas of math to students, many of whom may not remember (or were never taught) basic math facts and skills or even be reading at grade level. This substantial amount of knowledge and expertise is not even the hardest part about teaching. By the very nature of their job, teachers have to engage with dozens of students at any one time. Not only are they trying to teach these students skills and knowledge that will empower them for years to come, but they are also trying to manage these students and connect with them on a personal level. Unlike many jobs where one attends to a limited number of things at any given time, teaching brings demands related to instruction, managing classroom behavior, and building a cohesive classroom community simultaneously. And teachers do this all day every day. On top of that, their students have parents and caregivers, and they too demand time from teachers. And we have not even talked about ongoing technological challenges (e.g., cell phones, social media, generative artificial intelligence) that can enter the classroom in disruptive ways at any time.

Yes, teaching is hard. Since teaching is hard, and good teachers are hard to come by (or it takes time for teachers to develop themselves into good teachers), we need to do everything we can to recruit and retain good teachers. To do that, we need to understand the landscape as it exists now and what we need to change in order to have a sustainable, robust teaching workforce that can meet the needs of our society.

Characterizing Teacher Shortages over Time

The problem of teacher shortages goes back decades, but it has unfortunately grown worse in recent years. Even before the COVID-19 pandemic and definitely since then, we have had teacher shortages every year. Concerns about the impact of teacher shortages on schools escalated in the wake of the pandemic. Many teachers reached their breaking point, with teacher turnover rates reaching historic highs following the 2021–22 school year. The burnout rate for teachers rose during the first year of the pandemic and was markedly higher than that for other occupations. Yet there were already warning signs about the declining status of the teaching profession before the pandemic. Kraft and Lyon's 50-year study of the teacher workforce showed that interest in teaching, the number of newly prepared teachers, and job satisfaction had cratered in the years before the pandemic and only worsened in some instances.

Nationally we have tens of thousands of vacant positions and more than a quarter of a million underqualified teachers in our school systems. In the 2023–24 school year, the United States had at least 50,000 vacant positions and about 400,000 underqualified positions. While these numbers fluctuate from year to year and from state to state, they nevertheless indicate that, in many states and hundreds of school districts, it is difficult to find qualified teachers to teach, and sometimes it is impossible to find anyone to fill a vacant position at all. The best estimate of the national teacher vacancy rate is 2% or so, which is comparable to many other professions and even low relative to others. Teachers, however, are indispensable to society in a way that some other professionals are not.

Complicating this issue is the fact that we do not have a single national labor market for teachers in the United States. Teachers cannot simply move across state lines to teach because state standards differ. Having 50 states with varying requirements and substantial variations in salary translate into 50 labor markets across which movement is difficult. Some states have banded together to allow for easier movement across states, but it has not yet borne fruit. Moreover, teachers often have preferences for the types of schools in which to work, preferences that contribute to higher turnover rates and more vacancies in schools enrolling more students placed at risk by society and its institutions. Additionally, teachers teach specific subjects, so a math teacher may not make a good English teacher, and an English teacher may not be able teach biology well.

Simply put, we have tens of thousands of vacant positions and hundreds of thousands of underqualified teachers, but they are not distributed evenly across states, districts, or subject areas. Many schools and districts have no difficulty staffing their classrooms, and they may have dozens of applications for a single opening, and yet thousands of other schools and hundreds of districts struggle every year to replace teachers who leave for one reason or another. This is not a trivial puzzle that can be solved easily, as "solving" it requires us all to make changes and compromises that are fundamental to our society. Thus, while we offer a number of high-level recommendations—including reduced financial costs to becoming a teacher, raising teacher salaries, improving respect for teachers, and increasing teacher agency in deciding matters that affect their classroom instruction—much of the work to enact our vision will be quite localized if we are to end teacher shortages.

Policies to Increase Teacher Recruitment

One crucial part of the story is the supply side. Toward this end, we developed three main ways to increase teacher recruitment, either overall or for subgroups of teachers: financial incentives, licensure requirements, and alternative certification. There is a preponderance of evidence showing that financial incentives can be used to attract potential candidates into the teaching profession. We provided numerous examples of monetary-based policies and initiatives that increase interested candidates for teaching. Yet we also emphasized that these strategies are effective only at the margins; that is to say, they may shift a small number of people toward considering teaching as a viable occupation. Moreover, even to be marginally effective, incentives cannot be meager changes, as small amounts have little to no effects on recruitment. Overall, we believe it is better to substantially raise salary rather than work around the edges in the interest of building a robust foundation for the future of the teacher workforce.

In response to increasing teacher vacancies in numerous districts across the country, many states have taken drastic actions to quickly increase their teacher workforce, such as creating new license types, decreasing requirements, easing the transfer process of licensure from one state to another, creating expedited pathways to the profession, allowing retired teachers to teach again, and even recruiting veterans who otherwise lack the credentials to teach. Even with these changes that lower standards for entry into the profession and that provide many pathways to joining the profession, states and districts still struggle to meet demand for teachers. Moreover, while reducing barriers may increase supply in the short term for some schools and in some subject areas, these policies place additional and tremendous burdens on school districts to mentor and support these teachers, many of whom will leave at higher rates than teachers who come from traditional preparation programs.

On the other hand, additional requirements to become a teacher, such as edTPA, appear to deter candidates from becoming teachers, thereby reducing the teacher supply. As student learning is not always directly tied to licensure requirements for teachers, we need to learn more about what credentialing is effective and what is not as well as what cutoff points on licensure exams may be optimal for recruitment while balancing quality student learning. These decisions must further contend with the historical use of licensure exams to prevent some candidates from obtaining licenses, particularly Black and Hispanic candidates. In short, though maintaining minimum thresholds for who can become a teacher appears important for reducing transience in the teaching workforce, how high to set those standards so as not to weed out candidates who would otherwise make a strong future teacher is not altogether clear. Thus scholars and policymakers need know more about (1) how licensure exams would unnecessarily decrease the diversity of the incoming teacher workforce, (2) what cutoff points maximize the number of new teachers while minimizing ineffective teachers, and (3) what alternatives to retaking licensure tests could permit acceptable passage into the profession.

Last but not least, alternative pathways into the profession represent another set of policies and initiatives that could be leveraged to increase recruitment. Specifically, we are talking about alternative certification programs (ACPs), teacher residency programs (TRPs), Grow Your Own (GYO) programs, and teaching apprenticeship programs. By and large, the evidence suggests that these policies and initiatives can increase teacher recruitment with some caveats. First, ACPs have been able to recruit more candidates where traditional programs have not, and these candidates are also more likely to be people of color. Questions remains about the extent to which candidates who come from these programs actually remain in teaching, with significant variation in the quality of ACPs. Similarly, TRPs are also able to attract and recruit more candidates as well as increase the diversity of candidates. Preliminary and growing evidence of GYOs suggest they too can increase recruitment. These place-based programs that provide compensated clinical teaching experiences may be a good investment to recruit more prospective candidates into the profession. However, we note that the number of candidates joining the profession through GYOs tends to be small at this point, and we are only beginning to build up the evidence base for the efficacy of these programs.

To be clear, these policies will likely help to recruit new teachers, but together they will not be enough to address shortages in most districts. Instead of approaching teacher recruitment as the solution to teacher shortages, we ultimately think these strategies are most effective when targeted toward teacher critical shortage areas (i.e., STEM, special education, rural communities). We note that there are specific and direct steps that policymakers can take to diversify the teacher workforce and recruit STEM and special education teachers and that district leaders can take to improve rural teacher recruitment. Once again, it is important to note that there is no singular teacher labor market, so many of the initiatives and policies we can implement must be strategic to target the specified needs of the schools and districts where subgroups of teachers are needed. Overall, however, from our perspective and the evidence that now exists, we believe that each of the three main ways to recruit teachers can be leveraged in strategic ways to increase and diversify the teacher workforce. To ensure that beginning teachers remain in teaching at higher rates than they currently do, more robust recruitment efforts must also attend to the conditions that teachers experience when they enter the classroom.

We note, however, that these recruitment strategies for increasing the supply of teachers may be limited if the underlying conditions of teaching do not change. Just because there are more teachers coming into the profession after a concerted recruitment effort does not necessarily mean that a sufficient teacher workforce will stay at their schools year after year. This is precisely why recruitment and retention are two sides of the same coin when it comes to teacher workforce. We absolutely need to consider how to retain more teachers and to change teacher working conditions to ensure a robust teacher workforce. This leads us to the next sections where we consider changing the focus from teacher turnover to teacher retention and the policies and practices to increase teacher retention.

From Teacher Turnover to Teacher Retention

Chapter 4 made clear the increasingly granular ways researchers have come to understand which teachers are most at risk of turning over, which schools are most likely to experience elevated levels of turnover, and what broader policies and external factors shape these dynamics.

Just like shortages are not a problem that affect all schools equally, neither is teacher turnover. How schools respond to turnover should similarly reflect the localized dynamics regarding why teachers chose to stay or leave. Let us offer a few caveats here to focusing narrowly on teacher turnover. The argument we put forward—that ending teacher shortages requires affirmative strategies to create the schools where teachers want to stay rather than simply preventing some teachers from leaving—guides our thinking.

Researchers, ourselves included, have given too much attention to teacher turnover as opposed to teacher retention. There are a few interrelated issues that emerge from this focus. First, attending primarily to teachers who leave risks losing sight of the overwhelming majority of teachers who remain in teaching from one year to the next. We have shown that between 86% and 91% of teachers worked in the same school from one school year to the next. By focusing on the small fraction of teachers who leave, we often overlook the stories of the majority of teachers who commit their life's work to the profession. A helpful example of this type of research is Nieto's work on why people become teachers and what keeps them going.[1]

This type of research can provide a helpful corrective to the public discourse around teaching being framed by high levels of burnout and turnover. When the public narratives about teaching focus on the negative aspects of the work, young people may seriously question why they would consider joining a profession where so many people who are doing the job say they are considering leaving. Thus, focusing primary on turnover may have detrimental consequences for recruiting the next generation of teachers.

By focusing on the reasons that teachers report staying in their jobs, educational leaders and policymakers can take meaningful steps to make teaching a more sustainable profession. These efforts can be supported by concerted efforts from federal, state, and district policymakers to create work environments where teachers feel well supported. The goal is to make teaching a more attractive career by creating environments supportive of the values that drive teachers to enter the teaching profession in the first place.

Lastly, describing high teacher turnover levels as a long-standing feature of the teaching profession can distract from the growing evidence base on the policies and practices that can improve stability in the teacher workforce. More concerningly, it risks creating a sense of intractability that the problem of teacher shortages will never be addressed. We hope that our preceding chapters have provided a renewed sense of hopefulness for how, as a society, we value and support the work of teachers and can design systems that provide the needed levels of support for their work.

Policies and Practices to Increase Teacher Retention

There is no point in recruiting so many new teachers into the profession if we end up losing most of them a few years down the line. The amount of time and resources lost is detrimental to schools and districts as well as students. Educational leaders and policymakers need to do all they can to retain teachers for a healthy and robust teacher workforce. To this end, we have categorized policies to retain teachers into three main areas: (1) financial incentives, (2) preparation and support, and (3) working conditions. We note that the majority of these policies and practices are at the local level and can be enacted by school and district leaders.

Under financial incentives, we have two general buckets, bonuses and salary increase. Bonuses include extra pay for working in high-needs schools or teaching in high-shortage areas such as special education or STEM or for good performance from students (i.e., pay-for-performance or merit pay). By and large, the literature suggests that these bonus incentives are mostly effective in retaining teachers. In particular, bonus incentives for the most effective teachers can and do improve teacher retention. Likewise, a salary increase is also associated with an increase in teacher retention. However, we should note that the relationship is generally small (positive, but small), and when a salary increase is temporary and insubstantial, its effects are also small and will dissipate over time. A few states have increased the minimum salary by a substantial amount (to $50,000 in Arkansas and $40,000 in

Missouri), but we do not yet have evidence on how this increases teacher retention, particularly when it is unclear if and how the program will be funded (in the case of Missouri). In sum, the current evidence suggests that, dollar for dollar, bonus incentives and targeted incentives are better for retaining teachers than a flat salary increase but that more substantial salary increases may have other benefits tied to how such increases could be marketed.

We want to underscore the key point that money matters but that money is not the only thing that matters. To retain teachers, teacher preparation and their ongoing support also play a key role in teacher retention. With teacher preparation, there appears to be a trade-off between retention (as teachers who attended traditional preparation programs are more likely to stay than teachers who are alternatively certified) and recruitment (as alternatively certified teachers are more diverse in terms of race/ethnicity and socioeconomic background). At this point, it is unclear whether the preparation program itself is what increases retention rate (i.e., that traditional teacher preparation programs do something that increases the likelihood of teachers to stay from year to year) or teachers who tend to remain in the profession longer are more likely to seek standard credentials. Nevertheless, it is not the case that we must have just one or the other, but there may be optimal ways to incentivize candidates through either type of program depending on the short- and long-term needs of the schools and districts and the students that they serve.

We also note that programs with targeted missions and where student teachers are placed both contribute to teacher retention as well. In particular, student teachers who are placed in easier-to-staff schools to begin their learning as a teacher are more likely to be retained than those placed in hard-to-staff schools. Placing student teachers in supportive working environment when they are learning how to teach seems to have positive effects on their teaching ability and the likelihood that they will stay in teaching longer, even when they end up working in less supportive environments later on. Relatedly, we also have good evidence showing that supporting teachers when they begin their career and supporting them throughout their career could increase teacher retention. It seems obvious that providing teachers with mentor teachers in a profession where much of the learning is done on the job would help beginning teachers learn their craft, become better teachers, and stay on longer, but it is good to have concrete evidence to support the value of this type of program. Moreover, high-quality mentoring and induction programs are relatively cheaper than salary increases. Yet simply having a mentoring program does not ensure that it will be implemented well. Ongoing research can help us better understand how best to match mentors and mentees, how frequently they should meet, and whether there are specific aspects of new teachers' work that are most advantageous to address. Similarly, continued research is helping illuminate how in-service professional development and coaching can be designed in ways that benefit teachers' long-term career development.

Last but not least, the most obvious set of actions we can take at the school level and even the district level is to ameliorate teachers' challenging working conditions. Schools with better physical facilities (such as working air conditioners), fewer student disciplinary issues, and lower amounts of threats and violence to teachers have more teachers stay on a year-to-year basis. Since teachers spend many of their waking hours at work, it follows that they would want to work in schools with better working conditions. Happy and satisfied teachers are, by definition, less likely to be stressed and burnt out, leading to higher retention and better teaching. Even something as seemingly trivial as not having to buy classroom materials and resources to do their job matters for teacher retention.

Related to this, teachers who have stable teaching assignments and more autonomy in their classes or at their school are also more likely to stay. In this regard, principals and other school administrators can contribute importantly to retention by supporting teachers. Principals, in particular, have the power to positively shape teacher working conditions and can take various steps to support teachers. Teachers who feel supported by their administrators are notably more likely to stay in the same school. This support can include everything from knowing the principal will have their back if they have a conflict with a parent to feeling that the principal knows and values their professional aspirations and provides support for them to continue to develop. Teachers know that teaching is hard and that they can use all the help they can get, so when they work with an effective and supportive principal, they want to stay and teach for as long as they can.

Moreover, while it is important to think about policies and initiatives that would retain more teachers on the whole, it is also equally important to note that some of these policies and initiatives could and should be focused on early-career teachers, teachers of color, and teachers in hard-to-staff schools, including teachers in geographically isolated areas. Teachers in these categories are more at risk of leaving their school than their counterparts. School-level and district-level policymakers would do well to think about how their proposed actions and implementations would affect these teachers categorically. It is not the case that we do not know how to better retain teachers; in fact, we have robust empirical evidence that many actions can be taken to increase teacher retention.

Putting It All Together: The Goal of a Sustainable Teacher Workforce

When we put everything that we have discussed together, we argue that the policies to increase teacher recruitment and retention are interconnected. More than that, they are two sides of the same coin when it comes to what can be done to address teacher shortages. To start, financial incentives, whether in the form of bonus pay or a salary increase, are important for both recruitment and retention. For instance, teacher salary increases can make teaching a more attractive career to prospective teachers, while also making current teachers less likely to leave to move into another better-paying occupation. We should not expect to be able to keep the most talented teachers—those who have content expertise, know how to reach students, and can inspire the next generations—when we do not pay them well. Teachers should not have to work a second job to make ends meet. Teaching is hard, and teachers should be well compensated for it. While we can debate what qualifies as a living wage, as cost of living varies greatly from state to state, we should agree that teachers should be paid well, and as a society, we should make the commitment to pay teachers as well as we can. This is not the case where we should think about what minimal salary would put a warm body in front of a classroom but, rather, how a well-compensated occupation could attract the best and brightest.

From our perspective, it is not out of the question to have $50,000 be the starting salary for a full-time qualified teacher in 2026. A starting salary of $50,000 will do two key things for the teaching profession. First, for better or worse, money is important in our country, and rightly or wrongly, respect is attached to earning money. Setting the starting salary at this level indicates that teaching is a well-respected profession. Many teachers, ourselves included, did not go into teaching to become rich. A starting salary of $50,000, however, would put teaching firmly in middle-class status, with the exception of a select number of high-cost cities. Second, and relatedly, if we set this salary as the standard, it would let prospective teachers know that they can earn a good living wage anywhere in the country. While teaching may be a noble profession—and we would argue that it is since teachers are educating the next generations of doctors, scientists, artists, and technicians that our society needs—it is not the case that nobleness makes up for meager pay. Anyone who has expertise in a content area and has the training to teach students of varying abilities and backgrounds should know that they would be able to earn a respectable wage anywhere in the United States.

We note that attempts to raise teacher salaries now comes at a distinct historical juncture. Disenrollment from public schools is increasing. Homeschooling is the fastest growing type of schooling. Universal or near-universal school voucher programs have been adopted in a growing number of states, further incentivizing the exit from traditional public schools. At the federal level, drastic steps have been taken to limit the size and the scope of the US Department of Education during the second Trump administration. Moreover, a difference in public opinion between Democrats and Republicans on public education has only widened in the past decade, including opinion on teachers' unions and increasing teacher salaries.[2]

At the same time, fewer adults now consider teaching a prestigious occupation as did in the past. Still, Americans' opinion of their local public schools was higher in 2022 than it had been since 1974.[3] Two-thirds of Americans believe that teachers in their community have salaries that are too low and would be willing to pay higher property taxes if that meant teacher salaries could be increased.

That teachers still have a high level of support at the local level suggests that steps can be taken to increase teacher salaries across many school districts. This first step is needed not only to improve the teachers' material conditions but also to address larger questions of societal status. Increasing salaries symbolizes to current and prospective teachers that teaching matters and is worthy of much higher compensation. We believe higher salaries can go a long way in addressing shortages, particularly if salary increases are clearly communicated to prospective teachers.

Aside from increasing teacher salaries, there are multiple ways we can build and strengthen systems that genuinely center teachers at the core. These structures support the work of teachers, from teacher recruitment efforts and teacher preparation programs to the conditions of the schools where they work and to the professional organizations they join and professional development opportunities they have through their careers. To this last point specifically, we advocate for career models of teaching that recognize the importance of ongoing professional development to further develop teachers' instructional practice as well as opportunities to take on new responsibilities such as mentor training or leadership training. Additionally, we also suggest that students, communities, and society at large can do more to share the positive experiences had at school; there should be more accurate portrayals of teachers in the media as well as inspirational stories of teachers and how they change people's lives.

We do not pretend to have all the answers about how to enact our plans and suggestions. In fact, we cannot underscore enough that the complexity of shortages precludes a one-size-fits-all solution. To this end, we concur with recent recommendations for "bargaining for the common good," whereby teachers and their unions negotiate not only for their collective needs but for the needs of parents and working people too.[4] Because of their unique educative role in society, teachers are well positioned to speak about the conditions shaping their work and how society and its institutions can better provide for children and families so that students are ready to learn when they come to school. Supporting teachers' advocacy work is critical for the broader goal of ending teacher shortages given its potential to improve teachers' work environments in untold ways.

In sum, it is too low of a bar to simply reduce teacher turnover and adopt short-term approaches to addressing ongoing teacher staffing challenges. By focusing on the reasons teachers report staying in their jobs, educational leaders and policymakers can take meaningful steps to make teaching a more sustainable profession. These efforts can be supported by concerted efforts from federal, state, and district policymakers to create work environments where teachers feel well supported. The goal is to make teaching a more attractive career by creating environments supportive of the values that drive teachers to enter the teaching profession in the first place. Ending teacher shortages requires these affirmative strategies to create schools where teachers want to stay—not simply preventing some teachers from leaving.

NOTES

Introduction

1. Tuan D. Nguyen, Chanh B. Lam, and Paul Bruno, "What Do We Know About the Extent of Teacher Shortages Nationwide? A Systematic Examination of Reports of US Teacher Shortages," *AERA Open* 10 (2024): 23328584241276512.

2. Matthew A. Kraft and Melissa Arnold Lyon, "The Rise and Fall of the Teaching Profession: Prestige, Interest, Preparation, and Satisfaction over the Last Half Century," *American Educational Research Journal* 61, no. 6 (2024): 1192–236.

3. Richard M. Ingersoll, "Teacher Turnover and Teacher Shortages: An Organizational Analysis," *American Educational Research Journal* 38, no. 3 (2001): 499–534.

4. Grace Kena, William Hussar, Joel McFarland, Cristobal De Brey, Lauren Musu-Gillette, Xiaolei Wang, Jijun Zhang, et al., "The Condition of Education 2016. NCES 2016-144," National Center for Education Statistics, 2016.

5. Christopher Redding and Gary T. Henry, "Leaving School Early: An Examination of Novice Teachers' Within- and End-of-Year Turnover," *American Educational Research Journal* 56, no. 1 (2019): 204–36.

Chapter 1. The Teaching Procession or Teaching Profession?

Epigraph. Willard Slingerland Elsbree, *Teacher Turnover in the Cities and Villages of New York State.* No. 300 (Teachers College, Columbia University, 1928), 1.

1. Susan B. Carter and Elizabeth Savoca, "The 'Teaching Procession'? Another Look at Teacher Tenure, 1845–1925," *Explorations in Economic History* 29, no. 4 (1992): 401–16; David Labaree, "Career Ladders and the Early Public High School Teacher," in *American Teachers: Histories of a Profession at Work*, ed. Donald Warren (Macmillan, 1989); John L. Rury, "Who Became Teachers? The Social Characteristics of Teachers in American History," in *American Teachers: Histories of a Profession at Work*, ed. by Donald R. Warren, 9–48; David Tyack and Elisabeth Hansot, *Managers of Virtue: Public School Leadership in America, 1820–1980* (Basic Books, 1994); "Characteristics of Public and Private Elementary and Secondary School Teachers in the United States: Results from the 2017–18 National Teacher and Principal Survey, First Look," National Center for Education Statistics, September 2020. https://nces.ed.gov/surveys/ntps/summary/2020142rev.asp.

2. Linda Darling-Hammond, "Breaking the Legacy of Teacher Shortages," *Educational Leadership* 80, no. 2 (2022): 14–20.

3. John L. Rury and Jennifer Hurst, "The Segmentation of Teacher Professionalisation: The American Experience," in *The Status of the Teaching Profession*, ed. by Xavier Dumay and Katharine Burn (Routledge, 2022), 38–61.

4. Claudia Goldin, "Labor Markets in the Twentieth Century," in *The Cambridge Economic History of the United States*, ed. by Stanley L. Engerman and Robert E. Gallman (Cambridge University Press, 2000), 549–624; Laura Owen, "History of Labor Turnover in the US," April 30, 2004, in *H.Net Encyclopedia of Economic and Business History*, ed. Robert Whaples.

5. Labaree, "Career Ladders."

6. Judith Kafka, "In Search of a Grand Narrative: The Turbulent History of Teaching," in *Handbook of Research on Teaching*, ed. Drew H. Gitomer and Courtney A. Bell (American Educational Research Association, 2016), 69–126; Marjorie Murphy, *Blackboard Unions: The AFT and the NEA, 1900–1980* (Cornell University Press, 1990).

7. Kafka, "In Search of a Grand Narrative"; Kitae Sohn, "The Migration Patterns of US Female Teachers, 1860–80," *Social Science History* 39, no. 3 (2015): 339–60; Kathleen Weiler, *Country Schoolwomen: Teaching in Rural California, 1850–1950* (Stanford University Press, 1998).

8. Nancy Hoffman, *Woman's "True" Profession: Voices from the History of Teaching*, 2nd ed. (Harvard Education Press, 2003); Kafka, "In Search of a Grand Narrative"; Labaree, "Career Ladders"; Rury, "Who Became Teachers?"; David Tyack and Elizabeth Hansot, *Learning Together: A History of Coeducation in American Public Schools* (Yale University Press, 1990).

9. Labaree, "Career Ladders."

10. Jeremy T. Murphy, "From Teacher Improvement to Teacher Turnover: Unintended Consequences of School Reform in Quincy, Massachusetts, 1872–1893," *History of Education Quarterly* 61, no. 4 (2021): 503–33, 521.

11. Wayne E. Fuller, "The Teacher in the Country School," in *American Teachers: Histories of a Profession at Work*, ed. by Donald R. Warren (Macmillan, 1989), 98–117.

12. Lotus D. Coffman, *The Social Composition of the Teaching Population*, Columbia University Contributions to Education no. 41. (Teachers College Press, 1911); Labaree, "Career Ladders."

13. Tyack and Hansot, *Managers of Virtue*, 17–18.

14. Elsbree, *Teacher Turnover.*

15. Coffman, *Social Composition of the Teaching Population*; Labaree, "Career Ladders."

16. Coffman, *Social Composition of the Teaching Population*; Elsbree, *Teacher Turnover*; Labaree, "Career Ladders"; Sohn, "Migration Patterns of US Female Teachers."

17. William Graebner, "Retirement in Education: The Economic and Social Functions of the Teachers' Pension," *History of Education Quarterly* 18, no. 4 (1978): 397–417, 409.

18. Wayne J. Urban, *Why Teachers Organized* (Wayne State University Press, 1982).

19. Quoted in Graebner, "Retirement in Education," 408.

20. John Eiselmeier, *Report of the Commissioner of Education for the Year 1902* (Government Printing Office, 1903).

21. Diana D'Amico Pawlewicz, *Blaming Teachers: Professionalization Policies and the Failure of Reform in American History* (Rutgers University Press, 2020).

22. Graebner, "Retirement in Education"; Kafka, "In Search of a Grand Narrative."

23. Quoted (pp. 174–75) in Karen Leroux, "'Lady Teachers' and the Genteel Roots of Teacher Organization in Gilded Age Cities," *History of Education Quarterly* 46, no. 2 (2006): 164–91.

24. Kafka, "In Search of a Grand Narrative," 77.

25. Kafka, "In Search of a Grand Narrative"; Pawlewicz, *Blaming Teachers*; Jean Protsik, "History of Teacher Pay and Incentive Reforms," *Journal of School Leadership* 6, no. 3 (1996): 265–89; Urban, *Why Teachers Organized*.

26. Protsik, "History of Teacher Pay and Incentive Reforms."

27. Lief Esbenshade, "Breaking Down: Teacher Attrition from Publicly Available Resources," unpublished paper, EdArXiv, 2022. doi:10.31219/osf.io/e6cky.

28. Murphy, *Blackboard Unions*.

29. Joshua M. Cowen and Katharine O. Strunk, "The Impact of Teachers' Unions on Educational Outcomes: What We Know and What We Need to Learn," *Economics of Education Review* 48 (2015): 208–23; Murphy, *Blackboard Unions*.

30. Graebner, "Retirement in Education"; Janet S. Hansen, "An Introduction to Teacher Retirement Benefits," *Education Finance and Policy* 5, no. 4 (2010): 402–37.

31. Graebner, "Retirement in Education"; Raegen T. Miller, "Redefining Teacher Pensions: Strategically Defined Benefits for New Teachers and Fiscal Sustainability for All," Center for American Progress, 2011. https://files.eric.ed.gov/fulltext/ED535996.pdf.

32. Hansen, "Introduction to Teacher Retirement Benefits," 411.

33. Davison M. Douglas, *Jim Crow Moves North: The Battle over Northern School Segregation, 1865–1954* (Cambridge University Press, 2005); Kafka, "In Search of a Grand Narrative."

34. Pawlewicz, *Blaming Teachers*; Owen Thompson, "School Desegregation and Black Teacher Employment," *Review of Economics and Statistics* 104, no. 5 (2022): 962–80; Vanessa Siddle Walker, "Valued Segregated Schools for African

American Children in the South, 1935–1969: A Review of Common Themes and Characteristics," *Review of Educational Research* 70, no. 3 (2000): 253–85.

35. Richard D. Kahlenberg, "Teacher Tenure Has a Long History and, Hopefully, a Future," *Phi Delta Kappan* 97, no. 6 (2016): 16–21; Murphy, *Blackboard Unions.*

36. "1920s: The Condition of Teachers," California Federation of Teachers. https://www.cft.org/post/1920s-condition-teachers.

37. Dana Goldstein, *The Teacher Wars: A History of America's Most Embattled Profession* (Anchor Books, 2015).

38. Goldstein, *Teacher Wars*; Kahlenberg, "Teacher Tenure"; Pawlewicz, *Blaming Teachers.*

39. Raegen Miller and Robin Chait, "Teacher Turnover, Tenure Policies, and the Distribution of Teacher Quality," Center for American Progress, 2008. https://cdn.americanprogress.org/wp-content/uploads/issues/2008/12/pdf/teacher_attrition.pdf.

40. Pawlewicz, *Blaming Teachers*, 66.

41. Murphy, *Blackboard Unions.*

42. Cowen and Strunk, "Impact of Teachers' Unions"; Susan Moore Johnson, *Teacher Unions in Schools* (Temple University Press, 1984); Murphy, *Blackboard Unions.*

43. Richard M. Ingersoll, *Who Controls Teachers' Work? Power and Accountability in America's Schools* (Harvard University Press, 2006); Anthony C. LaBue, "Teacher Certification in the United States: A Brief History," *Journal of Teacher Education* 11, no. 2 (1960): 147–72.

44. Murphy, *Blackboard Unions*, 45.

45. Jal Mehta, *The Allure of Order: High Hopes, Dashed Expectations, and the Troubled Quest to Remake American Schooling* (Oxford University Press, 2013); Murphy, *Blackboard Unions*; Pawlewicz, *Blaming Teachers.*

46. Andrew Gitlin and David F. Labaree, "Historical Notes on the Barriers to the Professionalization of American Teachers: The Influence of Markets and Patriarchy," In *Teachers' Professional Lives*, ed. Ivor F. Goodson and Andy Hargreaves (Routledge, 2002), 96–116, 99.

47. Pawlewicz, *Blaming Teachers*, 36.

48. Gitlin and Labaree, "Historical Notes"; Pawlewicz, *Blaming Teachers.*

49. Pawlewicz, *Blaming Teachers.*

50. Murphy, *Blackboard Unions.*

51. Murphy, *Blackboard Unions*, 37.

52. Dan C. Lortie, *Schoolteacher: A Sociological Study* (University of Chicago Press, 2020); Murphy, *Blackboard Unions.*

53. David Labaree, "Power, Knowledge, and the Rationalization of Teaching: A Genealogy of the Movement to Professionalize Teaching," *Harvard Educational Review* 62, no. 2 (1992): 123–55; Pawlewicz, *Blaming Teachers.*

54. Gitlin and Labaree, "Historical Notes"; Marvin F. Wideen, Jolie A. Mayer-Smith, and Barbara J. Moon, "Knowledge, Teacher Development and Change," in *Teachers' Professional Lives*, ed. Ivor F. Goodson and Andy Hargreaves (Routledge, 2002), 195–12.

55. Gitlin and Labaree, "Historical Notes."

56. Labaree, "Power, Knowledge"; Rury and Hurst, "Segmentation of Teacher Professionalisation."

57. David L. Angus, *Professionalism and the Public Good: A Brief History of Teacher Certification* (Thomas B. Fordham Foundation, 2001); LaBue, "Teacher Certification in the United States" 161.

58. LaBue, "Teacher Certification in the United States."

59. Christina Collins, *Ethnically Qualified: Race, Merit, and the Selection of Urban Teachers, 1920–1980* (Teachers College Press, 2011); Kafka, "In Search of a Grand Narrative"; Ruth Jacknow Markowitz, *My Daughter, the Teacher: Jewish Teachers in the New York City Schools* (Rutgers University Press, 1993).

60. Angus, *Professionalism and the Public Good.*

Chapter 2. Schools in Crisis?

1. Tyler Mobra and Daniel Hamlin, "Emergency Certified Teachers' Motivations for Entering the Teaching Profession: Evidence from Oklahoma," *Education Policy Analysis Archives* 28, no. 109 (2020); Tuan D. Nguyen, Chanh B. Lam, and Paul Bruno, "What Do We Know About the Extent of Teacher Shortages Nationwide? A Systematic Examination of Reports of US Teacher Shortages," *AERA Open* 10 (2024): 23328584241276512; Madeline Will, "This State Is Giving New Teachers up to $20K to Stay on the Job. But There's a Catch," *Education Week*, November 30, 2023. https://www.edweek.org/leadership/this-state-is-giving-new-teachers-up-to-20k-to-stay-on-the-job-but-theres-a-catch/2023/11.

2. Christopher Redding and Tuan D. Nguyen, "Recent Trends in the Characteristics of New Teachers, the Schools in Which They Teach, and Their Turnover Rates," *Teachers College Record* 122 no. 7 (2020): 1–36; *Charles T. Clotfelter, Helen F. Ladd, and Jacob L. Vigdor, "Teacher Credentials and Student Achievement in High School: A Cross-Subject Analysis with Student Fixed Effects," *Journal of Human Resources* 45, no. 3 (2010): 655–81; *Li Feng and Tim R. Sass, "What Makes Special-Education Teachers Special? Teacher Training and Achievement of Students with Disabilities," *Economics of Education Review* 36 (2013): 122–34. *Heather C. Hill, Brian Rowan, and Deborah Loewenberg Ball, "Effects of Teachers' Mathematical Knowledge for Teaching on Student Achievement," *American Educational Research Journal* 42, no. 2 (2005): 371–406.

3. Gerard Robinson, "A Solution to America's K–12 STEM Teacher Shortage: Endowed Chairs," *The Conversation*, September 28, 2023. https://theconversation.com/a-solution-to-americas-k-12-stem-teacher-shortage-endowed-chairs-214436.

4. Toni Feder, "The US Is in Dire Need of STEM Teachers," *Physics Today* 75, no. 3 (2022): 25–27.

5. National Center for Education Statistics, "Forty-Four Percent of Public Schools Were Operating Without a Full Teaching Staff," press release, October 2022. https://ies.ed.gov/press-releases/nces-press-releases.

6. Carrie Jung, "One Challenge to Reopening Schools: Finding Enough Teachers," WBUR, December 21, 2020. https://www.wbur.org/news/2020/12/21/massachusetts-teacher-shortage; J. Poff, "New Mexico Turns to National Guard to Fill Substitute Teacher Shortage," *Washington Examiner*, January 27, 2022. https://www.washingtonexaminer.com/policy/newmexico-turns-to-national-guard-to-fill-substitute-teacher-shortage; Stephanie Sandoval, "Schools Are Asking Parents for Help amid Teacher Shortage," Scripps News, January 31, 2022; Tom Wiedmann, "Newark Public Schools Call on Retired Teachers for Emergency Help." TAPinto Newark, January 26, 2022. https://www.tapinto.net/towns/newark/sections/education/articles/newark-public-schools-call-on-retired-teachers-for-emergency-help.

7. Derek Thompson, "There Is No National Teacher Shortage," *The Atlantic*, August 24, 2022. https://www.theatlantic.com/newsletters/archive/2022/08/national-teacher-shortage-turnover-student-enrollment/671214/.

8. Nicole Hernandez, "Spokane Public Schools Trains New Teachers, Not Affected by Teacher Shortage," KREM, August 18, 2022. https://www.krem.com/article/news/education/sps-spokane-public-schools-contract-approval-new-teachers/293-8d557bd4-e223-4b1c-8f82-7e2d2dfd8ee4; April Thompson, "MSCS Says Teacher Shortage Not a Problem This School Year," WREG, August 7, 2023. https://wreg.com/news/local/mscs-says-teacher-shortage-not-a-problem-this-school-year/.

9. J. Reed, "Data Shows Strong Teacher Retention in Utah Despite Pandemic," AP News, April 18, 2021. https://apnews.com/article/education-utah-coronavirus-pandemic82869ee7a4995159c61459fd0dc71a79; "2021–13 Teacher Turnover, Shortage, and Vacancy Maps," Utah Legislative Auditor General's Office. https://public.tableau.com/app/profile/utah.legislative.auditor.general.s.office/viz/TeacherTurnoverShortageandVacancyMaps/DashboardAll.

10. Mimi Engel, Brian A. Jacob, and F. Chris Curran, "New Evidence on Teacher Labor Supply," *American Educational Research Journal* 51, no. 1 (2014): 36–72.

11. James Cowan, Dan Goldhaber, Kyle Hayes, and Roddy Theobald, "Missing Elements in the Discussion of Teacher Shortages," *Educational Researcher* 45, no. 8 (2016): 460–62; Emma García and Elaine Weiss, "Examining the Factors That Play a Role in the Teacher Shortage Crisis: Key Findings from EPI's 'Perfect Storm in the Teacher Labor Market' Series," Economic Policy Institute, 2020; Dan Goldhaber and Roddy Theobald, "Opinion: Sorting Out the Issues in the Teacher Shortage Crisis," The74million.org, September 22, 2016. https://www.the74million.org/article/article-opinion-sorting-out-the-issues-in-the-teacher

-shortage-crisis/; David Loewenberg, "Teacher Shortage? Depends Who You Ask," New America, 2019. http://newamerica.org/education-policy/edcentral/teacher-shortage-depends-who-you-ask/; Leib Sutcher, Linda Darling-Hammond, and Desiree Carver-Thomas, "Understanding Teacher Shortages: An Analysis of Teacher Supply and Demand in the United States," *Education Policy Analysis Archives* 27, no. 35 (2019). https://doi.org/10.14507/epaa.27.3696

12. García and Weiss, "Examining the Factors"; Sutcher et al., "Understanding Teacher Shortages."

13. Cowan et al., "Missing Elements"; Goldhaber and Theobald, "Opinion."

14. R. M. Ingersoll, "Is There Really a Teacher Shortage?," research report, Consortium for Policy Research in Education, September 2003.

15. "Identification of Critical Teacher Shortage Areas for 2022–23," Florida Department of Education, 2022. https://www.fldoe.org/core/fileparse.php/20042/urlt/7-2.pdf.

16. Donald Boyd, Daniel Goldhaber, Hamilton Lankford, and James Wyckoff, "The Effect of Certification and Preparation on Teacher Quality," *The Future of Children* 17, no. 1 (2007): 45–68; Thomas J. Kane, Jonah E. Rockoff, and Douglas O. Staiger, "What Does Certification Tell Us About Teacher Effectiveness? Evidence from New York City," *Economics of Education Review* 27, no. 6 (2008): 615–31. https://doi.org/10.1016/j.econedurev.2007.05.005.

17. Authors' calculation using data from the National Teacher and Principal Survey.

18. "Job Openings and Labor Turnover—October 2025," news release, Bureau of Labor Statistics, December 9, 2025. https://www.bls.gov/news.release/pdf/jolts.pdf.

19. Richard M. Ingersoll and Henry May, "The Magnitude, Destinations, and Determinants of Mathematics and Science Teacher Turnover," *Educational Evaluation and Policy Analysis* 34, no. 4 (2012): 435–64.

20. Bonnie Billingsley and Elizabeth Bettini, "Special Education Teacher Attrition and Retention: A Review of the Literature," *Review of Educational Research* 89, no. 5 (2019): 697–744.

21. Donald Boyd, Hamilton Lankford, Susanna Loeb, and James Wyckoff, "The Draw of Home: How Teachers' Preferences for Proximity Disadvantage Urban Schools," *Journal of Policy Analysis and Management* 24, no. 1 (2005): 113–32; Jacob Fowles, J. S. Butler, Joshua M. Cowen, Megan E. Streams, and Eugenia F. Toma, "Public Employee Quality in a Geographic Context: A Study of Rural Teachers," *American Review of Public Administration* 44, no. 5 (2014): 503–21; Michelle Reininger, "Hometown Disadvantage? It Depends on Where You're From: Teachers' Location Preferences and the Implications for Staffing Schools," *Educational Evaluation and Policy Analysis* 34, no. 2 (2012): 127–45.

22. Paul Bruno, "Pandemic-Era School Staff Shortages: Evidence from Unfilled Position Data in Illinois," unpublished paper, Social Science Research Network, posted 2023.

23. Danielle Sanderson Edwards, Matthew A. Kraft, Alvin Christian, and Christopher A. Candelaria, "Teacher Shortages: A Framework for Understanding and Predicting Vacancies," *Educational Evaluation and Policy Analysis* (2024): 01623737241235224.

24. D. Goldhaber, G. Falken, R. Theobald, "What Do Teacher Job Postings Tell Us about School Hiring Needs and Equity?," working paper no. 282-0323, National Center for Analysis of Longitudinal Data in Education Research, 2023.

25. Dan Goldhaber, Nate Brown, Nathaniel Marcuson, and Roddy Theobald, "School District Job Postings and Staffing Challenges Throughout the Second School Year During the COVID-19 Pandemic," *Educational Administration Quarterly* (2022): 0013161X241308512.

26. Joshua F. Bleiberg and Matthew A. Kraft, "What Happened to the K–12 Education Labor Market during COVID? The Acute Need for Better Data Systems," EdWorkingPaper no. 22-544, Annenberg Institute at Brown University, 2022; Tuan D. Nguyen, Chanh B. Lam, and Paul Bruno, "What Do We Know About the Extent of Teacher Shortages Nationwide? A Systematic Examination of Reports of US Teacher Shortages," *AERA Open* 10 (2024): 23328584241276512.

27. Jacey Fortin and Eliza Fawcett, "How Bad Is the Teacher Shortage? Depends Where You Live," *New York Times*, August 29, 2022.

Chapter 3. Where Shall They Come From?

1. Mimi Engel, "The Timing of Teacher Hires and Teacher Qualifications: Is There an Association?," *Teachers College Record* 114, no. 12 (2012): 1–29; John P. Papay and Matthew A. Kraft, "The Productivity Costs of Inefficient Hiring Practices: Evidence from Late Teacher Hiring," *Journal of Policy Analysis and Management* 35, no. 4 (2016): 791–817.

2. US Department of Education, National Center for Education Statistics, "Schools and Staffing Survey." https://nces.ed.gov/surveys/sass/tables/sass0708_034_t1n.asp. The table of data on this page is titled "Number and percentage of public school K-12 teachers, by survey years, workforce categories relative to a specific school, and employment background: 1987–88, 1990–91, 1993–94, 1999–2000, 2003–04, and 2007–08."

3. We are indebted to Richard Ingersoll's work on this point.

4. *Suzanne M. Wilson and Shannon L. Kelley, "Landscape of Teacher Preparation Programs and Teacher Candidates. Evaluating and Improving Teacher Preparation Programs," National Academy of Education, 2022.

5. North Cooc and Grace MyHyun Kim, "Racial and Ethnic Disparities in Adolescent Teaching Career Expectations," *American Educational Research Journal* 60, no. 5 (2023): 882–915.

6. Dan C. Lortie, *Schoolteacher: A Sociological Study* (University of Chicago Press, 2020).

7. Linda Darling-Hammond and Jeannie Oakes, *Preparing Teachers for Deeper Learning* (Harvard Education Press, 2021).

8. Donald Boyd, Pam L. Grossman, Karen Hammerness, R. Hamilton Lankford, Susanna Loeb, Morva McDonald, Michelle Reininger, Matthew Ronfeldt, and James Wyckoff, "Surveying the Landscape of Teacher Education in New York City: Constrained Variation and the Challenge of Innovation," *Educational Evaluation and Policy Analysis* 30, no. 4 (2008): 319–43; Daniel C. Humphrey and Marjorie E. Wechsler, "Insights into Alternative Certification: Initial Findings from a National Study," *Teachers College Record* 109, no. 3 (2007): 483–530.

9. Donald J. Boyd, Pam Grossman, Hamilton Lankford, Susanna Loeb, Nicholas M. Michelli, and Jim Wyckoff, "Complex by Design: Investigating Pathways into Teaching in New York City Schools," *Journal of Teacher Education* 57, no. 2 (2006): 155–66.

10. Christopher Redding and Thomas M. Smith, "Easy In, Easy Out: Are Alternatively Certified Teachers Turning Over at Increased Rates?," *American Educational Research Journal* 53, no. 4 (2016): 1086–125.

11. *A Nation Prepared: Teachers for the 21st Century: The Report of the Task Force on Teaching as a Profession* (Carnegie Forum on Education and the Economy, May 1986); *Tomorrow's Teachers: A Report of the Holmes Group* (Holmes Group, 1986).

12. Linda Darling-Hammond, Ruth Chung, and Fred Frelow, "Variation in Teacher Preparation: How Well Do Different Pathways Prepare Teachers to Teach?," *Journal of Teacher Education* 53, no. 4 (2002): 286–302; Richard Ingersoll, Lisa Merrill, and Henry May, "Retaining Teachers: How Preparation Matters," *Educational Leadership* 69, no. 8 (2012): 30–34; Redding and Smith, "Easy In, Easy Out"; Matthew Ronfeldt, Nathaniel Schwartz, and Brian A. Jacob, "Does Preservice Preparation Matter? Examining an Old Question in New Ways," *Teachers College Record* 116, no. 10 (2014): 1–46; Robert Vagi, Margarita Pivovarova, and Wendy Miedel Barnard, "Keeping Our Best? A Survival Analysis Examining a Measure of Preservice Teacher Quality and Teacher Attrition," *Journal of Teacher Education* 70, no. 2 (2019): 115–27.

13. Karen J. DeAngelis, Andrew F. Wall, and Jing Che, "The Impact of Preservice Preparation and Early Career Support on Novice Teachers' Career Intentions and Decisions," *Journal of Teacher Education* 64, no. 4 (2013): 338–55; William Viviani, Andrew Brantlinger, and Ashley Anne Grant, "Teacher Preparedness and Retention," *Teacher Education Quarterly* 50, no. 3 (2023): 54–77. There are competing explanations for this finding, including that alternatively certified teachers enter teaching less committed in the first place and that they are sorted into schools with more challenging conditions, thereby exacerbating their turnover rates. See Redding and Smith, "Easy In, Easy Out."

14. Ronfeldt et al., "Does Preservice Preparation Matter?"

15. *Dan Goldhaber, John M. Krieg, and Roddy Theobald, "Does the Match Matter? Exploring Whether Student Teaching Experiences Affect Teacher Effectiveness," *American Educational Research Journal* 54, no. 2 (2017): 325–59; *Matthew Ronfeldt, "Where Should Student Teachers Learn to Teach? Effects of Field Placement School Characteristics on Teacher Retention and Effectiveness," *Educational Evaluation and Policy Analysis* 34, no. 1 (2012): 3–26. Matthew Ronfeldt, "Links Among Teacher Preparation, Retention, and Teaching Effectiveness. Evaluating and Improving Teacher Preparation Programs," National Academy of Education, 2021.

16. *Kevin C. Bastian, Kristina M. Patterson, and Dale Carpenter, "Placed for Success: Which Teachers Benefit from High-Quality Student Teaching Placements?," *Educational Policy* 36, no. 7 (2022): 1583–611; Dan Goldhaber, John Krieg, and Roddy Theobald, "Effective Like Me? Does Having a More Productive Mentor Improve the Productivity of Mentees?," *Labour Economics* 63 (2020): 101792; *Matthew Ronfeldt, Emanuele Bardelli, Matthew Truwit, Hannah Mullman, Kevin Schaaf, and Julie C. Baker. "Improving Preservice Teachers' Feelings of Preparedness to Teach Through Recruitment of Instructionally Effective and Experienced Cooperating Teachers: A Randomized Experiment," *Educational Evaluation and Policy Analysis* 42, no. 4 (2020): 551–75; *Matthew Ronfeldt, Stacey L. Brockman, and Shanyce L. Campbell, "Does Cooperating Teachers' Instructional Effectiveness Improve Preservice Teachers' Future Performance?," *Educational Researcher* 47, no. 7 (2018): 405–18.

17. Dan Goldhaber, John Krieg, Roddy Theobald, and Marcelle Goggins, "Front End to Back End: Teacher Preparation, Workforce Entry, and Attrition," *Journal of Teacher Education* 73, no. 3 (2022): 253–70.

18. Goldhaber et al., "Front End to Back End."

19. Brendan Bartanen and Andrew Kwok, "From Interest to Entry: The Teacher Pipeline from College Application to Initial Employment," *American Educational Research Journal* 60, no. 5 (2023): 941–85. Vagi et al., "Keeping Our Best?

20. Dan Goldhaber, John Krieg, Roddy Theobald, and Stephanie Liddle. "Lost to the System? A Descriptive Exploration of Teacher Candidates' Career Paths," *Educational Researcher* 51, no. 4 (2022): 255–64; Goldhaber et al., "Front End to Back End."

21. James Cowan, Dan Goldhaber, Kyle Hayes, and Roddy Theobald, "Missing Elements in the Discussion of Teacher Shortages," *Educational Researcher* 45, no. 8 (2016): 460–62.

22. US Department of Education, Title II Reports: National Teacher Preparation Data. https://title2.ed.gov/Public/Home.aspx.

23. Donald Boyd, Hamilton Lankford, Susanna Loeb, and James Wyckoff, "The Draw of Home: How Teachers' Preferences for Proximity Disadvantage Urban Schools," *Journal of Policy Analysis and Management* 24, no. 1 (2005): 113–32; *Hamilton Lankford, Susanna Loeb, and James Wyckoff, "Teacher

Sorting and the Plight of Urban Schools: A Descriptive Analysis," *Educational Evaluation and Policy Analysis* 24, no. 1 (2002): 37–62; *Michelle Reininger, "Hometown Disadvantage? It Depends on Where You're From: Teachers' Location Preferences and the Implications for Staffing Schools," *Educational Evaluation and Policy Analysis* 34, no. 2 (2012): 127–45.

24. Dan Goldhaber, Katharine O. Strunk, Nate Brown, Andrea Chambers, Natsumi Naito, and Malcolm Wolff, "Teacher Staffing Challenges in California: Exploring the Factors That Influence Teacher Staffing and Distribution," technical report of the Getting Down to Facts II project, 2018.

25. Dan Goldhaber, John Krieg, and Roddy Theobald, "Knocking on the Door to the Teaching Profession? Modeling the Entry of Prospective Teachers into the Workforce," *Economics of Education Review* 43 (2014): 106–24; *John M. Krieg, Roddy Theobald, and Dan Goldhaber, "A Foot in the Door: Exploring the Role of Student Teaching Assignments in Teachers' Initial Job Placements," *Educational Evaluation and Policy Analysis* 38, no. 2 (2016): 364–88.

26. Bradley W. Bergey, John Ranellucci, and Avi Kaplan, "The Conceptualization of Costs and Barriers of a Teaching Career Among Latino Preservice Teachers," *Contemporary Educational Psychology* 59 (2019): 101794; *Christopher Redding and Dominique J. Baker, "Understanding Racial/Ethnic Diversity Gaps Among Early Career Teachers," *AERA Open* 5, no. 2 (2019): 2332858419848440.

27. Ranita Cheruvu, Mariana Souto-Manning, Tara Lencl, and Marisa Chin-Calubaquib, "Race, Isolation, and Exclusion: What Early Childhood Teacher Educators Need to Know About the Experiences of Pre-Service Teachers of Color," *Urban Review* 47 (2015): 237–65; *Conra D. Gist, "Voices of Aspiring Teachers of Color: Unraveling the Double Bind in Teacher Education," *Urban Education* 52, no. 8 (2017): 927–56; Sonya V. Scott and Louie F. Rodriguez, "'A Fly in the Ointment' African American Male Preservice Teachers' Experiences with Stereotype Threat in Teacher Education," *Urban Education* 50, no. 6 (2015): 689–717; *Christine E. Sleeter, "Preparing Teachers for Culturally Diverse Schools: Research and the Overwhelming Presence of Whiteness," *Journal of Teacher Education* 52, no. 2 (2001): 94–106.

28. Constance A. Lindsay, Erica Blom, and Alexandra Tilsley, "Diversifying the Classroom: Examining the Teacher Pipeline," Urban Institute, 2017.

29. Bartenan and Kwok, "From Interest to Entry."

30. Bartenan and Kwok, "From Interest to Entry"; David Blazar, Ramon Goings, Max Anthenelli, Seth Gershenson, and Wenjing Gao, "Disparate Pathways: Understanding Racial Disparities in Teaching," EdWorkingPaper no. 24-945, Annenberg Institute at Brown University, 2024.

31. Redding and Baker, "Understanding Racial/Ethnic Diversity Gaps."

32. Thomas S. Dee and Dan Goldhaber, "Understanding and Addressing Teacher Shortages in the United States," The Hamilton Project, 2017.

33. Cowan et al., "Missing Elements."

34. *Joshua D. Angrist and Jonathan Guryan, "Does Teacher Testing Raise Teacher Quality? Evidence from State Certification Requirements," *Economics of Education Review* 27, no. 5 (2008): 483–503; *Eric A. Hanushek and Richard R. Pace, "Who Chooses to Teach (and Why)?," *Economics of Education Review* 14, no. 2 (1995): 101–17; Charles F. Manski, "Academic Ability, Earnings, and the Decision to Become a Teacher: Evidence from the National Longitudinal Study of the High School Class of 1972," in *Public Sector Payrolls* (University of Chicago Press, 1987), 291–316.

35. Hanushek and Pace, "Who Chooses to Teach."

36. *Bobby W. Chung and Jian Zou, "Teacher Licensing, Teacher Supply, and Student Achievement: Nationwide Implementation of edTPA," EdWorkingPaper no. 21-440, Annenberg Institute at Brown University, 2021.

37. Christopher Redding, "Changing the Composition of Beginning Teachers: The Role of State Alternative Certification Policies," *Educational Policy* 36, no. 7 (2022): 1791–820.

38. *Randall Reback, "Entry Costs and the Supply of Public School Teachers," *Education Finance and Policy* 1, no. 2 (2006): 247–65.

39. *Christopher Redding and Tuan D. Nguyen, "The Effects of Race to the Top on Teacher Qualifications, Work Environments, and Job Attitudes," *Educational Evaluation and Policy Analysis* 47, no. 1 (2025): 237–62.

40. Dan Goldhaber, "Evidence-Based Teacher Preparation: Policy Context and What We Know," *Journal of Teacher Education* 70, no. 2 (2019): 90–101; K. Zeichner and V. Strauss. "The Disturbing Provisions About Teacher Preparation in No Child Left Behind Rewrite," *Washington Post*, December 15, 2015.

41. Yiting Chu and Weijia Wang, "The Urban Teacher Residency Model to Prepare Teachers: A Review of the Literature," *Urban Education* 59, no. 8 (2024): 2489–518; Matthew Truwit, Matthew Ronfeldt, and Emanuele Bardelli, "Exploring Whether and How Teacher Residencies Offer a Different Kind of Preparation," *AERA Open* 10 (2024): 23328584241231937.

42. Redding and Smith, "Easy In, Easy Out."

43. US Department of Education, Title II Reports: National Teacher Preparation Data. https://title2.ed.gov/Public/Home.aspx.

44. Jacqueline E. King and Jessica Yin, "The Alternative Teacher Certification Sector Outside Higher Education: 2022 Update," Center for American Progress, 2022.

45. Conra D. Gist, Margarita Bianco, and Marvin Lynn, "Examining Grow Your Own Programs Across the Teacher Development Continuum: Mining Research on Teachers of Color and Nontraditional Educator Pipelines," *Journal of Teacher Education* 70, no. 1 (2019): 13–25; Humphrey and Wechsler, "Insights into Alternative Certification"; *Christopher Redding, "Are Homegrown Teachers Who Graduate from Urban Districts More Racially Diverse, More Effective, and Less Likely to Exit Teaching?," *American Educational Research Journal* 59, no. 5 (2022): 939–74; Christine E. Sleeter and H. Richard Milner,

"Researching Successful Efforts in Teacher Education to Diversify Teachers," in *Studying Diversity in Teacher Education*, ed. Arnetha F. Ball and Cynthia A. Tyson (Rowman and Littlefield, 2011), 81–103.

46. King and Yin, *Alternative Teacher Certification Sector.*

47. Redding and Smith, "Easy In, Easy Out."

48. Jessica Cardichon, Linda Darling-Hammond, Man Yang, Caitlin Scott, Patrick M. Shields, and Dion Burns, "Inequitable Opportunity to Learn: Student Access to Certified and Experienced Teachers," Learning Policy Institute, 2020; Richard M. Ingersoll, "Teacher Turnover and Teacher Shortages: An Organizational Analysis," *American Educational Research Journal* 38, no. 3 (2001): 499–534; Brian A. Jacob, "The Challenges of Staffing Urban Schools with Effective Teachers," *The Future of Children* (2007): 129–153; John P. Papay, Andrew Bacher-Hicks, Lindsay C. Page, and William H. Marinell, "The Challenge of Teacher Retention in Urban Schools: Evidence of Variation from a Cross-Site Analysis," *Educational Researcher* 46, no. 8 (2017): 434–48.

49. Gist et al., "Examining Grow Your Own Programs"; Julia H. Kaufman, Benjamin K. Master, Alice Huguet, Paul Youngmin Yoo, Susannah Faxon-Mills, David Schulker, and Geoffrey E. Grimm, "Growing Teachers from Within: Implementation, Impact, and Cost of an Alternative Teacher Preparation Program in Three Urban School Districts," research report RR-A256-1, RAND Corporation, 2020.

50. Redding, "Changing the Composition of Beginning Teachers."

51. Redding and Smith, "Easy In, Easy Out."

52. Dee and Goldhaber, "Understanding and Addressing Teacher Shortages."

53. Robert A. Roth, "Emergency Certificates, Misassignment of Teachers, and Other 'Dirty Little Secrets,'" *Phi Delta Kappan* 67, no. 10 (1986): 725–27.

54. H. Ramirez, "The Shift from Hands-Off: The Federal Role in Supporting and Defining Teacher Quality," in *A Qualified Teacher in Every Classroom?*, ed. R. Hess, A. Rotherham, and K. Walsh K. (Harvard Education Press, 2004); Redding and Smith, "Easy In, Easy Out."

55. "Prevalence of Teachers without Full State Certification and Variation Across Schools and States," results in brief, US Department of Education, 2016.

56. E. García, M. Leung-Gagné, and S. K. Patrick, "The State of the Teacher Workforce: A State-by-State Analysis of the Factors Influencing Teacher Shortages, Supply, Demand, and Equality," Learning Policy Institute, 2023.

57. Cardichon et al., "Inequitable Opportunity to Learn."

58. Pedro Reyes, Michael Marder, Celeste Alexander, Janet Solis Rodriguez, and Annelies Rhodes, "Texas Educator Preparation Pathways Study," Texas Education Research Center, University of Texas at Austin, 2022.

59. Leib Sutcher, Linda Darling-Hammond, and Desiree Carver-Thomas, "Understanding Teacher Shortages: An Analysis of Teacher Supply and Demand in the United States," *Education Policy Analysis Archives* 27, no. 35 (2019).

60. Tuan D. Nguyen and Chris Doss, "Examining the Teacher Supply and Reserve Pool: Evidence from National Data," *Journal of Education Human Resources* 43, no. 3 (2025).

61. Goldhaber et al., "Front End to Back End"; Goldhaber et al., "Lost to the System?"

62. Sutcher et al., "Understanding Teacher Shortages."

63. Fredrick Flyer and Sherwin Rosen, "The New Economics of Teachers and Education," *Journal of Labor Economics* 15, no. 1, pt. 2 (1997): S104–S139.

64. Karen J. DeAngelis, "A Look at Returning Teachers," *Education Policy Analysis Archives* 21 (2013): 1–31; Jason A. Grissom and Michelle Reininger, "Who Comes Back? A Longitudinal Analysis of the Reentry Behavior of Exiting Teachers," *Education Finance and Policy* 7, no. 4 (2012): 425–54.

65. DeAngelis, "Look at Returning Teachers"; Grissom and Reininger, "Who Comes Back?"

66. Anna Moyer, "Has 'Who Comes Back' Changed? Teacher Reentry 2000–2019," *Educational Researcher* 51, no. 8 (2022): 544–46.

67. Andrene J. Castro, "Tensions Between What Principals Know and Do: The Role of Labor Market Conditions on Teacher Recruitment and Hiring," *Leadership and Policy in Schools* 21, no. 4 (2022): 756–79.

68. Christopher Redding and Gary T. Henry, "New Evidence on the Frequency of Teacher Turnover: Accounting for Within-Year Turnover," *Educational Researcher* 47, no. 9 (2018): 577–93.

69. Frank Perrone and Coby V. Meyers, "A Review of the Research on Teacher Hiring in the United States (2001–2021)," *Journal of Education Human Resources* (2023): e20220041; Castro, "Tensions Between What Principals Know and Do"; *Michael DeArmond, Betheny Gross, and Dan Goldhaber, "Is It Better to Be Good or Lucky? Decentralized Teacher Selection in 10 Elementary Schools," *Educational Administration Quarterly* 46, no. 3 (2010): 322–62; Mimi Engel and F. Chris Curran, "Toward Understanding Principals' Hiring Practices," *Journal of Educational Administration* 54, no. 2 (2016): 173–90.

70. DeArmond et al., "Is It Better to Be Good or Lucky?"

71. Cardichon et al., "Inequitable Opportunity to Learn."

72. Lora Cohen-Vogel, Li Feng, and La'Tara Osborne-Lampkin, "Seniority Provisions in Collective Bargaining Agreements and the 'Teacher Quality Gap,'" *Educational Evaluation and Policy Analysis* 35, no. 3 (2013): 324–43; *Dan Goldhaber, Lesley Lavery, and Roddy Theobald, "Inconvenient Truth? Do Collective Bargaining Agreements Help Explain the Mobility of Teachers Within School Districts?," *Journal of Policy Analysis and Management* 35, no. 4 (2016): 848–80; William S. Koski and Eileen L. Horng, "Facilitating the Teacher Quality Gap? Collective Bargaining Agreements, Teacher Hiring and Transfer Rules, and Teacher Assignment Among Schools in California," *Education Finance and Policy* 2, no. 3 (2007): 262–300; *Jessalynn James, Matthew A. Kraft, and John P. Papay, "Local Supply, Temporal Dynamics, and Unrealized

Potential in Teacher Hiring," *Journal of Policy Analysis and Management* 42, no. 4 (2023): 1010–44.

73. Mimi Engel, Marisa Cannata, and F. Chris Curran, "Principal Influence in Teacher Hiring: Documenting Decentralization over Time," *Journal of Educational Administration* 56, no. 3 (2018): 277–96; Perrone and Meyers, "Review of the Research on Teacher Hiring."

74. Marisa Cannata, Mollie Rubin, Ellen Goldring, Jason A. Grissom, Christine M. Neumerski, Timothy A. Drake, and Patrick Schuermann, "Using Teacher Effectiveness Data for Information-Rich Hiring," *Educational Administration Quarterly* 53, no. 2 (2017): 180–222; Perrone and Meyers, "Review of the Research on Teacher Hiring."

75. Christina Ellis, Susan Troncoso Skidmore, and Julie P. Combs, "The Hiring Process Matters: The Role of Person–Job and Person–Organization Fit in Teacher Satisfaction," *Educational Administration Quarterly* 53, no. 3 (2017): 448–74.

76. DeArmond et al., "Is It Better to Be Good or Lucky?"

77. Boyd et al., "Draw of Home"; Mimi Engel, Brian A. Jacob, and F. Chris Curran. "New Evidence on Teacher Labor Supply," *American Educational Research Journal* 51, no. 1 (2014): 36–72.

78. Reininger, "Hometown Disadvantage?"

79. Ingersoll, "Teacher Turnover and Teacher Shortages"; Jacob, "Challenges of Staffing"; Papay, "Challenge of Teacher Retention"; Nicole Simon and Susan Moore Johnson, "Teacher Turnover in High-Poverty Schools: What We Know and Can Do," *Teachers College Record* 117, no. 3 (2015): 1–36.

80. *Samantha Viano, Lam D. Pham, Gary T. Henry, Adam Kho, and Ron Zimmer, "What Teachers Want: School Factors Predicting Teachers' Decisions to Work in Low-Performing Schools," *American Educational Research Journal* 58, no. 1 (2021): 201–33.

81. Marisa Cannata, "Understanding the Teacher Job Search Process: Espoused Preferences and Preferences in Use," *Teachers College Record* 112, no. 12 (2010): 2889–934; Huriya Jabbar, Marisa Cannata, Emily Germain, and Andrene Castro, "It's Who You Know: The Role of Social Networks in a Changing Labor Market," *American Educational Research Journal* 57, no. 4 (2020): 1485–524.

82. Edward Liu and Susan Moore Johnson, "New Teachers' Experiences of Hiring: Late, Rushed, and Information-Poor," *Educational Administration Quarterly* 42, no. 3 (2006): 324–60.

83. DeArmond et al., "Is It Better to Be Good or Lucky?" Liu and Johnson, "New Teachers' Experiences of Hiring."

Chapter 4. The Revolving Door Keeps Spinning

1. *Gary T. Henry and Christopher Redding, "The Consequences of Leaving School Early: The Effects of Within-Year and End-of-Year Teacher Turnover," *Education Finance and Policy* 15, no. 2 (2020): 332–56. *Matthew Ronfeldt,

Susanna Loeb, and James Wyckoff, "How Teacher Turnover Harms Student Achievement," *American Educational Research Journal* 50, no. 1 (2013): 4–36.

2. Gary Barnes, Edward Crowe, and Benjamin Schaefer, "The Cost of Teacher Turnover in Five School Districts: A Pilot Study," National Commission on Teaching and America's Future, 2007; D. J. DeFeo et al., "The Cost of Teacher Turnover in Alaska," Center for Alaska Education Policy Research, University of Alaska at Anchorage, 2017.

3. *Luis A. Rodriguez, Tuan D. Nguyen, and Matthew G. Springer, "Revisiting Teaching Quality Gaps: Urbanicity and Disparities in Access to High-Quality Teachers Across Tennessee," *Urban Education* 60, no. 2 (2025): 467–504.

4. *Donald Boyd et al., "Teacher Layoffs: An Empirical Illustration of Seniority Versus Measures of Effectiveness," *Education Finance and Policy* 6, no. 3 (2011): 439–54; *Richard M. Ingersoll, "Teacher Turnover and Teacher Shortages: An Organizational Analysis," *American Educational Research Journal* 38, no. 3 (2001): 499–534.

5. *Tuan D. Nguyen et al., "The Correlates of Teacher Turnover: An Updated and Expanded Meta-Analysis of the Literature," *Educational Research Review* 31 (2020): 100355; *Tuan D. Nguyen and Matthew G. Springer. "A Conceptual Framework of Teacher Turnover: A Systematic Review of the Empirical International Literature and Insights from the Employee Turnover Literature," *Educational Review* 75, no. 5 (2023): 993–1028.

6. *Charles T. Clotfelter, Helen F. Ladd, and Jacob L. Vigdor, "Teacher Mobility, School Segregation, and Pay-Based Policies to Level the Playing Field," *Education Finance and Policy* 6, no. 3 (2011): 399–438; *Richard M. Ingersoll and Henry May, "The Magnitude, Destinations, and Determinants of Mathematics and Science Teacher Turnover," *Educational Evaluation and Policy Analysis* 34, no. 4 (2012): 435–64; *Christopher Redding and Tuan D. Nguyen, "Recent Trends in the Characteristics of New Teachers, the Schools in Which They Teach, and Their Turnover Rates," *Teachers College Record* 122, no. 7 (2020): 1–36.

7. *Morgaen L. Donaldson and Susan Moore Johnson, "The Price of Misassignment: The Role of Teaching Assignments in Teach For America Teachers' Exit from Low-Income Schools and the Teaching Profession," *Educational Evaluation and Policy Analysis* 32, no. 2 (2010): 299–323; E. Nah, "Factors Affecting the Retention of Effective Teachers" (PhD diss., Claremont Graduate University, 2015).

8. *Christopher J. Flinn, "Wages and Job Mobility of Young Workers," *Journal of Political Economy* 94, no. 3, pt. 2 (June 1986): S88–S110.

9. *Geoffrey D. Borman and N. Maritza Dowling, "Teacher Attrition and Retention: A Meta-Analytic and Narrative Review of the Research," *Review of Educational Research* 78, no. 3 (2008): 367–409.

10. Gianna Barbieri, Claudio Rossetti, and Paolo Sestito, "The Determinants of Teacher Mobility: Evidence Using Italian Teachers' Transfer Applications," *Economics of Education Review* 30, no. 6 (2011): 1430–444; *Jason A. Grissom, Jill

Nicholson-Crotty, and Lael Keiser, "Does My Boss's Gender Matter? Explaining Job Satisfaction and Employee Turnover in the Public Sector," *Journal of Public Administration Research and Theory* 22, no. 4 (2012): 649–73.

11. Michael P. Fogarty, Rhona Rapoport, and Robert N. Rapoport, *Sex, Career and Family* (Routledge, 2017); Susan Hanson, "Gender and Mobility: New Approaches for Informing Sustainability," *Gender, Place & Culture* 17, no. 1 (February 2010): 5–23.

12. Sharon Kukla-Acevedo, "Leavers, Movers, and Stayers: The Role of Workplace Conditions in Teacher Mobility Decisions," *Journal of Educational Research* 102, no. 6 (2009): 443–52; *Todd R. Stinebrickner, "An Analysis of Occupational Change and Departure from the Labor Force: Evidence of the Reasons That Teachers Leave," *Journal of Human Resources* (2002): 192–216.

13. Pamela Harrell et al., "No Teacher Left Behind: Results of a Five-Year Study of Teacher Attrition," *Action in Teacher Education* 26, no. 2 (2004): 47–59.

14. Mahmoud A. A. Elsayed and Christine H. Roch, "Former Teachers: Exits and Re-Entries," *Educational Policy* 37, no. 2 (2023): 279–307; *Jason A. Grissom and Michelle Reininger, "Who Comes Back? A Longitudinal Analysis of the Reentry Behavior of Exiting Teachers," *Education Finance and Policy* 7, no. 4 (2012): 425–54.

15. Soheyla Taie and Laurie Lewis, "Teacher Attrition and Mobility Results from the 2021–22 Teacher Follow-Up Survey to the National Teacher and Principal Survey | IES," Ed.gov, 2021. https://nces.ed.gov/use-work/resource-library/report/first-look-ed-tab/teacher-attrition-and-mobility-results-2021-22-teacher-follow-survey-national-teacher-and-principal?pubid=2024039.

16. *Matthew A. Kraft, William H. Marinell, and Darrick Shen-Wei Yee, "School Organizational Contexts, Teacher Turnover, and Student Achievement: Evidence from Panel Data," *American Educational Research Journal* 53, no. 5 (2016): 1411–449; Nicole Simon and Susan Moore Johnson, "Teacher Turnover in High-Poverty Schools: What We Know and Can Do," *Teachers College Record* 117, no. 3 (2015): 1–36; Ingersoll, "Teacher Turnover and Teacher Shortages."

17. Betty Achinstein and Julia Aguirre, "Cultural Match or Culturally Suspect: How New Teachers of Color Negotiate Sociocultural Challenges in the Classroom," *Teachers College Record* 110, no. 8 (2008): 1505–540; *Desiree Carver-Thomas and Linda Darling-Hammond, "Teacher Turnover: Why It Matters and What We Can Do About It," Learning Policy Institute, August 16, 2017; Ayana Kee Campoli, "Supportive Principals and Black Teacher Turnover: ESSA as an Opportunity to Improve Retention," *Journal of School Leadership* 27, no. 5 (2017): 675–700; Susan Kemper Patrick and Francisco Arturo Santelli, "Exploring the Relationship Between Demographic Isolation and Professional Experiences of Black and Latinx Teachers," *Journal of Education Human Resources* 40, no. 2 (2022): 138–68; Marcos Pizarro and Rita Kohli, "'I Stopped Sleeping': Teachers of Color and the Impact of Racial Battle Fatigue," *Urban Education* 55, no. 7 (2020): 967–91; Richard M. Ingersoll et al., "Five Trends

Shaping the Teaching Force," *State Education Standard* 22, no. 3 (2022): 6; Rita Kohli and Marcos Pizarro, "Fighting to Educate Our Own: Teachers of Color, Relational Accountability, and the Struggle for Racial Justice," *Equity & Excellence in Education* 49, no. 1 (2016): 72–84; Lynnette Mawhinney and Carol R. Rinke, *There Has to Be a Better Way: Lessons from Former Urban Teachers* (Rutgers University Press, 2019); Darrius A. Stanley, "'I Want to Leave ASAP': Black Women Teachers Discuss the Role of Administrative Support and Teacher Turnover," *Journal of School Leadership* 31, no. 3 (2021): 209–26; *Travis J. Bristol, "To Be Alone or in a Group: An Exploration into How the School-Based Experiences Differ for Black Male Teachers Across One Urban School District," *Urban Education* 53, no. 3 (2018): 334–54; Rita Kohli, "Lessons for Teacher Education: The Role of Critical Professional Development in Teacher of Color Retention," *Journal of Teacher Education* 70, no. 1 (2019): 39–50.

18. Nathan D. Jones, Adam Maier, and Erin Grogan, "The Extent of Late-Hiring and Its Relationship with Teacher Turnover: Evidence from Michigan," Society for Research on Educational Effectiveness, 2011; *Thomas M. Smith and Richard M. Ingersoll, "What Are the Effects of Induction and Mentoring on Beginning Teacher Turnover?," *American Educational Research Journal* 41, no. 3 (2004): 681–714.

19. Christopher Redding, "Are Homegrown Teachers Who Graduate from Urban Districts More Racially Diverse, More Effective, and Less Likely to Exit Teaching?," *American Educational Research Journal* 59, no. 5 (2022): 939–74.

20. Jennifer L. Steele et al., "The Distribution and Mobility of Effective Teachers: Evidence from a Large, Urban School District," *Economics of Education Review* 48 (2015): 86–101.

21. *Sean Kelly and Laura Northrop, "Early Career Outcomes for the 'Best and the Brightest': Selectivity, Satisfaction, and Attrition in the Beginning Teacher Longitudinal Survey," *American Educational Research Journal* 52, no. 4 (2015): 624–56; Ummuhan Yesil Dagli, "America's Public School Kindergarten Teachers' Job Turnover and Associated Factors," *Educational Sciences: Theory and Practice* 12, no. 4 (2012): 3121–34; *Tuan D. Nguyen and Jenna W. Kramer, "Constructing a Clear Definition of Neotraditional Students and Illuminating Their Financial Aid, Academic, and Non-Academic Experiences and Outcomes in the 21st Century," *Journal of Student Financial Aid* 52, no. 1 (2023): 2; Jason M. Miller and Peter Youngs, "Person-Organization Fit and First-Year Teacher Retention in the United States," *Teaching and Teacher Education* 97 (2021): 103226; Jason M. Miller, Peter Youngs, Frank Perrone, and Erin Grogan, "Using Measures of Fit to Predict Beginning Teacher Retention," *Elementary School Journal* 120, no. 3 (2020): 399–421.

22. Desiree Carver-Thomas and Linda Darling-Hammond, "Teacher Turnover: Why It Matters and What We Can Do About It," Learning Policy Institute, August 16, 2017. https://doi.org/10.54300/454.278.

23. Cara M. Djonko-Moore, "An Exploration of Teacher Attrition and Mobility in High Poverty Racially Segregated Schools," *Race Ethnicity and Education* 19, no. 5 (2016): 1063–87; Karen M. Jackson, "Influence Matters: The link Between Principal and Teacher Influence over School Policy and Teacher Turnover," *Journal of School Leadership* 22, no. 5 (2012): 875–901.

24. Richard M. Ingersoll, "The Teacher Shortage: Myth or Reality?," *Educational Horizons* 81, no. 3 (2003): 146–52.

25. *Dan Goldhaber, Betheny Gross, and Daniel Player, "Teacher Career Paths, Teacher Quality, and Persistence in the Classroom: Are Public Schools Keeping Their Best?," *Journal of Policy Analysis and Management* 30, no. 1 (November 2, 2010): 57–87; David Perda, "Transitions into and out of Teaching: A Longitudinal Analysis of Early Career Teacher Turnover" (PhD diss., University of Pennsylvania, 2013); Richard Murnane, Judith Singer, and James Kemple, *Who Will Teach? Policies That Matter* (Harvard University Press, 1991).

26. Stacy Johnson Erickson, "An Examination of the Relationship Between Professional Development and Teacher Turnover" (EdD diss., University of Oregon, 2007).

27. Debbie F. C. Harris-McIntyre, "The Impact of Teacher Induction Programs on the Retention of Novice Teachers" (PhD diss., Keiser University, 2014); Michelle Helms-Lorenz, Wim van de Grift, and Ridwan Maulana, "Longitudinal Effects of Induction on Teaching Skills and Attrition Rates of Beginning Teachers," *School Effectiveness and School Improvement* 27, no. 2 (2016): 178–204; William Kyle Ingle, "Teacher Quality and Attrition in a US School District," *Journal of Educational Administration* 47, no. 5 (2009): 557–85; Christina Catherine Luke, "The Effect of State Induction Policies on Novice Teacher Attrition" (PhD diss., State University of New York at Albany, 2014).

28. Vincent Connelly and Suzanne Graham, "Student Teaching and Teacher Attrition in Special Education," *Teacher Education and Special Education* 32, no. 3 (2009): 257–69; *D. Goldhaber, J. M. Krieg, and R. Theobald, "Does the Match Matter? Exploring Whether Student Teaching Experiences Affect Teacher Effectiveness," *American Educational Research Journal* 54, no. 2 (2017): 325–59; Cara M. Moore, "Why Do Teachers Quit? An Investigation of the Influence of School Environment and Teacher Characteristics on Discontent and Attrition" (PhD diss., Temple University, 2011).

29. *Susan Moore Johnson and Sarah E. Birkeland, "Pursuing a 'Sense of Success': New Teachers Explain Their Career Decisions," *American Educational Research Journal* 40, no. 3 (2003): 581–617; Sean Kelly, "An Event History Analysis of Teacher Attrition: Salary, Teacher Tracking, and Socially Disadvantaged Schools," *Journal of Experimental Education* 72, no. 3 (2004): 195–220.

30. *Joshua M. Cowen et al., "Teacher Retention in Appalachian Schools: Evidence from Kentucky," *Economics of Education Review* 31, no. 4 (2012): 431–41; Charles Olufemi Ogundimu, "Does the Mode of Entry into Teaching Matter in

Teacher Retention? A Discrete-Time Survival Analysis Modeling of New York City Public School Teachers" (PhD diss., Columbia University, 2014).

31. *Tuan D. Nguyen and Christopher Redding, "Changes in the Demographics, Qualifications, and Turnover of American STEM teachers, 1988–2012." *AERA Open* 4, no. 3 (2018): 2332858418802790; Daniel A. Sass et al., "Identifying Personal and Contextual Factors That Contribute to Attrition Rates for Texas Public School Teachers," *Education Policy Analysis Archives / Archivos Analíticos de Políticas Educativas* 20 (2012): 1–26.

32. *Thomas S. Dee and Dan Goldhaber, "Understanding and Addressing Teacher Shortages in the United States," The Hamilton Project, 2017; *Emma García and Elaine Weiss, "The Teacher Shortage Is Real, Large and Growing, and Worse than We Thought," Economic Policy Institute, 2019.

33. Bonnie S. Billingsley, "Recognizing and Supporting the Critical Roles of Teachers in Special Education Leadership," *Exceptionality* 15, no. 3 (2007): 163–76; *Bonnie Billingsley and Elizabeth Bettini, "Special Education Teacher Attrition and Retention: A Review of the Literature," *Review of Educational Research* 89, no. 5 (2019): 697–744.

34. *Mary T. Brownell and Paul T. Sindelar, "Preparing and Retaining Effective Special Education Teachers: Systemic Solutions for Addressing Teacher Shortages," policy brief, Collaboration for Effective Educator Development, Accountability and Reform, 2016; David J. Peyton, Kelly Acosta, Alexandria Harvey, Daisy J. Pua, Paul T. Sindelar, Loretta Mason-Williams, Jim Dewey, Tiffany L. Fisher, and Emily Crews, "Special Education Teacher Shortage: Differences Between High and Low Shortage States," *Teacher Education and Special Education* 44, no. 1 (2020): 088840642090661.

35. *Elizabeth Bettini et al., "Ethnoracial Diversity of the Special Educator Workforce over Time," *Exceptional Children* 91, no. 2 (2025): 144–65.

36. Betty Achinstein and Rodney T. Ogawa, "Change(d) Agents: School Contexts and the Cultural/Professional Roles of New Teachers of Mexican Descent," *Teachers College Record* 113, no. 11 (2011): 2503–551; Travis J. Bristol and Marcelle Mentor, "Policing and Teaching: The Positioning of Black Male Teachers as Agents in the Universal Carceral Apparatus," *Urban Review* 50 (2018): 218–34.

37. Richard M. Ingersoll, "The Teacher Shortage: Myth or Reality?," *Educational Horizons* 81, no. 3 (2003): 146–52.

38. Jennifer Imazeki, "Teacher Salaries and Teacher Attrition," *Economics of Education Review* 24, no. 4 (2005): 431–49; Tuan D. Nguyen, "Examining the Teacher Labor Market in Different Rural Contexts: Variations by Urbanicity and Rural States," *AERA Open* 6, no. 4 (2020): 2332858420966336.

39. Fred L. Pigge and Ronald N. Marso, "A Seven Year Longitudinal Multi-Factor Assessment of Teaching Concerns Development Through Preparation and Early Years of Teaching," *Teaching and Teacher Education* 13, no. 2 (1997): 225–35; *Thomas M. Smith and Richard M. Ingersoll, "What Are the Effects of

Induction and Mentoring on Beginning Teacher Turnover?," *American Educational Research Journal* 41, no. 3 (2004): 681–714.

40. *Christopher Redding and Thomas M. Smith, "Easy In, Easy Out: Are Alternatively Certified Teachers Turning Over at Increased Rates?," *American Educational Research Journal* 53, no. 4 (2016): 1086–1125; Sass et al., "Identifying Personal and Contextual Factors"; David A. Stuit and Thomas M. Smith, "Explaining the Gap in Charter and Traditional Public School Teacher Turnover Rates," *Economics of Education Review* 31, no. 2 (2012): 268–79; Michael Crouch and Tuan D. Nguyen, "Examining Teacher Characteristics, School Conditions, and Attrition Rates at the Intersection of School Choice and Rural Education," *Journal of School Choice* 15, no. 2 (2021): 268–94.

41. Anna Weiss, David Woo, and Tuan Nguyen, "More Alike or More Different over Time? Exploring Urban Charter and Public School Teachers' Characteristics and Working Conditions," *Journal of School Choice* 18, no. 2 (2024): 215–37.

42. Steve Bradley, Colin P. Green, and Gareth Leeves, "The Role of Pecuniary and Non-Pecuniary Factors in Teacher Turnover and Mobility Decisions," unpublished manuscript, Social Science Research Network, posted 2006; Donaldson and Johnson, "Price of Misassignment"; Jackson, "Influence Matters."

43. *F. Chris Curran, Samantha L. Viano, and Benjamin W. Fisher, "Teacher Victimization, Turnover, and Contextual Factors Promoting Resilience," *Journal of School Violence* 18, no. 1 (2019): 21–38.

44. *Ben Ost and Jeffrey C. Schiman, "Grade-Specific Experience, Grade Reassignments, and Teacher Turnover," *Economics of Education Review* 46 (2015): 112–26; Jack Buckley, Mark Schneider, and Yi Shang, "Fix It and They Might Stay: School Facility Quality and Teacher Retention in Washington, DC," *Teachers College Record* 107, no. 5 (2005): 1107–23; Todd Martin, "A Study of Middle School Principal Behaviors and Their Impact on Teacher Retention" (EdD diss., Gardner-Webb University, 2011).

45. Ingersoll and May, "Magnitude, Destinations, and Determinants."

46. Ummuhan Yesil Dagli, "America's Public School Kindergarten Teachers' Job Turnover and Associated Factors," *Educational Sciences: Theory and Practice* 12, no. 4 (2012): 3121–34.

47. Valeriy Lazarev et al., "The Texas Teacher Evaluation and Support System Rubric: Properties and Association with School Characteristics," Department of Education, Institute of Education Sciences, National Center for Education Evaluation and Regional Assistance, Regional Educational Laboratory Southwest, 2017; Tamala Boyd Shaw, "How Does Participating in a Teacher Leadership Program Impact Secondary Teachers' Retention, Instructional Capacity, and Influence on Other Teachers" (EdD diss., University of Memphis, 2016); Rusi Sun and Weijie Wang, "Transformational Leadership, Employee Turnover Intention,

and Actual Voluntary Turnover in Public Organizations," *Public Management Review* 19, no. 8 (2017): 1124–41.

48. Susan R. Wynn and Kathleen M. Brown, "Principal Leadership and Professional Learning Communities: What Beginning Teachers Value," *International Journal of Educational Reform* 17, no. 1 (2008): 37–63; Warren S. Eller, Carl B. Doerfler, and Kenneth J. Meier, "Teacher Turnover in Texas: Problems and Prospects," report, Texas Educational Excellence Project, 2000. Angela Urick, "The Influence of Typologies of School Leaders on Teacher Retention: A Multilevel Latent Class Analysis," *Journal of Educational Administration* 54, no. 4 (2016): 434–68.

49. Donaldson and Johnson, "Price of Misassignment."

50. *Matthew A. Kraft, William H. Marinell, and Darrick Shen-Wei Yee, "School Organizational Contexts, Teacher Turnover, and Student Achievement: Evidence from Panel Data," *American Educational Research Journal* 53, no. 5 (2016): 1411–49.

51. K. Mihaly, Master, Benjamin K., and Cate Yoon, " (Examining the Early Impacts of the Leading Educators Fellowship on Student Achievement and Teacher Retention," Rand Corporation, 2015; Matthew Ronfeldt and Kiel McQueen, "Does New Teacher Induction Really Improve Retention?," *Journal of Teacher Education* 68, no. 4 (2017): 394–410.

52. Steven Glazerman, Eric Isenberg, Sarah Dolfin, Martha Bleeker, Amy Johnson, Mary Grider, and Matthew Jacobus, "Impacts of Comprehensive Teacher Induction: Final Results from a Randomized Controlled Study. NCEE 2010–4027," National Center for Education Evaluation and Regional Assistance, 2010; Rebecca A. Schmidt, Aliya R. Pilchen, Katrina Laguarda, Haiwen Wang, and Deepa Patel, "Scaling Up Teacher Induction: Implementation and Impact on Teachers and Students. Evaluation of the New Teacher Center's i3 Scale-Up Grant, Revised Final Report," SRI Education, 2025.

53. Jonah E. Rockoff, "Does Mentoring Reduce Turnover and Improve Skills of New Employees? Evidence from Teachers in New York City," working paper 13868, National Bureau of Economic Research, 2008; Mike Coldwell, "Exploring the Influence of Professional Development on Teacher Careers: A Path Model Approach," *Teaching and Teacher Education* 61 (2017): 189–98. Lisa M. DiGaudio, "Implications of the School Improvement Engine for Teacher Retention and School Organizational Health" (PhD diss., Walden University, 2017).

54. *R. Mark Gritz and Neil D. Theobald, "The Effects of School District Spending Priorities on Length of Stay in Teaching," *Journal of Human Resources* 31, no. 3 (1996): 477–512; *Sheila Nataraj Kirby, Mark Berends, and Scott Naftel, "Supply and Demand of Minority Teachers in Texas: Problems and Prospects," *Educational Evaluation and Policy Analysis* 21, no. 1 (1999): 47–66; *C. Kirabo Jackson and Claire L. Mackevicius, "What Impacts Can We Expect from School Spending Policy? Evidence from Evaluations in the United States," *American Economic Journal: Applied Economics* 16, no. 1 (2024): 412–46.

55. Barbieri et al., "Determinants of Teacher Mobility"; *Li Feng, "Hire Today, Gone Tomorrow: New Teacher Classroom Assignments and Teacher Mobility," *Education Finance and Policy* 5, no. 3 (2010): 278–316.

56. Susanna Loeb and Linda Darling-Hammond, "How Teaching Conditions Predict Teacher Turnover in California Schools," *Peabody Journal of Education* 80, no. 3 (2005): 44–70; Thomas M. Smith, "How Do State-Level Induction and Standards-Based Reform Policies Affect Induction Experiences and Turnover Among New Teachers?," *American Journal of Education* 113, no. 2 (2007): 273–309; Holly Anne Lopez Stevens, "The Effects of Los Angeles Universal Preschool on Quality Preschool Teacher Retention in Los Angeles County" (EdD diss., University of California, Los Angeles, 2010).

57. Richard Ingersoll and Henry Tran, "Teacher Shortages and Turnover in Rural Schools in the US: An Organizational Analysis," *Educational Administration Quarterly* 59, no.2 (2023): 396–431.

58. *Susanna Loeb, Demetra Kalogrides, and Tara Béteille, "Effective Schools: Teacher Hiring, Assignment, Development, and Retention," *Education Finance and Policy* 7, no. 3 (2012): 269–304; Xiaoxia A. Newton, Rosario Rivero, Bruce Fuller, and Luke Dauter, "Teacher Stability and Turnover in Los Angeles: The Influence of Teacher and School Characteristics. Los Angeles School Infrastructure Project," working paper, Policy Analysis for California Education, 2011.

59. Debbie L. Hahs-Vaughn and Lisa Scherff, "Beginning English Teacher Attrition, Mobility, and Retention," *Journal of Experimental Education* 77, no. 1 (2008): 21–54.

60. Desiree Carver-Thomas and Linda Darling-Hammond, "Teacher Turnover: Why It Matters and What We Can Do About It," Learning Policy Institute, August 16, 2017. https://doi.org/10.54300/454.278.

61. Hamilton Lankford, Susanna Loeb, and James Wyckoff, "Teacher Sorting and the Plight of Urban Schools: A Descriptive Analysis," *Educational Evaluation and Policy Analysis* 24, no. 1 (2002): 37–62; *Michelle Reininger, "Hometown Disadvantage? It Depends on Where You're From: Teachers' Location Preferences and the Implications for Staffing Schools," *Educational Evaluation and Policy Analysis* 34, no. 2 (2012): 127–45.

62. *Li Feng and Tim R. Sass, "Teacher Quality and Teacher Mobility," *Education Finance and Policy* 12, no. 3 (2017): 396–418.

63. Susan Fairchild et al., "White and Black Teachers' Job Satisfaction: Does Relational Demography Matter?," *Urban Education* 47, no. 1 (2012): 170–97; Jason A. Grissom, Emily C. Kern, and Luis A. Rodriguez, "The 'Representative Bureaucracy' in Education: Educator Workforce Diversity, Policy Outputs, and Outcomes for Disadvantaged Students," *Educational Researcher* 44, no. 3 (2015): 185–92.

64. Anne S. Tsui and Charles A. O'Reilly III, "Beyond Simple Demographic Effects: The Importance of Relational Demography in Superior-Subordinate Dyads," *Academy of Management Journal* 32, no. 2 (1989): 402–23.

65. *Christopher Redding, "A Teacher like Me: A Review of the Effect of Student–Teacher Racial/Ethnic Matching on Teacher Perceptions of Students and Student Academic and Behavioral Outcomes," *Review of Educational Research* 89, no. 4 (2019): 499–535.

66. Jason A. Grissom, Jill Nicholson-Crotty, and Lael Keiser, "Does My Boss's Gender Matter? Explaining Job Satisfaction and Employee Turnover in the Public Sector," *Journal of Public Administration Research and Theory* 22, no. 4 (2012): 649–73; Debbi C. Harris, "Should I Stay or Should I Go? Comparing Teacher Mobility in Florida's Charter and Traditional Public Schools," *Peabody Journal of Education* 82, nos. 2–3 (2007): 274–310; *Jason A. Grissom and Lael R. Keiser, "A Supervisor like Me: Race, Representation, and the Satisfaction and Turnover Decisions of Public Sector Employees," *Journal of Policy Analysis and Management* 30, no. 3 (2011): 557–80.

67. *Jason A. Grissom, Sean Nicholson-Crotty, and James R. Harrington, "Estimating the Effects of No Child Left Behind on Teachers' Work Environments and Job Attitudes," *Educational Evaluation and Policy Analysis* 36, no. 4 (2014): 417–36; *Tuan D. Nguyen, Christopher Redding, Allison F. Gilmour, and Elizabeth Bettini, "No Child Left Behind and the Individuals with Disabilities Education Act: Examining Special Educators' Outcomes," *Remedial and Special Education* 45, no. 3 (2024): 139–51; *Christopher Redding and Tuan D. Nguyen, "The Effects of Race to the Top on Teacher Qualifications, Work Environments, and Job Attitudes," *Educational Evaluation and Policy Analysis* 47, no. 1 (2025): 237–62; *Min Sun, Andrew Saultz, and Yincheng Ye, "Federal Policy and the Teacher Labor Market: Exploring the Effects of NCLB School Accountability on Teacher Turnover," *School Effectiveness and School Improvement* 28, no. 1 (2017): 102–22.

68. *Matthew Shirrell, "The Effects of Subgroup-Specific Accountability on Teacher Turnover and Attrition," *Education Finance and Policy* 13, no. 3 (2018): 333–68.

69. Donald Boyd, Pam Grossman, Hamilton Lankford, Susanna Loeb, and James Wyckoff, "Who Leaves? Teacher Attrition and Student Achievement," working paper 14022, National Bureau of Economic Research, 2008.

70. Redding, "Teacher like Me."

71. DiGaudio, "Implications of the School Improvement Engine."

72. Linda Darling-Hammond et al., "Evaluating Teacher Evaluation," *Phi Delta Kappan* 93, no. 6 (2012): 8–15.

73. *Alex L. Rubenstein et al., "Surveying the Forest: A Meta-Analysis, Moderator Investigation, and Future-Oriented Discussion of the Antecedents of Voluntary Employee Turnover," *Personnel Psychology* 71, no. 1 (2018): 23–65.

74. Rodger W. Griffeth, Peter W. Hom, and Stefan Gaertner, "A Meta-Analysis of Antecedents and Correlates of Employee Turnover: Update, Moderator Tests, and Research Implications for the Next Millennium," *Journal of Management* 26, no. 3 (2000): 463–88.

75. Todd R. Stinebrickner, "Estimation of a Duration Model in the Presence of Missing Data," *Review of Economics and Statistics* 81, no. 3 (1999): 529–42.

76. Erling E. Boe, Sharon A. Bobbitt, Lynne H. Cook, Gema Barkanic, and Greg Maislin, "Teacher Turnover in Eight Cognate Areas: National Trends and Predictors," University of Pennsylvania, Graduate School of Education, Center for Research and Evaluation in Social Policy, 1998; Cynthia Martinez Garcia, John R. Slate, and Carmen Tejeda Delgado, "Salary and Ranking and Teacher Turnover: A Statewide Study," *International Journal of Education Policy and Leadership* 4, no. 7 (2009): 1–8.

77. Boe et al., "Teacher Turnover in Eight Cognate Areas"; Sean Kelly, "An Event History Analysis of Teacher Attrition: Salary, Teacher Tracking, and Socially Disadvantaged Schools," *Journal of Experimental Education* 72, no. 3 (2004): 195–220; *Eric A. Hanushek, John F. Kain, and Steven G. Rivkin, "Why Public Schools Lose Teachers," *Journal of Human Resources* 39, no. 2 (2004): 326–54; *Christopher Redding and Kelley A. Taksier, "Breaking Bad/Good Patterns and Consequences of Public School Teachers' Multiple Jobholding," EdWorkingPaper no. 23-811, Annenberg Institute at Brown University, 2023.

78. Redding and Taksier, "Breaking Bad/Good Patterns."

79. *Li Feng and Tim R. Sass, "The Impact of Incentives to Recruit and Retain Teachers in 'Hard-to-Staff' Subjects," *Journal of Policy Analysis and Management* 37, no. 1 (2018): 112–35; *Matthew G. Springer, Walker A. Swain, and Luis A. Rodriguez, "Effective Teacher Retention Bonuses: Evidence from Tennessee," *Educational Evaluation and Policy Analysis* 38, no. 2 (2016): 199–221.

80. Carycruz Bueno and Tim R. Sass, "The Effects of Differential Pay on Teacher Recruitment and Retention," working paper no. 219-0519, National Center for Analysis of Longitudinal Data in Education Research, 2019; *Charles T. Clotfelter et al., "Teacher Bonuses and Teacher Retention in Low-Performing Schools: Evidence from the North Carolina $1,800 Teacher Bonus Program," *Public Finance Review* 36, no. 1 (2008): 63–87. Feng and Sass, "Impact of Incentives"; Beng Huat See, Rebecca Morris, Stephen Gorard, and Nada El Soufi, "What Works in Attracting and Retaining Teachers in Challenging Schools and Areas?," *Oxford Review of Education* 46, no. 6 (2020): 678–97.

81. Eller et al., "Teacher Turnover in Texas."

82. "Pensions, Explained for Educators," National Education Association, April 18, 2022. https://www.nea.org/resource-library/pensions-explained-educators.

83. *Ben Backes, Dan Goldhaber, Cyrus Grout, Cory Koedel, Shawn Ni, Michael Podgursky, P. Brett Xiang, and Zeyu Xu, "Benefit or Burden? On the Intergenerational Inequity of Teacher Pension Plans," *Educational Researcher* 45, no. 6 (2016): 367–77; *Andrew G. Biggs, "The Long-Term Solvency of Teacher Pension Plans: How We Got to Now and Prospects for Recovery," *Educational Researcher* 52, no. 2 (2023): 98–115; *Robert M. Costrell, "The Three R's of Teacher

Pension Funding: Redistribution, Return, and Risk," *Educational Researcher* 52, no. 2 (2023): 91–97.

84. Costrell, "Three R's of Teacher Pension Funding."

85. Chad Aldeman, "The Pension Pac-Man: How Pension Debt Eats Away at Teacher Salaries," TeachersPensions.org and Bellwether Education Partners, 2016. https://bellwether.org/wp-content/uploads/2016/05/Teacher-Pension-Pac-Man_Web.pdf.

86. Backes et al., "Benefit or Burden."

87. Kathryn M. Doherty, Sandi Jacobs, and Trisha M. Madden, "No One Benefits: How Teacher Pension Systems Are Failing Both Teachers and Taxpayers," National Council on Teacher Quality, 2012.

88. *Joshua B. McGee and Marcus A. Winters, "How Pensions Contribute to the Premium Paid to Experienced Public School Teachers," *Educational Researcher* 46, no. 5 (2017): 250–58.

89. *Andrew C .Johnston, Jonah E. Rockoff, and James R. Harrington, "Pension Reform and Labor Supply: Retention and Productivity Under a Pension Cut," working paper 33673, National Bureau of Economic Research, 2025.

90. Kelly and Northrop, "Early Career Outcomes"; Kukla-Acevedo, "Leavers, Movers, and Stayers"; Redding and Smith, "Easy In, Easy Out."

91. *Barbara Biasi, "The Labor Market for Teachers Under Different Pay Schemes," *American Economic Journal: Economic Policy* 13, no. 3 (2021): 63–102; *Jonathan Roth, "Union Reform and Teacher Turnover: Evidence from Wisconsin's Act 10," Harvard Kennedy School, 2017.

92. Susanna Loeb, Luke C. Miller, and James Wyckoff, "Performance Screens for School Improvement: The Case of Teacher Tenure Reform in New York City," *Educational Researcher* 44, no. 4 (2015): 199–212.

93. Katharine O. Strunk, Nathan Barrett, and Jane Arnold Lincove, "When Tenure Ends: The Short-Run Effects of the Elimination of Louisiana's Teacher Employment Protections on Teacher Exit and Retirement," technical report, Education Research Alliance, 2017.

94. *Tuan D. Nguyen, Lam D. Pham, Michael Crouch, Matthew G. Springer, "The Correlates of Teacher Turnover: An Updated and Expanded Meta-Analysis of the Literature," *Educational Research Review* 31 (2020): 100355.

95. Donaldson and Johnson, "Price of Misassignment."

96. *Kevin C. Bastian and Sarah C. Fuller, "Educator Attrition and Mobility During the COVID-19 Pandemic," *Educational Researcher* 52, no. 8 (2023): 516–20.

97. *Christopher Redding and Gary T. Henry, "Leaving School Early: An Examination of Novice Teachers' Within- and End-of-Year Turnover," *American Educational Research Journal* 56, no. 1 (2019): 204–36.

98. Frank Perrone, Daniel Player, and Peter Youngs, "Administrative Climate, Early Career Teacher Burnout, and Turnover," *Journal of School Leadership* 29, no. 3 (2019): 191–209.

99. Ogundimu, "Does the Mode of Entry."

100. Ingersoll and May, "Magnitude, Destinations, and Determinants."

101. Sass et al., "Identifying Personal and Contextual Factors."

102. Dee and Goldhaber, "Understanding and Addressing Teacher Shortages."

103. Sass et al., "Identifying Personal and Contextual Factors."

104. Billingsley, "Recognizing and Supporting."

105. Bettini et al., "Ethnoracial Diversity."

106. *Loretta Mason-Williams et al., "Rethinking Shortages in Special Education: Making Good on the Promise of an Equal Opportunity for Students with Disabilities," *Teacher Education and Special Education* 43, no. 1 (2020): 45–62; *Tuan D. Nguyen, Elizabeth Bettini, Allison F. Gilmour, and Christopher Redding, "Examining the Supply of New Special Educators: Variations by Institutional Characteristics and For-Profit Status," *Remedial and Special Education* 46, no. 6 (2025): 456–67.

107. Strunk et al., "When Tenure Ends."

Chapter 5. Policies to Increase Teacher Recruitment

1. Richard M. Ingersoll and David Perda, "The Status of Teaching as a Profession," *Schools and Society* 3 (2008): 106–18.

2. Matthew A. Kraft and Melissa Arnold Lyon, "The Rise and Fall of the Teaching Profession: Prestige, Interest, Preparation, and Satisfaction over the Last Half Century," *American Educational Research Journal* 61, no. 6 (2024): 1192–236.

3. Akilah Alleyne, "Book Banning, Curriculum Restrictions, and the Politicization of US Schools," Center for American Progress, 2022. https://www.americanprogress.org/article/book-banning-curriculum-restrictions-and-the-politicization-of-us-schools; Rachel Roegman, Kevin Tan, Patrick Rice, and Jenna Mahoney, "Politics, Polarization, and Politicization of Social Emotional Learning and School Boards," *AASA Journal of Scholarship and Practice* 19, no. 2 (2022): 41–53.

4. Tuan D. Nguyen, Chanh B. Lam, and Paul Bruno, "What Do We Know About the Extent of Teacher Shortages Nationwide? A Systematic Examination of Reports of US Teacher Shortages," *AERA Open* 10 (2024): 23328584241276512; Patricia Saenz-Armstrong, "Data Brief: How Do Trends in Teacher Preparation Enrollment and Completion Vary by State?," National Council on Teacher Quality, 2023.

5. Brendan Bartanen and Andrew Kwok, "From Interest to Entry: The Teacher Pipeline from College Application to Initial Employment," *American Educational Research Journal* 60, no. 5 (2023): 941–85.

6. Sylvia A. Allegretto and Lawrence Mishel, "The Teacher Pay Gap Is Wider than Ever: Teachers' Pay Continues to Fall Further Behind Pay of Comparable Workers," Economic Policy Institute, 2016.

7. Peter J. Dolton, "Teacher Supply," in *Handbook of the Economics of Education*, vol. 2, ed. E. Hanushek and F. Welch (Elsevier, 2006), 1079–161.

8. Jennifer Whitfield, Manjari Banerjee, Hersh C. Waxman, Timothy P. Scott, and Mary Margaret Capraro, "Recruitment and Retention of STEM Teachers Through the Noyce Scholarship: A Longitudinal Mixed Methods Study," *Teaching and Teacher Education* 103 (2021): 103361.

9. Matthew D. Hendricks, "Towards an Optimal Teacher Salary Schedule: Designing Base Salary to Attract and Retain Effective Teachers," *Economics of Education Review* 47 (2015): 143–67.

10. Heather J. Hough and Susanna Loeb, "Can a District-Level Teacher Salary Incentive Policy Improve Teacher Recruitment and Retention?," policy brief 13-4, Policy Analysis for California Education, 2013.

11. Lorin W. Anderson and Jo Anne Craig Anderson, "A Study of Teacher Recruitment Programs Funded with Education Improvement Act (EIA) Revenues," white paper prepared for the South Carolina Education Oversight Committee, 2022. https://eoc.sc.gov/sites/eoc/files/Documents/Teacher%20Report%20Anderson/EIA%20Program%20Review_Anderson-08.19.2022.pdf.

12. *Gary T. Henry, Kevin C. Bastian, and Adrienne A. Smith, "Scholarships to Recruit the 'Best and Brightest' into Teaching: Who Is Recruited, Where Do They Teach, How Effective Are They, and How Long Do They Stay?," *Educational Researcher* 41, no. 3 (2012): 83–92.

13. Anne Podolsky and Tara Kini, "How Effective Are Loan Forgiveness and Service Scholarships for Recruiting Teachers?," policy brief, Learning Policy Institute, 2016.

14. *Jennifer L. Steele, Richard J. Murnane, and John B. Willett, "Do Financial Incentives Help Low-Performing Schools Attract and Keep Academically Talented Teachers? Evidence from California," *Journal of Policy Analysis and Management* 29, no. 3 (2010): 451–78.

15. Sherri Martinie, Tuan Nguyen, Tegan Nusser, Craig Spencer, and Rekha Natarajan, "The Recruitment and Retention of Mathematics Teachers in High-Need Schools," *Mathematics Teacher Education and Development* 25, no. 2 (2023): article 1; Patricia D. Morrell and Stephanie Salomone, "Impact of a Robert Noyce Scholarship on STEM Teacher Recruitment," *Journal of College Science Teaching* 47, no. 2 (2017): 16–21.

16. Whitfield et al., "Recruitment and Retention of STEM Teachers."

17. David J. Peyton, Wilhelmina van Dijk, and Loretta Mason-Williams, "Meeting the Moment: Impact of TEACH Grant on US Undergraduate Education Degree Completion in High-Need Content Areas," *Higher Education Policy* (2022). https://doi.org/10.1057/s41307-022-00263-3.

18. Podolsky and Kini, "How Effective Are Loan Forgiveness and Service Scholarships."

19. *Brian A. Jacob, Damon Jones, and Benjamin J. Keys, "The Value of Student Debt Relief and the Role of Administrative Barriers: Evidence from the

Teacher Loan Forgiveness Program," *Journal of Labor Economics* 42, no. S1 (2024): S261–S292.

20. *Jennifer L. Steele, Richard J. Murnane, and John B. Willett, "Do Financial Incentives Help Low-Performing Schools Attract and Keep Academically Talented Teachers? Evidence from California," *Journal of Policy Analysis and Management* 29, no. 3 (2010): 451–78.

21. Podolsky and Kini, "How Effective Are Loan Forgiveness and Service Scholarships."

22. Beng Huat See, Rebecca Morris, Stephen Gorard, Dimitra Kokotsaki, and Sophia Abdi, "Teacher Recruitment and Retention: A Critical Review of International Evidence of Most Promising Interventions," *Education Sciences* 10, no. 10 (2020): 262.

23. Nevada A.B. 7. https://www.leg.state.nv.us/App/NELIS/REL/79th2017/Bill/4613/Text.

24. Arizona S.B. 1042. https://www.azleg.gov/legtext/53leg/1r/bills/sb1042p.pdf.

25. Arizona S.B. 1159. https://www.azleg.gov/legtext/55leg/2R/laws/0337.pdf.

26. Kentucky S.B. 49. https://apps.legislature.ky.gov/law/acts/23RS/documents/0054.pdf.

27. Dan Goldhaber, "Everyone's Doing It, but What Does Teacher Testing Tell Us About Teacher Effectiveness?," *Journal of Human Resources* 42, no. 4 (2007): 765–94.

28. Leslie Fenwick and AACTE's Dean-in-Residence, "The History, Current Use, and Impact of Entrance and Licensure Examinations Cut Scores on the Teacher-of-Color Pipeline: A Structural Racism Analysis," American Association of Colleges for Teacher Education, 2021; Linda Tyler, "Toward Increasing Teacher Diversity: Targeting Support and Intervention for Teacher Licensure Candidates," Educational Testing Service, 2011.

29. *Eric A. Hanushek and Richard R. Pace, "Who Chooses to Teach (and Why)?," *Economics of Education Review* 14, no. 2 (1995): 101–17.

30. Nevada A.B. 7.

31. Arizona S.B. 1159; *Richard Buddin and Gema Zamarro, "Teacher Qualifications and Student Achievement in Urban Elementary Schools," *Journal of Urban Economics* 66, no. 2 (2009): 103–15; *Dan Goldhaber and Michael Hansen, "Race, Gender, and Teacher Testing: How Informative a Tool Is Teacher Licensure Testing?," *American Educational Research Journal* 47, no. 1 (2010): 218–51.

32. *Alexis Orellana and Marcus A. Winters, "Licensure Tests and Teacher Supply," *Journal of Human Resources* 60, no. 6 (2025), https://doi.org/10.3368/jhr.0324-13465R2. A different study using Arkansas data found a positive correlation between Praxis II and student achievement, but the magnitudes were small and the results only correlational. James V. Shuls and Julie R. Trivitt, "Teacher Effectiveness: An Analysis of Licensure Screens," *Educational Policy* 29, no. 4

(2015): 645–75. A more recent study also finds that the Praxis I and Praxis II would exclude effective and ineffective teachers. James V. Shuls, "Raising the Bar on Teacher Quality: Assessing the Impact of Increasing Licensure Exam Cut-Scores," *Educational Policy* 32, no. 7 (2018): 969–92.

33. Andrew Bacher-Hicks, Olivia L. Chi, and Alexis Orellana, "Two Years Later: How COVID-19 Has Shaped the Teacher Workforce," *Educational Researcher* 52, no. 4 (2023): 219–29.

34. Ariel Tichnor-Wagner, Andrew Bacher-Hicks, and Olivia L. Chi, "Motivations to Enter the Teaching Profession During the COVID-19 Pandemic: Insights from Emergency License Holders in Massachusetts," *Teaching and Teacher Education* 158 (2025): 104968; Olivia L. Chi, Andrew Bacher-Hicks, Ariel Tichnor-Wagner, and Sidrah Baloch, "Teacher Licensure and Workforce Quality: Insights from the First Wave of COVID-Era Emergency Licenses in Massachusetts," *Educational Evaluation and Policy Analysis* (2025). https://doi.org/10.3102/01623737251329345.

35. *Bobby W. Chung and Jian Zou, "Occupational Licensing in US Public Schools: Nationwide Implementation of Teacher Performance Assessment," *Journal of Public Economics* 244 (2025): 105328.

36. Christine D. Clayton, "Voices from Student Teachers in New York: The Persistence of a Subtractive Experience of the edTPA as a Licensure Exam for Initial Certification," *Education Policy Analysis Archives* 26 (2018), http://dx.doi.org/10.14507/epaa.26.2888; Lama Bergstrand Othman, Rowand Robinson, and Nancy F. Molfenter, "Emerging Issues with Consequential Use of the edTPA: Overall and Through a Special Education Lens," *Teacher Education and Special Education* 40, no. 4 (2017): 269–77; Kristen A. Gilbert and Nai-Cheng Kuo, "Ethical, Legal, and Pedagogical Issues in edTPA," *Critical Education* 10, no. 8 (2019): 1–17; Adam Kuranishi and Celia Oyler, "I Failed the edTPA," *Teacher Education and Special Education* 40, no. 4 (2017): 299–313; Sungmin Moon, Stacey L. Carpenter, Alexandria K. Hansen, Leslie Bushong, and Julie A. Bianchini, "Examining the Effects of Undergraduate STEM Teacher Recruitment and Teacher Education Programs on Preservice Secondary Science and Mathematics Teacher Readiness and Teacher Performance Assessment (edTPA) Scores," *School Science and Mathematics* 121, no. 8 (2021): 452–65; Linda Darling-Hammond and Maria E. Hyler, "The Role of Performance Assessment in Developing Teaching as a Profession," *Rethinking Schools* 27, no. 4 (2013): 10–15; Mistilina Sato, "What Is the Underlying Conception of Teaching of the edTPA?," *Journal of Teacher Education* 65, no. 5 (2014): 421–34.

37. Dan Goldhaber, James Cowan, and Roddy Theobald, "Evaluating Prospective Teachers: Testing the Predictive Validity of the edTPA," *Journal of Teacher Education* 68, no. 4 (2017): 377–93.

38. Bobby W. Chung and Jian Zou, "Teacher Licensing, Teacher Supply, and Student Achievement: Nationwide Implementation of edTPA," EdWorkingPaper no. 21-440, Annenberg Institute at Brown University, May 2023.

39. Drew H. Gitomer, José Felipe Martínez, Dan Battey, and Nora E. Hyland, "Assessing the Assessment: Evidence of Reliability and Validity in the edTPA," *American Educational Research Journal* 58, no. 1 (2021): 3–31.

40. *Li Feng and Tim R. Sass, "The Impact of Incentives to Recruit and Retain Teachers in 'Hard-to-Staff' Subjects," *Journal of Policy Analysis and Management* 37, no. 1 (2018): 112–35; Andrew Kwok and Tuan D. Nguyen, "What Matters and for Whom? Exploring Characteristics of Teacher Residency Programs and Their Relationship to Participant Perceptions." EdWorkingPaper no. 24-901, Annenberg Institute at Brown University, January 2024; Susanna Loeb and Jeannie Myung, "Economic Approaches to Teacher Recruitment and Retention," in *The Economics of Education: A Comprehensive Overview*, 2nd ed., ed. Steve Bradley and Colin Green (Academic Press, 2020), 403–14; Anne Podolsky, Tara Kini, Joseph Bishop, and Linda Darling-Hammond, "Solving the Teacher Shortage: How to Attract and Retain Excellent Educators," Learning Policy Institute, 2016.

41. Christopher Redding and Thomas M. Smith, "Easy In, Easy Out: Are Alternatively Certified Teachers Turning Over at Increased Rates?," *American Educational Research Journal* 53, no. 4 (2016): 1086–125.

42. Christopher Redding, "Changing the Composition of Beginning Teachers: The Role of State Alternative Certification Policies," *Educational Policy* 36, no. 7 (2022): 1791–820.

43. Bergstrand et al., "Emerging Issues."

44. Patricia D. Morrell and Stephanie Salomone, "Impact of a Robert Noyce Scholarship on STEM Teacher Recruitment," *Journal of College Science Teaching* 47, no. 2 (2017): 16–21.

45. Julian Vasquez Heilig and Su Jin Jez, "Teach For America: A Review of the Evidence," unpublished paper, Education and the Public Interest Center, University of Colorado Boulder, and Education Policy Research Unit, Arizona State University, 2010; David Labaree, "Teach For America and Teacher Ed: Heads They Win, Tails We Lose," *Journal of Teacher Education* 61, nos. 1–2 (2010): 48–55.

46. *Donald Boyd, Pamela Grossman, Karen Hammerness, Hamilton Lankford, Susanna Loeb, Matthew Ronfeldt, and James Wyckoff, "Recruiting Effective Math Teachers: Evidence from New York City," *American Educational Research Journal* 49, no. 6 (2012): 1008–47; Linda Darling-Hammond, Deborah J. Holtzman, Su Jin Gatlin, and Julian Vasquez Heilig, "Does Teacher Preparation Matter? Evidence About Teacher Certification, Teach For America, and Teacher Effectiveness," *Education Policy Analysis Archives/Archivos Analíticos de Políticas Educativas* 13 (2005): 1–48; *Thomas J. Kane, Jonah E. Rockoff, and Douglas O. Staiger, "What Does Certification Tell Us About Teacher Effectiveness? Evidence from New York City," *Economics of Education Review* 27, no. 6 (2008): 615–31; Ildiko Laczko-Kerr and David C. Berliner, "The Effectiveness of 'Teach For America' and Other Under-Certified Teachers," *Education Policy*

Analysis Archives 10 (2002); *Hanley S. Chiang, Melissa A. Clark, and Sheena McConnell, "Supplying Disadvantaged Schools with Effective Teachers: Experimental Evidence on Secondary Math Teachers from Teach For America," *Journal of Policy Analysis and Management* 36, no. 1 (2017): 97–125; *Steven Glazerman, Daniel Mayer, and Paul Decker, "Alternative Routes to Teaching: The Impacts of Teach For America on Student Achievement and Other Outcomes," *Journal of Policy Analysis and Management* 25, no. 1 (2006): 75–96.

47. Andrew Morgan Brantlinger and Ashley Anne Grant, "The First-School Retention of Black and Latinx Community-Insiders and Elite College Graduates: Implications for the Recruitment, Selection, and Training of Urban Mathematics Teachers," *Education Policy Analysis Archives* 30, no. 111 (2022).

48. *Julia H. Kaufman, Benjamin K. Master, Alice Huguet, Paul Youngmin Yoo, Susannah Faxon-Mills, David Schulker, and Geoffrey E. Grimm, "Growing Teachers from Within: Implementation, Impact, and Cost of an Alternative Teacher Preparation Program in Three Urban School Districts," RAND Corporation, 2020.

49. LaRon A. Scott, "Experience of Black Male Special Education Teachers: Are Alternative Licensure Programs the Desired Route for Recruitment and Preparation?," *Education and Urban Society* 51, no. 3 (2019): 332–50.

50. Lauren Worley, and Nicolas Zerbino, "Teacher Residencies Offer Compelling Solution to Staffing Shortages, Although at a Large Investment," Brookings Institution, 2023. https://www.brookings.edu/articles/teacher-residencies-offer-compelling-solution-to-staffing-shortages-although-at-a-large-cost/.

51. Cortney Rowland, Tamara Azar, Tabitha Grossman, and Gabriela Mottesi, "State Policies to Support Teacher Residencies: An Overview," National Center for Teacher Residencies, 2024.

52. Yiting Chu and Weijia Wang, "The Urban Teacher Residency Model to Prepare Teachers: A Review of the Literature," *Urban Education* 59, no. 8 (2024): 2489–518.

53. Darling-Hammond et al., "Does Teacher Preparation Matter?"

54. Jennifer Pankowski and Joan T. Walker, "Using Simulation to Support Novice Teachers' Classroom Management Skills: Comparing Traditional and Alternative Certification Groups," *Journal of the National Association for Alternative Certification* 11, no. 1 (2016): 3–20.

55. *John P. Papay, Martin R. West, Jon B. Fullerton, and Thomas J. Kane, "Does an Urban Teacher Residency Increase Student Achievement? Early Evidence from Boston," *Educational Evaluation and Policy Analysis* 34, no. 4 (2012): 413–34.

56. Barnett Berry, Diana Montgomery, and Jon Snyder, "Urban Teacher Residency Models and Institutes of Higher Education: Implications for Teacher Preparation," Center for Teaching Quality, 2008.

57. Nancy Burstein, Sue Sears, and Anne Wilcoxen, "Examining the Effectiveness of a Special Education Residency Program in Increasing the

Recruitment and Retention of Teachers in Urban Schools," *Teacher Education Quarterly* 50, no. 1 (2023): 28–52.

58. Robert Shand, Naureen Madhani, and Kimberly Austin, "Teacher Residencies as an Approach to Teacher Diversity: Promising Strategies for Recruiting and Retaining Black Educators," *Issues in Teacher Education* 32, no. 1 (2023): 74–101.

59. Crystal Chen Lee, Sibel Akin, and A. Lin Goodwin, "Teacher Candidates' Intentions to Teach: Implications for Recruiting and Retaining Teachers in Urban Schools," *Journal of Education for Teaching* 45, no. 5 (2019): 525–39.

60. Jesse Solomon, "The Boston Teacher Residency: District-Based Teacher Education," *Journal of Teacher Education* 60, no. 5 (2009): 478–88.

61. John E. Henning, "A Sustainable Teacher Residency: Designing Paid Internships for Teacher Education," *School-University Partnerships* 11, no. 3 (2018): 1–16.

62. Kwok and Nguyen. "What Matters and for Whom?"

63. Andrew Kwok, Megan Svajda-Hardy, Valerie Hill-Jackson, and Shaun Hutchins, "Exploring a Teacher Residency as a Recruitment and Retention Strategy for High-Need Districts," *Journal of Education* 204, no. 3 (2024): 608–20.

64. Cathy Yun and Karen DeMoss, "Sustainable Strategies for Funding Teacher Residencies: Lessons from California," Learning Policy Institute, 2020.

65. Amaya Garcia, "Grow Your Own Teachers: A 50-State Scan of Policies and Programs," New America, 2020.

66. Conra D. Gist, "Shifting Dominant Narratives of Teacher Development: New Directions for Expanding Access to the Educator Workforce Through Grow Your Own Programs," *Educational Researcher* 51, no. 1 (2022): 51–57.

67. Bergstrand et al., "Emerging Issues."

68. Meredith Galloway, "Human Resources Special Education Teacher Recruitment: Utilizing Grow Your Own," *Journal of Transformative Leadership & Policy Studies* 8, no. 2 (2019): 65–87.

69. Iesha Jackson and Doris L. Watson, "Retention Starts with Preparation: Preparing Black and Latinx Teachers Through Alternative Routes to Licensure," College of Education, University of Nevada–Las Vegas, 2018.

70. Danielle Sanderson Edwards and Matthew A. Kraft, "Grow Your Own: An Umbrella Term for Very Different Localized Teacher Pipeline Programs," EdWorkingPaper no. 24-895, Annenberg Institute at Brown University, 2024.

71. Anderson and Anderson, "Study of Teacher Recruitment Programs"; Henry et al., "Scholarships to Recruit."

72. Podolsky and Kini, "How Effective Are Loan Forgiveness and Service Scholarships."

73. Donald Boyd, Hamilton Lankford, Susanna Loeb, and James Wyckoff, "The Draw of Home: How Teachers' Preferences for Proximity Disadvantage Urban Schools," *Journal of Policy Analysis and Management* 24, no. 1 (2005):

113–32; Michelle Reininger, "Hometown Disadvantage? It Depends on Where You're From: Teachers' Location Preferences and the Implications for Staffing Schools," *Educational Evaluation and Policy Analysis* 34, no. 2 (2012): 127–45.

74. Shand et al., "Teacher Residencies."

75. Roy Jones, Winston Holton, and Mark Joseph, "Call Me Mister: Black Male Grow Your Own Program," *Teacher Education Quarterly* 46, no. 1 (2019): 55–68; Aram Ayalon, "A Model for Recruitment and Retention of Minority Students to Teaching: Lessons from a School-University Partnership," *Teacher Education Quarterly* 31, no. 3 (2004): 7–23; Katrina Liu, Shaoan Zhang, Chelsea Desalvo, and Malayka Cornejo, "Recruit, Prepare, and Retain Teachers of Color in Nevada," College of Education, University of Nevada–Las Vegas, 2017.

76. Whitfield et al., "Recruitment and Retention of STEM Teachers."

77. Feng and Sass, "Impact of Incentives."

78. Bergstrand et al., "Emerging Issues."

79. Brantlinger and Grant, "First-School Retention."

80. Saba Bireda and Robin Chait, "Increasing Teacher Diversity: Strategies to Improve the Teacher Workforce," Center for American Progress, 2011; Weade James, LaRon Scott, and Peter Temple, "Strategies Used by Historically Black Colleges and Universities to Recruit Minority Teacher Education Candidates," *Teacher Educators' Journal* 13 (2020): 76–104.

81. Ana María Villegas and Danné E. Davis, "Approaches to Diversifying the Teaching Force: Attending to Issues of Recruitment, Preparation, and Retention," *Teacher Education Quarterly* 34, no. 4 (2007): 137–47.

82. Andrea Beesley, Kim Atwill, Pamela Blair, and Zoe Barley, "Strategies for Recruitment and Retention of Secondary Teachers in Central Region Rural Schools," Mid-continent Research for Education and Learning, 2008.

83. Jackson and Watson, "Retention Starts with Preparation."

84. Morrell and Salomone, "Impact of a Robert Noyce Scholarship."

85. Carla McClure and Cynthia Reeves, "Rural Teacher Recruitment and Retention Review of the Research and Practice Literature," Appalachia Educational Laboratory, 2004; Henry Tran, Suzy Hardie, Simone Gause, Peter Moyi, and Rose Ylimaki, "Leveraging the Perspectives of Rural Educators to Develop Realistic Job Previews for Rural Teacher Recruitment and Retention," *Rural Educator* 41, no. 2 (2020): 31–46.

86. Mary T. Brownell, Anne M. Bishop, and Paul T. Sindelar, "NCLB and the Demand for Highly Qualified Teachers: Challenges and Solutions for Rural Schools," *Rural Special Education Quarterly* 24, no. 1 (2005): 9–15; Megan Burton, Kara Brown, and Amy Johnson, "Storylines About Rural Teachers in the United States: A Narrative Analysis of the Literature," *Journal of Research in Rural Education* 28, no. 12 (2013), 1–18; Jacob Fowles, J. S. Butler, Joshua M. Cowen, Megan E. Streams, and Eugenia F. Toma, "Public Employee Quality in a Geographic Context: A Study of Rural Teachers," *American Review of Public Administration* 44, no. 5 (2014): 503–21; Patricia Cahape Hammer, Georgia

Hughes, Carla McClure, Cynthia Reeves, and Dawn Salgado, "Rural Teacher Recruitment and Retention Practices: A Review of the Research Literature, National Survey of Rural Superintendents, and Case Studies of Programs in Virginia," Appalachia Educational Laboratory, 2005; James Shuls and Robert Maranto, "Show Them the Mission: A Comparison of Teacher Recruitment Incentives in High Need Communities." *Social Science Quarterly* 95, no. 1 (2014): 239–52.

87. Podolsky and Kini, "How Effective Are Loan Forgiveness and Service Scholarships."

88. Martinie et al., "Recruitment and Retention of Mathematics Teachers"; Katie N. Smith, "The North Carolina Teaching Fellows Program: A Case Study of the Use of Forgivable Loans in Recruiting Future STEM Teachers," *Journal of Student Financial Aid* 50, no. 3 (2021).

89. *Roddy Theobald, Zeyu Xu, Allison Gilmour, Lisa Lachlan-Hache, Elizabeth Bettini, and Nathan Jones, "The Impact of a $10,000 Bonus on Special Education Teacher Shortages in Hawai'i," *Educational Evaluation and Policy Analysis* (2023): 01623737241310905.

90. Whitfield et al., "Recruitment and Retention of STEM Teachers."

91. Glazerman et al., "Alternative Routes to Teaching."

92. Labaree, "Teach for America and Teacher Ed."

93. Barnett Berry and Patrick M. Shields, "Solving the Teacher Shortage: Revisiting the Lessons We've Learned." *Phi Delta Kappan* 98, no. 8 (2017): 8–18; Roneeta Guha, Maria E. Hyler, and Linda Darling-Hammond, "The Teacher Residency: A Practical Path to Recruitment and Retention," *American Educator* 41, no. 1 (2017): 31–34.

94. Hannah Putman and Kate Walsh, "State of the States 2021: Teacher Preparation Policy," National Council on Teacher Quality, 2021; Shuls and Maranto, "Show Them the Mission."

95. Steven S. Christensen, Randall S. Davies, Scott P. Harris, Joseph Hanks, and Bryan Bowles, "Teacher Recruitment: Factors That Predict High School Students' Willingness to Become Teachers," *Education Sciences* 9, no. 4 (2019): 282.

96. Dayna DeFeo, Diane Hirshberg, and Alexandra Hill, "It's More than Just Dollars: Problematizing Salary as the Sole Mechanism for Recruiting and Retaining Teachers in Rural Alaska," Proceedings from the Alaska Native Studies Conference, 2016; Charles DaVon Ross, "Recruitment and Retention: An Exploratory Study of the Influence of Salary on Virginia Teachers" (EdD diss., Virginia State University, 2023).

Chapter 6. Policies to Increase Teacher Retention

1. *Tuan D. Nguyen, "Linking School Organizational Characteristics and Teacher Retention: Evidence from Repeated Cross-Sectional National Data," *Teaching and Teacher Education* 97 (2021): 103220.

2. Gary Barnes, Edward Crowe, and Benjamin Schaefer, "The Cost of Teacher Turnover in Five School Districts: A Pilot Study," National Commission on Teaching and America's Future, 2007; Dayna DeFeo, Diane Hirshberg, and Alexandra Hill, "It's More than Just Dollars: Problematizing Salary as the Sole Mechanism for Recruiting and Retaining Teachers in Rural Alaska," Proceedings from the Alaska Native Studies Conference, 2016); *Matthew Ronfeldt, Susanna Loeb, and James Wyckoff, "How Teacher Turnover Harms Student Achievement," *American Educational Research Journal* 50, no. 1 (2013): 4–36; *Lucy C. Sorensen and Helen F. Ladd, "The Hidden Costs of Teacher Turnover," *AERA Open* 6, no. 1 (2020): 2332858420905812.

3. *Charles T. Clotfelter, Helen F. Ladd, and Jacob L. Vigdor, "Teacher Credentials and Student Achievement in High School: A Cross-Subject Analysis with Student Fixed Effects," *Journal of Human Resources* 45, no. 3 (2010): 655–81.

4. *Li Feng and Tim R. Sass, "The Impact of Incentives to Recruit and Retain Teachers in 'Hard-to-Staff' Subjects," *Journal of Policy Analysis and Management* 37, no. 1 (2018): 112–35.

5. *Carycruz Bueno and Tim R. Sass, "The Effects of Differential Pay on Teacher Recruitment and Retention," working paper no. 219-0519, National Center for Analysis of Longitudinal Data in Education Research, 2019.

6. *Matthew G. Springer, Walker A. Swain, and Luis A. Rodriguez, "Effective Teacher Retention Bonuses: Evidence from Tennessee," *Educational Evaluation and Policy Analysis* 38, no. 2 (2016): 199–221.

7. *Thomas S. Dee and James Wyckoff, "Incentives, Selection, and Teacher Performance: Evidence from IMPACT," *Journal of Policy Analysis and Management* 34, no. 2 (2015): 267–97.

8. Tuan D. Nguyen, Lam D. Pham, Michael Crouch, and Matthew G. Springer, "The Correlates of Teacher Turnover: An Updated and Expanded Meta-Analysis of the Literature," *Educational Research Review* 31 (2020): 100355; *Lam D. Pham, Tuan D. Nguyen, and Matthew G. Springer, "Teacher Merit Pay: A Meta-Analysis," *American Educational Research Journal* 58, no. 3 (2021): 527–66.

9. Holli Gottschall Bayonas and Fain Barke, "Guilford County Schools Mission Possible Program," SERVECenter, University of North Carolina, Greensboro, 2010; Won Seok Choi, "The Effect of Alternative Compensation Programs on Teacher Retention and Student Achievement: The Case of Q Comp in Minnesota" (PhD diss., University of Minnesota, 2015); *James Cowan and Dan Goldhaber, "National Board Certification and Teacher Effectiveness: Evidence from Washington," Center for Education Data & Research, 2015; Lisa M. DiGaudio, "Implications of the School Improvement Engine for Teacher Retention and School Organizational Health" (PhD diss., Walden University, 2017); *Eleanor S. Fulbeck, "Teacher Mobility and Financial Incentives: A Descriptive Analysis of Denver's ProComp," *Educational Evaluation and Policy Analysis* 36, no. 1 (2014): 67–82; *Steven Glazerman, Ali Protik, Bing-ru Teh, Julie

Bruch, and Jeffrey Max, "Transfer Incentives for High-Performing Teachers: Final Results from a Multisite Randomized Experiment. Executive Summary," National Center for Education Evaluation and Regional Assistance, US Department of Education, 2013; *Steven Glazerman and Allison Seifullah, "An Evaluation of the Chicago Teacher Advancement Program (Chicago TAP) After Four Years. Final Report," Mathematica Policy Research Inc., 2012; *Dara Shifrer, Ruth López Turley, and Holly Heard, "Do Teacher Financial Awards Improve Teacher Retention and Student Achievement in an Urban Disadvantaged School District?," *American Educational Research Journal* 54, no. 6 (2017): 1117–53; *Matthew G. Springer, Michael J. Podgursky, Jessica L. Lewis, Mark W. Ehlert, Timothy J. Gronberg, Laura S. Hamilton, Dennis W. Jansen, et al., "Texas Educator Excellence Grant (TEEG) Program: Year Two Evaluation Report. Policy Evaluation Report," National Center on Performance Incentives, 2008; *Matthew G. Springer, Jessica L. Lewis, Mark W. Ehlert, Michael J. Podgursky, Gary D. Crader, Lori L. Taylor, Timothy J. Gronberg, Dennis W. Jansen, Omar S. Lopez, and David A. Stuit, "District Awards for Teacher Excellence (DATE) Program: Final Evaluation Report. Policy Evaluation Report," National Center on Performance Incentives, 2010.

10. Kevin Booker and Steven Glazerman, "Effects of the Missouri Career Ladder Program on Teacher Mobility," Mathematica Policy Research Inc., 2009.

11. *James Cowan and Dan Goldhaber, "Do Bonuses Affect Teacher Staffing and Student Achievement in High Poverty Schools? Evidence from an Incentive for National Board Certified Teachers in Washington State," *Economics of Education Review* 65 (2018): 138–52.

12. Allison F. Gilmour, Roddy Theobald, and D. Jones Nathan, "Economic Interventions as Policy Levers for Attracting and Retaining Special Education Teachers," in *Handbook of Research on Special Education Teacher Preparation*, ed. Erica D. McCray, Elizabeth Bettini, Mary T. Brownell, James McLeskey, Paul T. Sindelar (Routledge, 2023), 190–212.

13. Li Feng, "Opportunity Wages, Classroom Characteristics, and Teacher Mobility," *Southern Economic Journal* 75, no. 4 (2009): 1165–90.

14. *Charles T. Clotfelter, Helen F. Ladd, and Jacob L. Vigdor, "Teacher Mobility, School Segregation, and Pay-Based Policies to Level the Playing Field," *Education Finance and Policy* 6, no. 3 (2011): 399–438.

15. *Matthew D. Hendricks, "Does It Pay to Pay Teachers More? Evidence from Texas," *Journal of Public Economics* 109 (2014): 50–63.

16. Nguyen et al., "Correlates of Teacher Turnover."

17. Debbi C. Harris, "The Promises and Pitfalls of Alternative Teacher Compensation Approaches," Education Policy Research Unit, Division of Educational Leadership and Policy Studies, College of Education, Arizona State University, 2007; Li Feng, "Compensating Differentials in Teacher Labor Markets," in *The Economics of Education: A Comprehensive Overview*, ed. Steve Bradley and Colin Green (Academic Press, 2020), 415–30; Sheila Nataraj Kirby,

Mark Berends, and Scott Naftel, "Supply and Demand of Minority Teachers in Texas: Problems and Prospects," *Educational Evaluation and Policy Analysis* 21, no. 1 (1999): 47–66.

18. Erling E. Boe, Sharon A. Bobbitt, Lynne H. Cook, Gema Barkanic, and Greg Maislin, "Teacher Turnover in Eight Cognate Areas: National Trends and Predictors," Center for Research and Evaluation in Social Policy, Graduate School of Education, University of Pennsylvania, 1998; Cynthia Martinez Garcia, John R. Slate, and Carmen Tejeda Delgado, "Salary and Ranking and Teacher Turnover: A Statewide Study," *International Journal of Education Policy and Leadership* 4, no. 7 (2009): 1–8; Sean Kelly, "An Event History Analysis of Teacher Attrition: Salary, Teacher Tracking, and Socially Disadvantaged Schools," *Journal of Experimental Education* 72, no. 3 (2004): 195–220; Hyun-Seok Shin, "Estimating Future Teacher Supply: Any Policy Implications for Educational Reform?," *International Journal of Educational Reform* 4, no. 4 (1995): 422–33.

19. Bueno and Sass, "Effects of Differential Pay"; Beng Huat See, Rebecca Morris, Stephen Gorard, and Nada El Soufi, "What Works in Attracting and Retaining Teachers in Challenging Schools and Areas?," *Oxford Review of Education* 46, no. 6 (2020): 678–97.

20. *Gema Zamarro, Andrew Camp, Josh McGee, Taylor Wilson, and Miranda Vernon, "Teacher Salary Raises and Turnover: Evidence from the First Year of the Arkansas LEARNS Act," EdWorkingPaper no. 24-972, Annenberg Institute at Brown University, 2024.

21. Maria Donovan Fitzpatrick, "How Much Are Public School Teachers Willing to Pay for Their Retirement Benefits?," *American Economic Journal: Economic Policy* 7, no. 4 (2015): 165–88; *Maria D. Fitzpatrick, "Pension-Spiking, Free-Riding, and the Effects of Pension Reform on Teachers' Earnings," *Journal of Public Economics* 148 (2017): 57–74; Andrew C. Johnston, "Teacher Preferences, Working Conditions, and Compensation Structure," discussion paper no. 13121, Institute of Labor Economics, 2020.

22. *Barbara Biasi, "Higher Salaries or Higher Pensions? Inferring Preferences from Teachers' Retirement Behavior," unpublished paper, Social Science Research Network, 2019.

23. *Barbara Biasi, "Salaries, Pensions, and the Retention of Public-Sector Employees: Evidence from Wisconsin Teachers," working paper, 2024.

24. *Matthew M. Chingos and Martin R. West, "Which Teachers Choose a Defined Contribution Pension Plan? Evidence from the Florida Retirement System," *Education Finance and Policy* 10, no. 2 (2015): 193–222.

25. *Cory Koedel and P. Brett Xiang, "Pension Enhancements and the Retention of Public Employees," *ILR Review* 70, no. 2 (2017): 519–51.

26. Dan Goldhaber and Cyrus Grout, "Which Plan to Choose? The Determinants of Pension System Choice for Public School Teachers," *Journal of Pension Economics & Finance* 15, no. 1 (2016): 30–54.

27. *Dan Goldhaber, Cyrus Grout, and Kristian L. Holden, "Pension Structure and Employee Turnover: Evidence from a Large Public Pension System," *ILR Review* 70, no. 4 (2017): 976–1007.

28. Goldhaber and Grout, "Which Plan to Choose?"

29. Joshua Furgeson, Robert P. Strauss, and William B. Vogt, "The Effects of Defined Benefit Pension Incentives and Working Conditions on Teacher Retirement Decisions," *Education Finance and Policy* 1, no. 3 (2006): 316–48.

30. Shawn Ni, Michael Podgursky, and Xiqian Wang, "Teacher Pension Plan Incentives, Retirement Decisions, and Workforce Quality," *Journal of Human Resources* 57, no. 1 (2022): 272–303.

31. Shawn Ni, Michael Podgursky, and Xiqian Wang, "Teacher Pension Enhancements and Staffing in an Urban School District," *Journal of Pension Economics & Finance* 21, no. 4 (2022): 613–33.

32. Chad Aldeman and Andrew J. Rotherham, "Teacher Pension Plans: How They Work, and How They Affect Recruitment, Retention, and Equity," Bellwether Education Partners, 2019.

33. Guili Zhang and Nancy Zeller, "A Longitudinal Investigation of the Relationship Between Teacher Preparation and Teacher Retention," *Teacher Education Quarterly* 43, no. 2 (2016): 73–92; *Matthew Ronfeldt, "Links Among Teacher Preparation, Retention, and Teaching Effectiveness. Evaluating and Improving Teacher Preparation Programs," National Academy of Education, 2021.

34. Debbie F. C. Harris-McIntyre, "The Impact of Teacher Induction Programs on the Retention of Novice Teachers" (MA thesis, Keiser University, 2014); Michelle Helms-Lorenz, Wim van de Grift, and Ridwan Maulana, "Longitudinal Effects of Induction on Teaching Skills and Attrition Rates of Beginning Teachers," *School Effectiveness and School Improvement* 27, no. 2 (2016): 178–204; William Kyle Ingle, "Teacher Quality and Attrition in a US School District," *Journal of Educational Administration* 47, no. 5 (2009): 557–85; Christina Catherine Luke, "The Effect of State Induction Policies on Novice Teacher Attrition" (PhD diss., State University of New York at Albany, 2014).

35. Fitzpatrick, "Pension-Spiking."

36. Matthew Ronfeldt and Michelle Reininger, "More or Better Student Teaching?," *Teaching and Teacher Education* 28, no. 8 (2012): 1091–106.

37. Robin R. Henke, Xianglei Chen, and Sonya Geis, "Progress Through the Teacher Pipeline: 1992–93 College Graduates and Elementary Secondary School Teaching as of 1997," National Center for Education Statistics, 2000; Richard M. Ingersoll, Lisa Merrill, and Henry May, "What Are the Effects of Teacher Education and Preparation on Beginning Teacher Attrition?," CPRE research report 82, Consortium for Policy Research in Education, 2014.

38. Fitzpatrick, "Pension-Spiking."

39. Matthew Ronfeldt, "Where Should Student Teachers Learn to Teach? Effects of Field Placement School Characteristics on Teacher Retention and Effectiveness," *Educational Evaluation and Policy Analysis* 34, no. 1 (2012): 3–26.

40. Sarah Warshauer Freedman and Deborah Appleman, "'What Else Would I Be Doing?': Teacher Identity and Teacher Retention in Urban Schools," *Teacher Education Quarterly* 35, no. 3 (2008): 109–26.

41. Sarah Warshauer Freedman and Deborah Appleman, "'In It for the Long Haul'—How Teacher Education Can Contribute to Teacher Retention in High-Poverty, Urban Schools," *Journal of Teacher Education* 60, no. 3 (2009): 323–37.

42. Furgeson, Strauss, and Vogt, "Effects of Defined Benefit Pension Incentives."

43. Brad Olsen and Lauren Anderson, "Courses of Action: A Qualitative Investigation into Urban Teacher Retention and Career Development," *Urban Education* 42, no. 1 (2007): 5–29.

44. Richard M. Ingersoll and Michael Strong, "The Impact of Induction and Mentoring Programs for Beginning Teachers: A Critical Review of the Research," *Review of Educational Research* 81, no. 2 (2011): 201–33; Tuan D. Nguyen and Matthew G. Springer, "A Conceptual Framework of Teacher Turnover: A Systematic Review of the Empirical International Literature and Insights from the Employee Turnover Literature," *Educational Review* 75, no. 5 (2023): 993–1028.

45. Matthew A. Cannady, "Modeling Teacher Attrition: Teacher Characteristics and Working Conditions" (PhD diss., Boston College, 2011); Benjamin K. Master and Cate Yoon, "Examining the Early Impacts of the Leading Educators Fellowship on Student Achievement and Teacher Retention," RAND, 2015; Thomas M. Smith, "How Do State-Level Induction and Standards-Based Reform Policies Affect Induction Experiences and Turnover Among New Teachers?," *American Journal of Education* 113, no. 2 (2007): 273–309; Peter D. Wiens, Annie Chou, David Vallett, and Jori S. Beck, "New Teacher Mentoring and Teacher Retention: Examining the Peer Assistance and Review Program," *Educational Research: Theory and Practice* 30, no. 2 (2019): 103–10.

46. *Matthew Ronfeldt and Kiel McQueen, "Does New Teacher Induction Really Improve Retention?," *Journal of Teacher Education* 68, no. 4 (2017): 394–410.

47. Sam Brill and Abby McCartney, "Stopping the Revolving Door: Increasing Teacher Retention," *Politics & Policy* 36, no. 5 (2008): 750–74.

48. *Jonah E. Rockoff, "Does Mentoring Reduce Turnover and Improve Skills of New Employees? Evidence from Teachers in New York City," working paper 13868, National Bureau of Economic Research, 2008.

49. *Steven Glazerman, Eric Isenberg, Sarah Dolfin, Martha Bleeker, Amy Johnson, Mary Grider, and Matthew Jacobus, "Impacts of Comprehensive Teacher Induction: Final Results from a Randomized Controlled Study," NCEE 2010-4027, National Center for Education Evaluation and Regional Assistance, 2010.

50. *Rebecca A. Schmidt, Aliya R. Pilchen, Katrina Laguarda, Haiwen Wang, and Deepa Patel, "Scaling Up Teacher Induction: Implementation and Impact on

Teachers and Students. Evaluation of the New Teacher Center's i3 Scale-Up Grant, Revised Final Report," SRI International, 2025.

51. Desiree Carver-Thomas and Linda Darling-Hammond, "Teacher Turnover: Why It Matters and What We Can Do About It," Learning Policy Institute, 2017.

52. Sheryn Waterman and Ye He, "Effects of Mentoring Programs on New Teacher Retention: A Literature Review," *Mentoring & Tutoring: Partnership in Learning* 19, no. 2 (2011): 139–56.

53. *Matthew A. Kraft, David Blazar, and Dylan Hogan, "The Effect of Teacher Coaching on Instruction and Achievement: A Meta-Analysis of the Causal Evidence," *Review of Educational Research* 88, no. 4 (2018): 547–88.

54. Susan Moore Johnson and Sarah E. Birkeland, "Pursuing a 'Sense of Success': New Teachers Explain Their Career Decisions," *American Educational Research Journal* 40, no. 3 (2003): 581–617. Hiershenee B. Luesse, Joseph E. Luesse, Jordan Lawson, Mathew J. Camp, and Karina G. Diaz, "The Academy for Teachers Professional Development Program. A Model to Support Teacher Retention," *Cogent Education* 9, no. 1 (2022): 2140540; Mike Smet, "Professional Development and Teacher Job Satisfaction: Evidence from a Multilevel Model," *Mathematics* 10, no. 1 (2021): 51.

55. Mike Coldwell, "Exploring the Influence of Professional Development on Teacher Careers: A Path Model Approach," *Teaching and Teacher Education* 61 (2017): 189–98; Stacy Johnson Erickson, "An Examination of the Relationship Between Professional Development and Teacher Turnover" (EdD diss., University of Oregon, 2007).

56. Kasey P. S. Goodpaster, Omolola A. Adedokun, and Gabriela C. Weaver, "Teachers' Perceptions of Rural STEM Teaching: Implications for Rural Teacher Retention," *Rural Educator* 33, no. 3 (2012): 9–22.

57. Susan Moore Johnson and Sarah E. Birkeland, "Pursuing a "Sense of Success": New Teachers Explain Their Career Decisions," *American Educational Research Journal* 40, no. 3 (2003): 581–617.

58. Susan Moore Johnson, *Where Teachers Thrive: Organizing Schools for Success* (Harvard Education Press, 2020).

59. Tray Geiger and Margarita Pivovarova, "The Effects of Working Conditions on Teacher Retention," *Teachers and Teaching* 24, no. 6 (2018): 604–25.

60. *Matthew A. Kraft, William H. Marinell, and Darrick Shen-Wei Yee, "School Organizational Contexts, Teacher Turnover, and Student Achievement: Evidence from Panel Data," *American Educational Research Journal* 53, no. 5 (2016): 1411–49.

61. Susan R. Wynn and Kathleen M. Brown, "Principal Leadership and Professional Learning Communities: What Beginning Teachers Value," *International Journal of Educational Reform* 17, no. 1 (2008): 37–63; Warren S. Eller, Carl B. Doerfler, and Kenneth J. Meier, "Teacher Turnover in Texas: Problems and Prospects," Texas Educational Excellence Project, 2000; Angela Urick,

"Examining US Principal Perception of Multiple Leadership Styles Used to Practice Shared Instructional Leadership," *Journal of Educational Administration* 54, no. 2 (2016): 152–72.

62. Cara M. Djonko-Moore, "An Exploration of Teacher Attrition and Mobility in High Poverty Racially Segregated Schools," *Race Ethnicity and Education* 19, no. 5 (2016): 1063–87; Richard M. Ingersoll, "Teacher Turnover and Teacher Shortages: An Organizational Analysis," *American Educational Research Journal* 38, no. 3 (2001): 499–534.

63. *F. Chris Curran, Samantha L. Viano, and Benjamin W. Fisher, "Teacher Victimization, Turnover, and Contextual Factors Promoting Resilience," *Journal of School Violence* 18, no. 1 (2019): 21–38; Richard M. Ingersoll and Henry May, "The Magnitude, Destinations, and Determinants of Mathematics and Science Teacher Turnover," *Educational Evaluation and Policy Analysis* 34, no. 4 (2012): 435–64; Kraft et al., "School Organizational Contexts."

64. Dorothy Espelage, Eric M. Anderman, Veda Evanell Brown, Abraham Jones, Kathleen Lynne Lane, Susan D. McMahon, Linda A. Reddy, and Cecil R. Reynolds, "Understanding and Preventing Violence Directed Against Teachers: Recommendations for a National Research, Practice, and Policy Agenda," *American Psychologist* 68, no. 2 (2013): 75–87; Susan D. McMahon, Frank C. Worrell, Linda A. Reddy, Andrew Martinez, Dorothy L. Espelage, Ron A. Astor, Eric M. Anderman, et al. "Violence and Aggression Against Educators and School Personnel, Retention, Stress, and Training Needs: National Survey Results," *American Psychologist* 79, no. 7 (2024): 903–19; Susan D. McMahon, Andrew Martinez, Dorothy Espelage, Chad Rose, Linda A. Reddy, Kathleen Lane, Eric M. Anderman, Cecil R. Reynolds, Abraham Jones, and Veda Brown, "Violence Directed Against Teachers: Results from a National Survey," *Psychology in the Schools* 51, no. 7 (2014): 753–66.

65. *Jason A. Grissom and Brendan Bartanen, "Strategic Retention: Principal Effectiveness and Teacher Turnover in Multiple-Measure Teacher Evaluation Systems," *American Educational Research Journal* 56, no. 2 (2019): 514–55.

66. Kathleen M. Brown and Susan R. Wynn, "Finding, Supporting, and Keeping: The Role of the Principal in Teacher Retention Issues," *Leadership and Policy in Schools* 8, no. 1 (2009): 37–63; Matthew T. Frahm and Marie Cianca, "Will They Stay or Will They Go? Leadership Behaviors That Increase Teacher Retention in Rural Schools," *Rural Educator* 42, no. 3 (2021); Amy L. Hughes, John J. Matt, and Frances L. O'Reilly, "Principal Support Is Imperative to the Retention of Teachers in Hard-to-Staff Schools," *Journal of Education and Training Studies* 3, no. 1 (2015): 129–34.

67. Christopher Redding and Thomas M. Smith, "Easy In, Easy Out: Are Alternatively Certified Teachers Turning Over at Increased Rates?," *American Educational Research Journal* 53, no. 4 (2016): 1086–125; Jimmy Shaw and Jodi Newton, "Teacher Retention and Satisfaction with a Servant Leader as Principal," *Education* 135, no. 1 (2014): 101–6.

68. *Donald Boyd, Pam Grossman, Marsha Ing, Hamilton Lankford, Susanna Loeb, and James Wyckoff, "The Influence of School Administrators on Teacher Retention Decisions," *American Educational Research Journal* 48, no. 2 (2011): 303–33.

69. Linet Arthur and Simon Bradley, "Teacher Retention in Challenging Schools: Please Don't Say Goodbye!," *Teachers and Teaching* 29, nos. 7–8 (2023): 753–71; Jeffrey Casely-Hayford, Christina Björklund, Gunnar Bergström, Per Lindqvist, and Lydia Kwak, "What Makes Teachers Stay? A Cross-Sectional Exploration of the Individual and Contextual Factors Associated with Teacher Retention in Sweden," *Teaching and Teacher Education* 113 (2022): 103664; Bruce Fuller, Anisah Waite, and David Torres Irribarra, "Explaining Teacher Turnover: School Cohesion and Intrinsic Motivation in Los Angeles," *American Journal of Education* 122, no. 4 (2016): 537–67.

70. Christopher Redding, Marisa Cannata, and Jason M. Miller, "System Learning in an Urban School District: A Case Study of Intra-District Learning," *Journal of Educational Change* 19 (2018): 77–101.

71. Nguyen, "Linking School Organizational Characteristics."

72. Todd Martin, "A Study of Middle School Principal Behaviors and Their Impact on Teacher Retention" (EdD diss., Gardner-Webb University, 2011); Cara M. Moore, "Why Do Teachers Quit? An Investigation of the Influence of School Environment and Teacher Characteristics on Discontent and Attrition" (PhD diss., Temple University, 2011).

73. Jack Buckley, Mark Schneider, and Yi Shang, "Fix It and They Might Stay: School Facility Quality and Teacher Retention in Washington, DC," *Teachers College Record* 107, no. 5 (2005): 1107–23.

74. *Ben Ost and Jeffrey C. Schiman, "Grade-Specific Experience, Grade Reassignments, and Teacher Turnover," *Economics of Education Review* 46 (2015): 112–26.

75. Nguyen et al., "Correlates of Teacher Turnover."

76. Susanna Loeb, Linda Darling-Hammond, and John Luczak, "How Teaching Conditions Predict Teacher Turnover in California Schools," in *Rendering School Resources More Effective*, ed. James W. Guthrie, Matthew G. Springer (Routledge, 2013), 44–70; Holly Anne Lopez Stevens, "The Effects of Los Angeles Universal Preschool on Quality Preschool Teacher Retention in Los Angeles County" (EdD, diss., University of California, Los Angeles, 2010).

77. Ummuhan Yesil Dagli, "America's Public School Kindergarten Teachers' Job Turnover and Associated Factors," *Educational Sciences: Theory and Practice* 12, no. 4 (2012): 3121–34; Richard M. Ingersoll, "Teacher Turnover and Teacher Shortages: An Organizational Analysis," *American Educational Research Journal* 38, no. 3 (2001): 499–534.

78. Ronfeldt, "Links Among."

79. Kathryn Ado, "From Pre-Service to Teacher Leader: The Early Development of Teacher Leaders," *Issues in Teacher Education* 25, no. 1 (2016): 3–21; John Buchanan, Anne Prescott, Sandra Schuck, Peter Aubusson, and Paul Burke,

"Teacher Retention and Attrition: Views of Early Career Teachers," *Australian Journal of Teacher Education (Online)* 38, no. 3 (2013): 124–41; Karen J. DeAngelis, Andrew F. Wall, and Jing Che, "The Impact of Preservice Preparation and Early Career Support on Novice Teachers' Career Intentions and Decisions," *Journal of Teacher Education* 64, no. 4 (2013): 338–55; Christopher Redding and Tuan D. Nguyen, "Recent Trends in the Characteristics of New Teachers, the Schools in Which They Teach, and Their Turnover Rates," *Teachers College Record* 122, no. 7 (2020): 1–36.

80. D. Jean Clandinin, Julie Long, Lee Schaefer, C. Aiden Downey, Pam Steeves, Eliza Pinnegar, Sue McKenzie Robblee, and Sheri Wnuk, "Early Career Teacher Attrition: Intentions of Teachers Beginning," *Teaching Education* 26, no. 1 (2015): 1–16; Jason M. Miller and Peter Youngs, "Person-Organization Fit and First-Year Teacher Retention in the United States" *Teaching and Teacher Education* 97 (2021): 103226; Lee Schaefer, Charles Aiden Downey, and D. Jean Clandinin, "Shifting from Stories to Live By to Stories to Leave By: Early Career Teacher Attrition," in *Journeys in Narrative Inquiry* (Routledge, 2019), 113–29.

81. Tanya Ovenden-Hope, Sonia Blandford, Tim Cain, and Bronwen Maxwell, "RETAIN Early Career Teacher Retention Programme: Evaluating the Role of Research Informed Continuing Professional Development for a High Quality, Sustainable 21st Century Teaching Profession," *Journal of Education for Teaching* 44, no. 5 (2018): 590–607; Benjamin Kutsyuruba, Lorraine Godden, and Leigha Tregunna, "Early-Career Teacher Attrition and Retention: A Pan-Canadian Document Analysis Study of Teacher Induction and Mentorship Programs," Faculty of Education, Queens University, 2013.

82. Richard Ingersoll, Henry May, and Gregory Collins, "Recruitment, Employment, Retention and the Minority Teacher Shortage," *Education Policy Analysis Archives* 27, no. 37 (2019).

83. Nguyen et al., "Correlates of Teacher Turnover."

84. Sharon Kukla-Acevedo, "Leavers, Movers, and Stayers: The Role of Workplace Conditions in Teacher Mobility Decisions," *Journal of Educational Research* 102, no. 6 (2009): 443–52; Xiaoxia A. Newton, Rosario Rivero, Bruce Fuller, and Luke Dauter, "Teacher Stability and Turnover in Los Angeles: The Influence of Teacher and School Characteristics," Policy Analysis for California Education Working Paper, 2011; Daniel A. Sass, Belinda Bustos Flores, Lorena Claeys, and Bertha Pérez, "Identifying Personal and Contextual Factors That Contribute to Attrition Rates for Texas Public School Teachers," *Education Policy Analysis Archives/Archivos Analíticos de Políticas Educativas* 20 (2012): 1–26.

85. Christopher Redding and Tuan D. Nguyen, "Greener Than Ever? A Look at the Newest Teachers in Our Public Schools," *Phi Delta Kappan* 103, no. 3 (2021): 8–12.

86. Judith Torres, Janet Santos, Nancy L. Peck, and Lydia Cortes, "Minority Teacher Recruitment, Development, and Retention," Northeast and Islands Regional Educational Laboratory, 2004.

87. Hughes et al., "Principal Support Is Imperative."

88. Barnett Berry, Diana Montgomery, Curtis Rachel, Mindy Hernandez, Judy Wurtzel, and Jon Snyder, "Creating and Sustaining Urban Teacher Residencies: A New Way to Recruit, Prepare, and Retain Effective Teachers in High-Needs Districts," Aspen Institute, 2008; Nancy Burstein, Sue Sears, and Anne Wilcoxen, "Examining the Effectiveness of a Special Education Residency Program in Increasing the Recruitment and Retention of Teachers in Urban Schools," *Teacher Education Quarterly* 50, no. 1 (2023): 28–52; Desiree Carver-Thomas, "Diversifying the Teaching Profession: How to Recruit and Retain Teachers of Color," Learning Policy Institute, 2018; Iesha Jackson and Doris L. Watson, "Retention Starts with Preparation: Preparing Black and Latinx Teachers Through Alternative Routes to Licensure," *Policy Issues in Nevada Education* 4, no. 1 (2021): 1; Andrew Kwok, Megan Svajda-Hardy, Valerie Hill-Jackson, and Shaun Hutchins, "Exploring a Teacher Residency as a Recruitment and Retention Strategy for High-Need Districts," *Journal of Education* 204, no. 3 (2024): 608–20.

89. Tuan Nguyen, "Teacher Attrition and Retention in Kansas: A Case Study of Geographically Rural States with Persistent Teacher Shortages," *Online Journal of Rural Research & Policy* 15, no. 1 (2020): 1.

90. Andrea Beesley, Kim Atwill, Pamela Blair, and Zoe Barley, "Strategies for Recruitment and Retention of Secondary Teachers in Central Region Rural Schools," Mid-continent Research for Education and Learning, 2008; Matthew K. Boggan, Teresa Jayroe, and Ben Alexander, "Best Practices Article: Hitting the Target with Transition to Teaching in Mississippi's Poorest School Districts: High Retention Rates Through Program Support, Resources, and Strategic Recruitment," *Journal of the National Association for Alternative Certification* 11, no. 1 (2016): 21–29; Patricia Cahape Hammer, Georgia Hughes, Carla McClure, Cynthia Reeves, and Dawn Salgado, "Rural Teacher Recruitment and Retention Practices: A Review of the Research Literature, National Survey of Rural Superintendents, and Case Studies of Programs in Virginia," Appalachia Educational Laboratory at Edvantia (NJ1), 2005; James Shuls and Robert Maranto, "Show Them the Mission: A Comparison of Teacher Recruitment Incentives in High Need Communities," *Social Science Quarterly* 95, no. 1 (2014): 239–52.

91. Jennifer L. Seelig and Katie M. McCabe, "Why Teachers Stay: Shaping a New Narrative on Rural Teacher Retention," *Journal of Research in Rural Education* 37, no. 8 (2021).

92. Matthew Ronfeldt and Kiel McQueen, "Does New Teacher Induction Really Improve Retention?," *Journal of Teacher Education* 68, no. 4 (2017): 394–410.

93. Marsha Smith Davis, "An Investigation of Factors Related to Teacher Retention in Small Rural School Districts in Montana" (EdD diss., Montana State University, 2002).

94. Kirk Banghart, "Teacher Recruitment and Retention in Rural Colorado," *State Education Standard* 21, no. 1 (2021): 29–32.

95. Kasey P. S. Goodpaster, Omolola A. Adedokun, and Gabriela C. Weaver, "Teachers' Perceptions of Rural STEM Teaching: Implications for Rural Teacher Retention," *Rural Educator* 33, no. 3 (2012): 9–22; *Bonnie Billingsley and Elizabeth Bettini, "Special Education Teacher Attrition and Retention: A Review of the Literature," *Review of Educational Research* 89, no. 5 (2019): 697–744; Laveria F. Hutchison, "Addressing the STEM Teacher Shortage in American Schools: Ways to Recruit and Retain Effective STEM Teachers," *Action in Teacher Education* 34, nos. 5–6 (2012): 541–50.

96. *Tuan D. Nguyen, "Linking School Organizational Characteristics and Teacher Retention: Evidence from Repeated Cross-Sectional National Data," *Teaching and Teacher Education* 97 (2021): 103220.

Chapter 7. An Aspirational Model for Ending Teacher Shortages

1. Prasiddha Shakya, "What Happens When We Pay Our Teachers More? Evidence from New Jersey Public Schools," EdWorkingPaper no. 24-1104, Annenberg Institute at Brown University, 2024.

2. Frederick Hess, "How to Pay Teachers $84,000 a Year—Without Raising Taxes," *Forbes*, July 25, 2023. https://www.forbes.com/sites/frederickhess/2023/07/25/how-to-pay-teachers-84000-a-year-without-raising-taxes/.

3. Eileen Lai Horng, "Teacher Tradeoffs: Disentangling Teachers' Preferences for Working Conditions and Student Demographics," *American Educational Research Journal* 46, no. 3 (2009): 690–717.

4. Linda Darling-Hammond, Dion Burns, Carol Campbell, A. Lin Goodwin, Karen Hammerness, Ee-Ling Low, Ann McIntyre, Mistilina Sato, and Ken Zeichner, *Empowered Educators: How High-Performing Systems Shape Teaching Quality Around the World* (John Wiley & Sons, 2017).

5. Sarah H. Sparks, "Fictional Teachers on TV Can Skew Public Perception," *Education Week*, October 4, 2024. https://www.edweek.org/teaching-learning/fictional-teachers-on-tv-can-skew-public-perception/2024/10.

6. James N. Dertouzos and Steven Garber, "Is Military Advertising Effective? An Estimation Methodology and Applications to Recruiting in the 1980s and 90s," RAND Corporation, 2003; Jason M. Ward, Jeffery B. Wenger, Irineo Cabreros, Daniel Schwam, Craig A. Bond, and Samual Absher, "A Revised Recruiting Resource Model for Achieving the Army Personnel Strategy," RAND Corporation, 2023.

7. *Eric S. Taylor and John H. Tyler, "The Effect of Evaluation on Teacher Performance," *American Economic Review* 102, no. 7 (2012): 3628–51.

8. Darling-Hammond et al., *Empowered Educators.*

9. Darling-Hammond et al., *Empowered Educators.*

10. Marilyn M. Cohn and Robert B. Kottkamp, *Teachers: The Missing Voice in Education* (State University of New York Press, 1993); Richard M. Ingersoll,

Who Controls Teachers' Work? Power and Accountability in America's Schools (Harvard University Press, 2009).

11. Ingersoll, *Who Controls Teachers' Work?*

12. Melissa Arnold Lyon, "Current Perspectives on Teacher Unionization, and What They're Missing," *Educational Policy* 37, no. 5 (2023): 1420–43.

13. Matthew Di Carlo, "What Do Teachers Think About How Teachers' Unions Affect Schools?," Albert Shanker Institute, May 30, 2018. https://www.shankerinstitute.org/blog/what-do-teachers-think-about-how-teachers-unions-affect-schools.

14. Ingersoll, *Who Controls Teachers' Work?*

15. Morgaen L. Donaldson, Susan Moore Johnson, Cheryl L. Kirkpatrick, Will Marinell, Jennifer L. Steele, and Stacy Agee Szczesiul, "Angling for Access, Bartering for Change: How Second-Stage Teachers Experience Differentiated Roles in Schools," *Teachers College Record* 110, no. 5 (2008): 1088–114; Jonathan Eckert, Jasmine Ulmer, Edit Khachatryan, and Patrick Ledesma, "Career Pathways of Teacher Leaders in the United States: Adding and Path-Finding New Professional Roles," *Professional Development in Education* 42, no. 5 (2016): 687–709; Mark A. Smylie and Jonathan Eckert, "Beyond Superheroes and Advocacy: The Pathway of Teacher Leadership Development," *Educational Management Administration & Leadership* 46, no. 4 (2018): 556–77.

16. Darling-Hammond et al., *Empowered Educators.*

17. Darling-Hammond et al., *Empowered Educators.*

18. Andy Hargreaves and Dennis Shirley, "The Far Side of Educational Reform," Canadian Teachers' Federation (NJ3), 2011.

19. Adam Lefstein and Hamutal Perath, "Empowering Teacher Voices in an Education Policy Discussion: Paradoxes of Representation," *Teaching and Teacher Education* 38 (2014): 33–43.

20. Lefstein and Perath, "Empowering Teacher Voices."

21. Yihua Hong and Kavita Kapadia Matsko, "Looking Inside and Outside of Mentoring: Effects on New Teachers' Organizational Commitment," *American Educational Research Journal* 56, no. 6 (2019): 2368–407.

22. Henry Tran, Kathleen Cunningham, Valerie Yelverton, Dave Osworth, and Suzy Hardie, "How Can School Leaders Retain Teachers? The Relative Importance of Different Administrative Supports for Teacher Retention in Different Types of Schools," *NASSP Bulletin* 107, no. 3 (2023): 185–217.

23. Tran et al., "How Can School Leaders Retain Teachers?"; Susan R. Wynn and Kathleen M. Brown, "Principal Leadership and Professional Learning Communities: What Beginning Teachers Value," *International Journal of Educational Reform* 17, no. 1 (2008): 37–63.

24. Henry Tran, "Revolutionizing School HR Strategies and Practices to Reflect Talent Centered Education Leadership," *Leadership and Policy in Schools*, 21, no. 2 (2022), 238–52.

25. *Robin Jacob, Roger Goddard, Minjung Kim, Robert Miller, and Yvonne Goddard, "Exploring the Causal Impact of the McREL Balanced Leadership Program on Leadership, Principal Efficacy, Instructional Climate, Educator Turnover, and Student Achievement," *Educational Evaluation and Policy Analysis* 37, no. 3 (2015): 314–32.

26. *Brendan Bartanen, Jason A. Grissom, and Laura K. Rogers. "The Impacts of Principal Turnover," *Educational Evaluation and Policy Analysis* 41, no. 3 (2019): 350–74; David E. DeMatthews, David S. Knight, and Jinseok Shin, "The Principal-Teacher Churn: Understanding the Relationship Between Leadership Turnover and Teacher Attrition," *Educational Administration Quarterly* 58, no. 1 (2022): 76–109.

Conclusion

1. Sonia Nieto, *What Keeps Teachers Going?* (Teachers College Press, 2003).

2. *David M. Houston, "Polarization, Partisan Sorting, and the Politics of Education," *American Educational Research Journal* 61, no. 3 (2024): 508–40.

3. Phi Delta Kappa, 2022 poll. https://pdkpoll.org/wp-content/uploads/2022/08/2022toplineresults.pdf.

4. Melissa Arnold Lyon, "Current Perspectives on Teacher Unionization, and What They're Missing," *Educational Policy* 37, no. 5 (2023): 1420–43.

INDEX